The Telecom Manager's Survival Guide

The Essential Reference for Telecommunications Systems, Solutions, and Cost Control

Stephen W. Medcroft

AMACOM

American Management Association

New York • Atlanta • Brussels • Chicago • Mexico City
San Francisco • Shanghai • Tokyo • Toronto • Washington, D. C.

Special discounts on bulk quantities of AMACOM books are available to corporations, professional associations, and other organizations. For details, contact Special Sales Department, AMACOM, a division of American Management Association, 1601 Broadway, New York, NY 10019.
Tel.: 212-903-8316. Fax: 212-903-8083.
Web site: www.amacombooks.org

This publication is designed to provide accurate and authoritative information in regard to the subject matter covered. It is sold with the understanding that the publisher is not engaged in rendering legal, accounting, or other professional service. If legal advice or other expert assistance is required, the services of a competent professional person should be sought.

Library of Congress Cataloging-in-Publication Data

Medcroft, Stephen, 1967–
    The telecom manager's survival guide : the essential reference for telecommunications systems, solutions, and cost control / Stephen W. Medcroft.
        p.   cm.
Includes bibliographical references and index.
        ISBN 0-8144-0719-6
    1. Telecommunication—Management. 2. Small business—Management.
I. Title.

    HE7661.M43 2003
    384'.068—dc21   2003011075

Printing number

10 9 8 7 6 5 4 3 2 1

Acknowledgments

Thank you to my wife, Keli, for your support, encouragement, and input. Thank you to our children for putting up with me spending so much time again locked away in a room, working.

Thank you Jacquie Flynn and the team at AMACOM Books for listening to an idea and seeing that it became a book. I look forward to a long and productive relationship with you.

Thank you to everyone who has been part of my career in telecommunications. There are too many to name you all, but if you have ever been my employer, colleague, customer, consultant, friend, or supporter, I mean you.

Table of Contents

List of Illustrations

Introduction

Benjamin Englewood steps across the threshold of his office in Kent, Washington, an industrial suburb of Seattle. It's November. The sun is not yet above the eastern horizon and none of his coworkers are in the office. He enjoys this short time before everyone else arrives because it gives him a moment to organize his day; to put into his day planner a list of tasks to accomplish, goals to achieve, a schedule to keep.

He pulls open his laptop computer and, as it boots up, fills a tall, thermos-style mug with cool water from a cooler down the hall.

Seventeen emails await him. All are new because he cleared his in box before leaving work the previous day. Scanning the subject headings he can see that some mean urgent trouble, some mean less urgent trouble, and the rest are of the fifty-a-day, dispense-with-in-a-couple-of-minutes kind; questions about reports, follow-ups on old issues, a notice about a change in the corporate benefits package.

As he reads the first, he can hear the thrum of feet and idle conversation behind him as life begins to flow through the veins of the office.

The rate of his heart's beating rises a percentage.

One of the urgent emails is from the inside sales group on the third floor. Eight of the sixteen phones the inside sales reps use are randomly flashing lights and sounds and appear to be completely useless to the salespeople. The email is tagged with a small flame symbol and, in clear and concise business-appropriate language, tells Benjamin it is his duty to attend to this issue first: for the sake of their customers who will be expecting help from the inside sales group, for the sake of the company that will lose profit by the fistful if he is slow to act, and for the poor employees who will not be able to earn the commissions they need to support their families.

He should do this first, even though another email makes a similar pull at him to organize a new voice mail tree to support a marketing effort put on by the product group (they forgot to mention the need three weeks ago when it was dreamt up and now, because the product is being released today, need the voice mail tree programmed and working by open of business this morning). He looks around his desk. There are several phones on a workbench along one wall of his office. He has been trying to clean and repair them to save the company their $350 replacement cost. There is a stack of local and long-distance phone bills that need to be approved for the accounts payable department. He should audit them for mistakes and make sure the carriers are true to their stated pricing but he knows he will not have time. So, as long as the dollars on the bottom line feel right, he'll scrawl his initials on the cover page and send them on to be paid.

On his calendar he sees that he has a project meeting for the new Interactive Voice Response system the dealer-distribution channel wants in by third quarter. It will help his company's distributors track orders on an automated basis through the telephone, just as a bank allows people to check on their accounts through a telephone-based system, and will be a fun project to work on. It requires a lot of internal management and coordination with the manufac-turer and the programmer to get it right. Benjamin will be spending three hours with the team this afternoon.

The rate of Benjamin's heart increases a few more percentage points.

There is also an appointment with the PBX vendor this morning. Good, he thinks, maybe he can get them to look at the eight phones with him. That many dead at one time probably means a problem with a station card in the phone system.

He thinks through the order of his day; optimistic that he will handle it all quickly.

On his laptop, he brings up the control software for the voice mail system just as someone steps into the room behind him.

"Hey Ben."

"Good morning," Ben says over his shoulder, his attention still on the screen. The phone on his desk starts to ring.

"Can I ask you a question about my calling card?"

Ben turns to the visitor. "Sure. Hang on," and swings to answer the phone.

"Are you ready for the call or not?"

"Call?" he asks, distracted by a rapid series of five beeps emitted from his computer; an urgent email has arrived and popped to the top of his email in-box list.

"The call with Campucom, Ben. About the merger of the two networks." The subject of the new email screams in capital letters for him to come up to the third floor inside sales department. IMMEDIATELY!!! "Come on man, I don't mean to be a jerk but we've been working on this for weeks and you said you'd be ready this morning to test the new frame-relay circuit to Delaware."

Ben presses his fingers to his temples. "I remember. Let me get down to the switch room and call you from there." Ben's second line starts to ring as the caller considers. "Fine. Five minutes, okay? I've only got the tester available until eight."

Ben hangs up the first call and pauses a blessed moment. The first line begins to ring again.

"Listen, about my calling card," the voice from behind inquires just as Ben pressed the line 2 button on his phone. He lifts his hand to the visitor and gives him the "one minute" signal.

"Hello."

"Is this Benjamin Englewood?"

"Yes," he answers weakly, anticipating the tone of the call.

"Hi Ben. This is Chuck over at MCI and I understand you're the right person to talk about your long-distance service. Now, as you know . . ."

Benjamin Englewood's heart rate rises another few percentage points, into dangerous territory now, as he cradles the phone to his cheek and lowers his head to his desk top.

1.1 Does Ben's Morning Seem Familiar to You at All?

Why are you reading this book? Are you a telecommunications manager? Is your experience like Ben's? And is this role your full-time responsibility? Or do you fulfill other duties to your company? Are you the owner? The controller? The receptionist or an administrative assistant? The (fill-in-the-blank)?

I'm glad. Because I need you as my partner for this journey. It is for you that I have written this book. I borrowed, consulted, and created with the most effective telecommunications people I know to create a system for managing a small- to medium-sized business' telecommunications.

Since about 1990 I have been fortunate enough to sit across an office desk, conference table, picnic bench, the corner of a cubicle, a restaurant or lunch-room table, and talk about the telecommunications issues of one-hundred businesses. Each one seemed unique. Some were service-oriented, such as restaurants, car-rental companies, and hotels. Others were manufacturers, such as bakers, beer bottlers, and tortilla makers. Still others were professional firms—lawyers, accountants, consultants, and architects. Other businesses include research firms, real estate brokers, loan consultants, and title companies. I have spent time with manufacturer's reps, dealer distributors, value-added resellers (VARs), vendors, telemarketers, independent marketers, and multilevel marketers.

I met once with a company that manufactured and distributed a line of clothing and accessories for fans of Renaissance festivals. I also worked closely with a phone-sex company.

The point being that there have been hundreds of different faces across the table. Despite all that diversity in business, I discovered striking similarities when the companies were dissected in strictly telecommunications terms.

Businesses need telephone lines to communicate with their customers. The dial tone we buy from the phone company may come in a variety of packages and prices, but in the end what we all need is the ability to make calls and receive calls.

Most businesses also need to make long-distance phone calls. Or provide toll-free long-distance calls for their customers. Many companies depend upon similar voice mail setups to handle calls when the business is closed or not available. They also have to deal with the business issues that come along with our ever-growing dependence on computers: networking, email, and Internet connectivity.

What a challenge the role of telecom manager has become in an age of open competition for every telecom service you use, thanks to several rounds of Federal Communications Commission (FCC) deregulation. Are there too many telecommunications services and products to choose from today?

Although it was a simpler time when there was only one true choice for telephone service, look at all that has happened since the first waves of deregulation. We now pay a small fraction of the cost for long-distance calls. Local phone companies now have direct competition, driving down price and bringing dozens of new product choices to the market. Technology, driven by competitive capitalism, has brought cheaper and cleaner basic service. Wireless networks—pagers, cell phones, wireless local area networks (LANs), microwave local loops—have a colossal impact on our working lives. Open competition among companies has brought cheap, high-speed Internet access to your door.

Now, with all this choice, these constantly emerging and dying companies and technologies, you are faced with a much more confusing marketplace and a tougher job than ever.

There are questions that have to be asked constantly: Are you doing the right thing for your company with its telecommunications? Are you running the ideal phone system for your business? Have you leveraged new technology to drive the expense of telecommunications down to the benefit of your bottom line? Is your wide area network (WAN) running on the cleanest, most efficient, and secure type of lines possible? Is some wily long-distance or local telephone company making huge profits off your budget? Is your business paying for the financial mistakes of a predecessor?

Let's discover the answer to these questions together in the pages ahead.

1.2   Why This Book Will Help You

This book presents you and your business with the job of professional telecommunications manager and captures the day-to-day processes and activities that make the best business telecom managers successful.

In other words, this book details, as simply as possible, a system for managing the telecommunications of your business.

In some areas of this book, you may find purely educational material—the descriptions and teaching of telecom technologies—not as finely detailed and technical as it could be. Is it necessary for you to know the bit counts for asynchronous transfer mode and how, as a network-carrier protocol, it compares to its cousin signaling system seven? Is it necessary to know what an LGE module in a Newbridge channel bank is used for?

Not to be effective.

To be effective, it is necessary to have a good general understanding of the technology you're using. It's mostly important to understand the application, the viable use of a certain technology, more than it is important to understand its inner workings.

1.3   What This Book Is Meant to Be

In this book, you will read about the four roles of a telecom manager. You'll be given tools to evaluate all the telecommunications technology in use in your business today, to break down carrier and vendor invoicing to its elements, and to understand the technology behind what they provide so you can make critical judgments as to the quality of their service.

This book will show you how to do the following:

- **Create a telecom database:** Create a telecom book for your business—a database to track and record everything you learn.
- **Vendor-prepared evaluations:** A way to have evaluations prepared for you by vendors and carriers that you can use to make tangible improvements in every aspect of your business' experience with telecommunications—all with a hawkish financial eye.
- **Solicit proposals:** Solicit proposals for improvements while bypassing some of the salesperson/prospective customer dynamics that rule the telecom landscape.
- **Track and manage projects and systems:** Effectively track and manage both projects and day-to-day trouble with the telecommunications services and systems used by your business.
- **Create an effective telecommunications system:** A system that can be adopted, in whole or in part, by you and your business or organization, so you can make the most effective use of the latest the telecommunications industry has to offer so you may dominate your market and destroy your competition.

1.4 What This Book Is Not Meant to Be

There are many books devoted to the dictionary of the telecommunications industry, volumes filled with thousands of terms for you to sift through that may or may not be relevant to your business. I recommend you buy one and stick it on a shelf, where, when opportunity demands, it can be your trusted guide. I have not tried to write a book competitive with, for example, CMP Media's *Newton's Telecommunications Directory.* Of course, there is a glossary in the back of the book to give you quick access to terms you must know in this field.

The Telecom Manager's Mission Statement

It all starts here. I believe in the power of mission statements. Having a defining sentence to capture the ideal spirit of the work to be done has great value to a telecommunications manager.

First of all, it could be said that for many businesses, big and small, the role of telecommunications manager is not clearly defined within the structure of the business. The responsibility for decisions that govern the telecommunications health of most business is spread across accounting departments, corporate officers, technical, or even clerical staff.

If you are to properly take on the role, you first need a clear definition of the boundaries of that role. That role is to accomplish the mission of a good telecom manager. This should be:

> Leverage telecommunications technology and services to the greatest possible benefit and competitive advantage of the business—at the lowest cost.

Let's dissect that statement.

Leverage telecommunications technology and services . . . This phrase is careful not to say "leverage the latest technology" because, in more cases than my industry would care to admit, the latest technology is neither the most capable or financially effective choice for business. An effective telecom manager understands the technology well enough to make a good distinction between bells and whistles that are good for them and those that are not.

. . . to the greatest possible benefit and competitive advantage . . . In business, you are in competition with someone. So ask yourself: What is the business benefit this technology or service brings? Will it improve the productivity of your staff and employees? Will it provide a service to your customers that will favor you over competitors?

. . . at the lowest cost. When you separate the fiscal and physical responsibilities of telecommunications, you are committing an error.

I recently viewed the Web site of a telecommunications consulting firm that specializes in bill auditing. They suggest that as much as 75 percent of all utility bills, including telephone service bills, have errors on them.

It is important to understand that many of the dollars wasted on telecommunications spending are hidden in small increments. The difference between $0.10 per minute and a promised $0.075 per minute is $250 on a $1,000 monthly long-distance bill. The difference between one hour of labor and two on a visit from your telephone vendor could be a hundred dollars or more. The difference between getting a quote up front for a new piece of equipment and trusting the vendor to be fair when you blindly order a new telephone for your office could be 30 percent or 40 percent.

Adopting a clear mission statement for the role of telecommunications management is a good first step in getting your telecom house in order. From here, the practical work begins.

2

The Four Primary Roles of Telecommunications Management

Are you a full-time telecom manager? Most people I have met who deal with the telecom equipment and service for their business or organization do not have that luxury. You're probably responsible for the accounts, for information technology (IT), for operations, or for who knows what else—maybe even the whole company.

For organizations large enough, however, full-time telecom management is a professional practice. As such, it has its professionals, complete with their established standards, their knowledge base, education, and experience.

In a way, this book is an attempt to give you the tools to operate the telecom of your business at their professional level. So, what does that mean?

I had a chance to browse the Internet recently and paused at an employment service Web site. For grins, I typed in the words "telecom manager" to see what would come back. What is this professional specialty worth? These two postings jumped out at me.

US — NY — New York City — SENIOR TELECOM MANAGER NEEDED FOR BILLION DOLLAR BANK!!

This is an international network of companies controlled by a billion dollar family, comprising banking and telecommunications. We have branches located in the U.S., Europe, the Middle East, Latin America, and the Caribbean. A Senior Telecom Manager is needed to restructure the infrastructure.

Technical requirements are at least 5–7 years of experience working with PBX, NEC 2400 switches, and CISCO 2000/3000 series switches. Knowledge of IPC phone systems will be a huge plus.

The salary is negotiable upon experience, with an excellent 401k plan and benefits that are given after the first day of employment!

ADDITIONAL INFORMATION
Salary: $76,000 to $100,000 per year
Position Type: Full Time, Employee

Voice Telecommunications Manager

ABC Company, Inc., is currently seeking a Voice Telecommunications Manager for our corporate headquarters. The position currently has one direct report. This is an outstanding opportunity with a growing company!

PRIMARY RESPONSIBILITIES:
Define and develop support policies. Serve as a point of contact for inquiries relating to telecommunications issues. Resolve all telecommunication issues, or work with Director, Network, to resolve more complex issues, and Assist Director, Network, in scheduling tasks and implementing projects relating to telecommunications. Work on various projects as assigned by management.

REQUIREMENTS:

Four years' experience with Nortel switches. To perform this job successfully, individual must have working knowledge of Microsoft Office, Windows NT, & 2000; excellent understanding and experience with Meridian Mail, Call Pilot, and Symposium; and experience of Witness, Banners, Blue Pumpkin is a plus.

COMPETENCIES:

- **Analytical:** Synthesizes complex or diverse information; collects and researches data.
- **Oral communication:** Speaks clearly and persuasively in positive or negative situations.
- **Written communication:** Writes clearly and informatively.
- **Project management:** Develops project plans; coordinates projects; communicates changes and progress; completes projects on time and budget; manages project team activities.
- **Technical skills:** Pursues training and development opportunities; strives to continuously build knowledge and skills; shares expertise with others.
- **Problem solving:** Identifies and resolves problems in a timely manner; gathers and analyzes information skillfully; develops alternative solutions; works well in group problem-solving situations.
- **Customer service:** Manages difficult or emotional customer situations; responds to requests for service and assistance.
- **Managing people:** Develops subordinates' skills and encourages growth; fosters quality focus in others; improves processes, products, and services.
- **Quality management:** Looks for ways to improve and promote quality; demonstrates accuracy and thoroughness.
- **Dependability:** Commits to long hours of work when necessary to reach goals.

* * *

If the first words that come to your mind when you read through these job postings are: overwhelming, daunting, and out-of-reach, then you are not alone.

Yet this is how the professional telecom manager role is defined at the high end. But it does not need to be. The job can be defined more simply, in more reachable language. To ask you to accept that you can take on, even as a part-time role, the character of a professional telecom manager, we must first break the job down into four manageable parts:

- Trouble resolution
- Project management
- Billing audit and review
- Strategic planning

In case this is not an assumed or established fact for your business, the telecom manager role needs to be specifically assigned to someone in your organization. There are many tangible benefits to doing this: by having one person be the expert on "all things telecom," the time it takes to re- solve issues is greatly shortened because the person responsible is the most current on all your telecom issues. This is especially critical when money is involved.

Before I was named the telecom manager for Digital Data Systems in Las Vegas, Nevada, every employee knew the phone number to our telephone vendor. They would call at all hours to complain of any abstract problem on the lines, such as sticky buttons with their phone or random static on the lines. They felt they were doing the company a favor by participating in the running of the most important business system the business owned. Trouble was, they did not understand the charges and fees ($100 plus for overtime hours worked by the vendor) associated with such late-night calls.

Assigning a sole telecom manager who will audit your company thoroughly as a first step to understanding the telecom needs of your business will help avoid some of the overspending that happens every day. Companies unwit- tingly pay for services they never requested, are not using, or don't need all the time. As you go through the process, you may uncover a nugget or two in your own business.

I have a dramatic example: I sold a network of telephone systems to the City of Redmond, Washington. I remember a conversation with the telecom manager in which she had found that she was paying for a telephone number she did not recognize. She couldn't find it listed on any of her inter- nal records. No employee had been assigned the number as best as she could tell. When she called it, it rang as a pager.

She checked her pager lists as she waited for a call back. Nothing.

Then the call came. The number, as it happened, rang to the pager hanging on the belt of a technician. A phone company technician. Not only had her local phone company been incorrectly billing her for several years for service she discovered her predecessor had disconnected, they had reissued the number to themselves!

Here's another one to consider: A computer consultant in Phoenix used to support one of the larger banks in town. He had occasion to come across a closet full of working telephone numbers that he could not justify against any of the people or equipment in the bank. The phone company couldn't tell where the lines went beyond the closet. No one at the bank owned up to them either. It may have been that, whenever someone felt they needed a line for a modem or a fax machine, they called the phone company (instead of their telecom manager) and ordered a new one, which resulted in a closet of telephone numbers.

Not knowing where they went, but sure they were not authorized, the consultant had the local phone company cancel all the lines. The result to his employer was approximately $10,000 saved. The result to his coworkers were a few angry people who lost their modem or fax, which he promptly replaced in a way that was more effective for the business.

Designate the role of telecommunications manager to someone if you haven't already. And be sure to communicate to the rest of your organization the best way to reach that person when needed.

2.1 Trouble Resolution

As the telecom manager, you are responsible for any and all trouble that occurs with any aspect of your business' telecom. If there is static on a telephone line, you'll need to know how to resolve it, who to call, and how to follow up to see that the job is completed. If the bill from your long-distance carrier reflects charges three times the agreed-upon rate per minute for calls, it will fall upon you to negotiate a credit and get the billing fixed. If a telephone hanging on the warehouse wall stops working, an antennae on a company cellular telephone falls off, or a pager battery dies, expect to be pressed into service.

The best telecom managers accomplish this role with the following steps.

Create and Manage a Trouble Ticket System

This system can help track and resolve telecom issues and problems. For example, if someone needs a phone repaired, they are usually asked to submit a request to create the trackable action of having a repair made.

A trouble-reporting system of some kind breeds accountability. Your employee or coworker has taken the initiative to make a request. The trouble ticket could be a verbal request or a voice mail or email asking for help. It could be as formal as a form the telecom manager creates.

Whatever the trouble ticket's incarnation, the telecom manager's role is to respond, which could mean on-the-spot action. It could mean placing an order with a third party, an item that can now be scheduled for follow-up. It could mean scheduling or creating a to-do task item to go to the person's desk and attempt to fix or replace the phone. It may mean clarifying the request before any action can be taken. But by making the requests formal, the telecom manager creates a manageable, measurable structure to this one aspect of their role—something to track, something to report back on, something to keep the request clear.

To keep pace with all these requests, some form of scheduling apparatus needs to be used. A white board in the telecom manager's office with a list of open requests has been enough for some. It could be a Franklin System Day Planner, which I use to track everything I am responsible for. You may use something similar. Or software to automate the task.

How would you handle trouble resolution?

Create Help Desk–Type Single-Number Support for the Company

Chris Robson is an account executive out of one of the branch offices I work with. One morning in March, he was about to close escrow on his new house. He needed to call his wife and conference with the title company to deal with a few last-minute details. Unfortunately, he had forgotten how to build a three-way conference call on his telephone. He learned it in new user training when the vendor installed the system seven months before but hasn't needed it much since. Where will he get help?

For most businesses with professional telecom managers, the answer is a single-number help desk: one number any employee with a telecom issue can call and know they will get a response. Often- times, it is the extension number of the telecom manager. Or it could be an extension on the phone system separate from his own that can be forwarded to anywhere he is working that day. The number could ring to an alternative person, or it could ring to a voice mail box that, in turn, pages him.

The single-number approach doesn't have to mean voice calls only. A special email box could be set up for users in distress to contact the telecom manager, and a fax machine set up for requests.

It could be an escalating list of contacts—phone numbers, emails, pagers, cell phones—of anyone in the chain of responsibility.

The point to your business is that such a contact list is published, available, and leads to the correct person or department.

Provide Training and End-User Education

Life can be good when you buy a brand new telephone system. It's like picking out a new car. We get all the latest gadgets and features we want. The dealership shines it up inside and out for the moment we drive it off the lot. Everything is perfect.

In the phone-system world, the time of installation (if your vendor is competent) can mirror that new car experience. The vendor sets everything up just the way you want it. You get that new voice mail system your employees have harped about for the past year. You finally get to use direct inward dialing as do most of the businesses you deal with; now everyone in your company has a private telephone number that rings right to their desk. Your receptionist loves you because her work load is greatly reduced with most of the calls bypassing the main desk so she can focus on volunteer and career-building tasks.

The day the new system is ready to be switched on for the first time (called *cutover*), a team of trainers from the vendor sets up shop in the conference room of your office. All your coworkers are scheduled to go in for an hour at a time, in class groups of five to eight. In class, they receive their user manual and a walk-through on the new system. They are shown how to use the five most common features on their phones: place and answer calls, build a conference, transfer, intercom. The trainer guides them through setting up their voice mail box for the first time and how to retrieve, save, and delete messages.

The front desk personnel, the ones who field most of the calls for the company, are given a class twice as long as other users.

The day after the installation of a new telephone system, everyone is on the same page.

Then someone forgets everything they learned and botches up the greeting in their voice mail. Or they can't figure out how to program speed dials. Or an employee leaves and a new hire comes in. Then what? Is the vendor coming back in to train individuals weeks, months, or years after the original sale? (The answer is no, by the way.)

You must prepare for the inevitability of needing to bring new employees up to the same level as older ones on the telecommunications infrastructure we have in place for them to use. Retraining those who, inevitably, forget everything they learned the first time when it suddenly becomes important to them again will also be necessary.

To fulfill this responsibility, the user guides that come with most telephone and voice mail systems are extremely helpful. They cover anything that a user might want to do. Some (especially voice mail user guides) have tear-off keys that can be kept close at hand for an employee to refer to in the time of need. In reality though, most users lose or simply forget they have guides. The simplest thing to do may be to get additional copies of training material from the vendor when they give the original training classes; many vendors create a special training cheat-sheet that covers the top five features of phones and voice mail.

If you have inherited systems installed before your time, and cannot locate the original training or user guides, call and ask the vendor for such material. It may also be worth paying for an hour or two of a trainer's labor to give you the basics of how to train users on their phone systems.

For any telecommunications-related project that will affect your users, be sure that training is included as an elemental part of any proposal you request. If you're going to be installing an automated attendant, for example, giving an overview of the new technology and how it will affect the business will help the project gain acceptance by the employees of your company.

Another method of keeping the end-user training alive is to share with everyone any problems that come up. Chris Robson wasn't the only person to ask how to make a conference call in our branch offices. It happens once or twice a day. Because I took a minute to explain the process once to Chris, how simple would it be to type a short explanation and email it to everyone in the company? Easy if not abused.

If all end users receive the same information, they are less likely to need support for the same issues.

And use of phones, voice mail, and basic telephone service is not the only training you need to be prepared to give. Cover the company's policies on personal calls on work time, calling cards, cell phone usage, and long-distance spending.

In the telecom world, a small misunderstanding on behalf of your employees can be costly. Not long ago, David Stephenson called me in a fury. He had just received a $3,300 phone bill from AT&T for calls made the previous month from his corporate office. They were charging him fifty-four cents per minute. My employer at the time, McLeodUSA, charged him six cents. And we were the elected carrier for corporate.

We went to Dave's office and called AT&T. After forty minutes of holding and going back and forth between customer service for AT&T and Qwest, Dave's local telephone company, AT&T came back with the statement that they had a legal sale. As far as they were concerned, their salesperson had called one of the Dallas retail stores and talked to an employee there (the employee was new and spoke only broken English). They had a recording of this employee on file (which they are going to play for us) authorizing them to change the long-distance carrier to AT&T.

But why, we asked the call-center agent, would we elect to switch from a six cents per minute plan to a fifty-four cents per minute plan?

"Oh, the fifty-four cents is a mistake. Our salesperson would have set you up at $0.075."

"But they didn't."

"It must be a mistake. We can fix that."

"But this employee was never authorized to make the change."

"According to FCC rules, because we verified the sale through a third party, and recorded it, we have a legal sale." And therefore the right to charge Dave for services he, as the only authorized telecom manager, did not request.

"But this employee was never authorized to make the change." I was trying to convey to the agent that Dave had been *slammed,* the industry term when someone changes your long-distance service without your permission.

"Okay sir. Then what we'll do is adjust your rate to what you would have paid to your current carrier. You just need to provide us with a copy of your most recent billing from them."

So, one-and-a-half hours invested and the net result is that Dave, because he knew his rights, will only be paying as much to AT&T as he would have to McLeodUSA. Except that now he is forced to send money to a company he did not choose to do business with. All because an employee at a retail store in Dallas said yes to a telemarketer over the phone.

Get your employees out of the phone business. Assert to all that every communication about telecommunications needs to be filtered to the telecom manager. It is the only way to protect your business in a structure that is complicated and favors carriers from fraud and unethical practices.

Measurable

With each of the four areas of responsibility, the effective telecom manager looks to provide accountability to his company for the work that he does. Accountability in the form of some kind of statistics that show his effect on the business.

For the task of trouble resolution, the number of requests and duration of time for their completion, as an average, could be used as statistics. Does it take four hours, on average, from the time trouble is reported to see it completely taken care of? Forty-eight hours? Whatever your turnaround time, improving it is a demonstration of your value.

It would be simple to ask employees, when submitting a trouble request to the telecom manager, to note the time of their request. And the telecom manager to note the time complete. This information could be tracked on a simple spreadsheet. As you grow in experience in dealing with trouble—learning who to call in what situation or understanding your rights with carriers and how better to assert them—you'll become more effective at dealing with trouble. As the company learns to involve you at the beginning, issues will practically resolve themselves.

2.2 Project Management

It happened to Don Barton when he first toured his new Claremont Hotel with an owner's eye for the first time; he realized he wanted to provide a better grade of service than was possible with the telecommunications system in place and so he set about making a change.

It happened to Benjamin Englewood, the telecommunications manager from the opening of the book, when the sales and marketing team wanted a new voice mail menu for customers calling about a new product.

It happened to David Stephenson of TTS, Inc., when AT&T sent him a bill for $3,000 and he learned his company's vulnerability to abuse by carriers. He knew he would need to reaudit every store's phone bills, every long distance charge, every cell phone and pager account to be sure there were no other financial loopholes for his money to fall through.

It happened to Herb Rosen of Trans-West Telephone Company when the competitive local phone company he had worked with on a couple of customer accounts asked to perform an analysis of his telephone lines. He needed to pull together copies of phone bills for them. They would look at his account records with the current local phone company. If they could structure his service more effectively and show him ways to save money, he might become their customer.

It has happened to many a business when its vendor told them they have finally outgrown the capability of their current telephone system.

It has happened whenever the CEO talks to a friend who just switched all his truck drivers in his beer distribution company from cellular telephones to Nextel's hybrid phone that also gives a two-way radio functionality.

I'm talking about major projects related to telecommunications. I'm talking about change. Changes that create events that now must be organized, controlled, managed, and successfully implemented.

There are four realities that drive businesses to change their current telecom structure.

1. **Innovation:** Development in the telecommunications field is best defined as hyperfast. In just 15 years, telecommunications have progressed from basic, though feature-rich, business telephone systems, to virtual, PC-screen–based multimedia call centers that can process phone calls, emails, faxes, and Web chat sessions into the same call-center agent.

   The last fifteen years have seen the telecommunications industry deregulated so that its consumers have choices in not only their long-distance carrier, but their local phone company as well. The implementation of new and exciting technologies allow us to communicate more effectively — such as voice mail systems, integrated switched digital networking (ISDN) telephone service, PCS telephone networks, wireless communications, nationwide data networks, and (of course) the booming growth in the capacity of the Internet.

   These innovations succeed because they come with proven abilities to enhance the productivity of businesses and can demonstrate specific advantages over the way we're doing things (or the way our competitors are doing things) today.

2. **Life of a system:** The average business telephone system has a useable life span of five to eight years. Cellular phones and pagers somewhat less. The use-

able life of fax machines, modems in computers, routers, channels service units, and channel banks—all manner of telecommunications technology—is based upon materials and technologies that have finite use. Our businesses outlast the equipment's physical life and the life of its practical applicability.

3. **Growth:** When you opened the doors to your company with only a handful of employees, including your spouse, you bought a phone system that could grow to accommodate sixteen people and thought you were hedging a bet against the future. Then the business took off and before you knew it, you were hiring the seventeenth employee with more to come. The system could no longer handle you.

4. **Financial reasons:** Upon careful review of all telecommunications spending, many telecom managers may come to understand that they are paying more than the market is offering for local telephone service, long-distance service, Internet access, the hosting of their Web site, their frame relay network between their three offices, their cellular calling plans, and their annual maintenance contract on the phone system. All this could easily have happened in the space of the eighteen months since they last performed an audit. The cost for telecommunications services, because of the incredible dollars spent by businesses each year, and the economics of open competition, drive the retail price of almost everything related to telecom down. How long do you think it will be until long distance is a penny a minute or a free feature added to local phone service? How long before business telephone systems become something you download off the Internet for next to no cost and run on your local LAN?

These pressures, in the real world, translate directly into opportunity to manage projects for you, the effective telecom manager. The distinction between the roles of project management and trouble resolution is the proactive nature of projects. Sure, some projects come on the tails of trouble events (replacing a phone system in a location that has accidentally been burned to the ground, for example). Therefore, the discipline to handle each role would be different. Whereas it takes calm and quick reaction, access to information and resources at a moments notice, and confidence to resolve trouble, it takes more patience and research and careful forethought and planning to successfully implement new projects.

Because projects are such a part of the telecom manager's life, I feel we should come to the following understanding of what the role means to us.

Manage Implementation of New Services and Equipment

Each new project will need to be broken into components to be managed effectively. Evaluating the need of the project is the first step; if you outgrew your phone system, what will be your future needs for growth for any new proposal? Are there other concerns about the old system that need to be addressed with the new one? What is the budget?

Soliciting proposals would be the next logical step. If the project is to implement a new voice response system to allow your customers to call in and check on their accounts without going to a live person, you'll want to qualify companies capable of providing the service. You may find an appropriate vendor through word of mouth, by looking them up in directories, finding a company with a similar system and asking them for a referral, or by just relying on your existing vendor. Either way, with a good needs analysis done, you'll be able to interview vendors and solicit adequate proposals to accomplish the project.

You'll also be responsible for seeing that the appropriate vendor or technology is selected to fill the need of the project.

The final, and toughest part, is seeing the project implemented correctly. You may have to ride the schedules of your vendor, coordinate with the employees of your company, work out training schedules, and answer last-minute questions affecting the installation.

Are you equipped to organize and manage your own telecommunications projects? It shouldn't be too difficult to figure out what needs to be done, right? Many projects will come with all the information needed to see them through. If you are approached by the salesperson of a telecom company asking you to consider a proposal he wishes to make, that company should be prepared to provide you with all the supporting information you need to decide the merit of their proposal. If the owner of your company wants you to see if that Nextel two-way cell phone service is cost-effective for your company, you go to Nextel, get all the pricing and service information you need, make a selection from their options, and allow their implementation process to take over.

What about those projects that are a little beyond your scope? Or projects that require specific expertise in times when you just don't want to take a vendor's word for it? Or, for that matter, projects that are going to require more hours than you have to spare?

Don Barton knew that his concept to revamp the telecommunications services offered at his hotel was beyond his scope of expertise. He had two choices: become an expert at telecom or hire someone to come in and manage the project. In his case, using a telecommunications consultant who was a contract employee, to work on behalf of his hotel was the more viable choice. The budget for his system ($150,000 plus) justified the expense of the consultant and ensured he would get an unbiased approach to vendor selection.

There is a network of professional telecommunications consultants out there and it makes sense to bring them in to help with this critical role of telecom management. But caveat emptor—consultancy in itself is a mostly unregulated industry. You expect to hire a consultant to work on your behalf, to protect your interests. Some telecom consultants have businesses that are structured so that they receive commissions or kickbacks from a variety of local telephone companies, long-distance carriers, Internet service providers, wide-area network (WAN) carriers, and sometime equipment vendors. They may still solicit you as a client and perform similar analysis of your needs and recommendations of solutions; even billing you for their time. But, because they glean revenue from the vendors and carriers they recommend to their clients, you can't be sure you received a truly unbiased representation of what companies are best suited to fulfill the needs of your project.

A true consultant makes money only from the client. The consultant is paid by the hour or on some flat-fee negotiated with you for the project as a whole. He or she has no bias or prejudice toward one vendor or carrier and focuses only on understanding your needs, expressing them to proposing companies, and working for the best possible deal for your business. A true consultant should be willing to stick with the recommendation and see it implemented by helping to manage it through to completion.

So ask careful questions and know exactly what type of "consultant" you're hiring before you put the faith of your company and its project into him or her.

Measurable

To be seen as effective in your role of managing projects, there must be some way to report progress. The simplest way would be to use project management software or report. All tasks are laid against a timeline at the beginning of new events. The elements are assigned to those responsible (vendor, you, a colleague). Each task is given a deadline. Some tasks must be completed before others can be attempted. This kind of project-management tool allows you, and anyone who needs to view the report, to understand the progress being made against the original goal.

2.3 Billing Audit and Review

Auditing and reviewing your company's telecommunications spending is the role where professional, effective telecom managers pay for themselves. More than any other role, this is where they prove their worth, justify their salary by catching mistakes and fraud in billing, and drive costs down by playing competitive carriers against each other.

Mistakes and fraud happen. Take local phone service, for example. I recently performed an audit for a Phoenix business with seventeen retail locations. Each store had five telephone lines; a main phone number with two additional lines that main number rolled to, one fax line, and one modem line. On its local phone bill, the company was being charged for a forwarding feature on the first and second telephone line. The forwarding feature was valuable to the company and originally installed so that if the business had to shut down temporarily (fire, an employee emergency that left the location unmanned), telephone calls to the main phone number could be redirected to another location. In that case, you would need to forward the main line, right? Anyone calling the store would call the main telephone number. So you would never need to forward the second line—it only serves as a place for a second call to the main phone number to roll to.

This customer was paying three dollars per location for the extra forwarding feature. For seven years, $4,200 worth of this business' hard-earned cash was thrown away on a feature that was not necessary and will never be needed.

Look at all the potential trouble that can happen on the long distance side of the house. Employees use telephones to make personal calls that cost you money. Shady long-distance telephone companies still "slam" businesses by the thousands every day. Remember Dave's bill? Because a new employee in a branch a thousand miles away said yes to something a telemarketer asked, Dave incurred a $3,000 AT&T bill.

Such mistakes may not be intentional, yet typically favor the carrier. And the unscrupulous perpetration of these mistakes succeed because of one major principle: most businesses either don't have the time or the understanding of telecom to properly audit its phone bill and subsequently just write a check for whatever the phone company tells the company it owes.

Vendor billings are not implacable either. Vendors who perform work for you may charge two hours when their technician was visiting for one and a half. You may find on a vendor invoice that you were mistakenly charged more for a telephone you bought than your original purchase contract states you should.

On the fraud side of things, there are many scams by fraud artists: someone may steal a calling card PIN (personal identification number) and share it with all his friends so they can all call back to their country of origin on your dime. A prison inmate could call your toll-free number, say he's an operator with MCI, and ask your front desk person to transfer him to extension 9 (or 90 or 9 and a series of numbers). If she does this, it could effectively give him access to an outside line off your phone system to make a call to wherever he chooses, for however long he chooses, without the ability to be detected by you until after the fact.

By monitoring the invoices that come in for all telecommunications, asking questions, and challenging anything that's out of line, you can have a positive effect on the bottom line.

The examples cited previously list hard-dollar savings that can be accounted for immediately. The not-so-obvious, but probably most effective, way to look for savings is to view telecom spending statistically. Anticipate bills and their amounts and keep a hawkish eye open for anomalies.

For example, many long-distance carriers, when signing you on, give the option for you to receive summary reports of your bills to accompany the detailed pages you normally see. Such a summary report may break your total spending down by which telephone line in your office the calls are accounted to. If you had eight main lines and normally use all eight to make long-distance calls, and on one month's summary bill the fifth line had no calls ascribed to it, you may surmise that there is a problem with your fifth telephone line. If the charges applied against one of the lines is three times greater than the others, then you will be looking through the detail of the bill and figuring out why. Is the line a modem that was connected to a long-distance telephone number for four days straight? Are there a disproportionate amount of international calls being made from that line? Again, it's the anomalies we look for, red flags that lead us to investigate further.

The ability to look at vendor and carrier bills and see if they are out of line with what you expect is dependent upon understanding exactly what they should look like, which leads to the core elements in the role of billing audit and review.

Inventory All Company Telecom Services and Equipment

Sometimes I come away from an appointment with a prospect, a customer, or a client a little afraid for them for how little they understand the telecommunications infrastructure in their business. I ask "How many phone lines do you have?" to be answered, "I'm not sure exactly, about twenty I guess."

What is the cost of having one telephone line more than you truly need to support the communications of your business? In Phoenix, it could be $35 per line. That's $360 in one year, not counting taxes. What's the effect of paying twenty cents per minute for long-distance calls within the United States instead of the eight cents you were promised by your carrier? If you're writing a $500 check per month to that carrier (before taxes and fees), approximately $300 of it is overcharge. Per month!

The effective telecom manager accumulates the information they'll need to base decisions from here on out.

I suggest you build a "telecom book," a repository of all the elements of your telecom infrastructure and the information to support it all. This book will be an important reference whenever issues arise and a starting point for the billing audit and review process on a monthly basis. In many cases your telecom book should actually be a book—a three-ring binder with tabs to separate the different types of information.

As an alternative, you could build a spreadsheet on your computer and create a series of forms to hold the information. If you are enterprising enough, you may even develop a database with a tool such as Microsoft Access. However you accomplish it, your "book" should carry the following information (to help, I have designed some basic paper forms (shown throughout the book) to help you organize this information. Feel free to copy the form or create something similar yourself. If you'd like electronic versions of these forms, so you can make modifications or print them at will, email me at *stevemedcroft@mcleodusa.net* and I will gladly forward you the original copies):

- **Phone service:** A listing of all your local telephone lines (land lines), every phone number, the type of service it delivers, and organizational information to support it. It is important to note whether the line is connected to the telephone system and what line position it correlates to. Also list any hunt group programming, modem and fax line designations, and so on. On your form, include the monthly cost (before taxes) for each line. If the line is routed through to a specific destination or used for a special purpose, list that here (an example would be a line that rings through to a specific department; you may note it as "accounting—main line"). Note any special features you may also be paying for.

- **Wireless inventory:** Every wireless device your company owns (cell phones, pagers, wireless email devices, wireless modems) and who it is assigned to. Include the carrier who provides it and the monthly cost.

- **Calling cards:** Make a list of all company cards and who they have been assigned to. When were they issued? What are the calling instructions and any security code or PIN? Keep the information on file in case a user either loses the card or so you can help effectively if he or she are experiencing trouble.

- **Maintain a complete inventory of your telephone system:** A phone system has only one responsibility: to share the communications assets of the business (telephone lines, voice mail system, long-distance service) with the users in the business (via telephone interface).

    In its construction, a telephone system is similar to a computer comprising modular components. A computer is assembled within a case that contains all the equipment. Inside, there is a power supply, hardware to store information, a motherboard for interconnecting all the pieces, and various cards and connectors that provide plugs for the keyboard, mouse, monitor, and so on. The beauty of computers is that they can be built with many optional configurations to accommodate the needs of the user.

    Without software, though, computers are no more than a box full of shiny green, gold, and silver trinkets. Software brings the computer to life; software to write with, to do accounting, to run businesses, and to play games.

    Your phone system, whether a small key system or a larger PBX, is similar. Somewhere (on a wall or in a closet probably), there is a case that contains all the brains of the phone's computer. It has a power supply. Inside is the hard drive or memory chips to store the systems programming information (what extension number represents which phone). There is a motherboard to allow all the pieces to communicate with each other. And there are modules or cards that slide into the main cabinet that provide the connections to the devices attached to your phone system: telephones, telephone lines, possibly a system that collects records of calls made for you to produce reports on, any fax machines, modems, or other telephone devices.

Each of these modules or cards interface to a specific type of device. You will see line cards to connect your standard business lines to. There could be a T1 card if you use such a high-speed telephone line. In some phone systems, the telephone sets communicate with the base system using a proprietary digital language so a special digital station card has to be used. Standard telephone devices (home style telephones, fax machines, modems) use analog telephone signals and require analog station cards. If you order direct inward dial telephone service from your local phone company, you will probably need a special module or card to make use of the service.

Each of these cards has a certain capacity, a maximum number of circuits or stations it supports. Based upon the capability of the system's processor and the physical number of cards of different types that can be loaded into the system, your phone system has a maximum capacity of its own. Having an inventory and understanding its total capacity will help you more effectively troubleshoot problems with your phone system.

For example, if eight phones go dead at the same time and your phone system station cards have eight ports, look to your inventory to see which card the phones are connected to. Chances are, in that scenario, one of your station cards has failed. List each currently installed card. Map which telephone line is connected to which port (position on a card). Map which telephone extension or device correlates to every station card position.

- **Data lines:** Do you have more than one location for your business? If so, what systems interconnect— computer, telephone, video conference? Do you have a frame relay network? ISDN service used for high-speed modem traffic? Point-to-point T1s or 56k leased lines? Are you running a virtual private network (VPN) using Internet connections? If the answers are yes to any of these questions, account for each of the circuits in your WAN: their location, detail about their capacity, the carrier, and so on.

- **Data equipment:** Each of the circuits just described has a point of entry at each location of your business and must be terminated at a specific type of equipment. Account for every connection point and the device that makes it happen: who is the manufacturer, the vendor, what model and make, what options the manufacturer offers are loaded on it?

- **Account for every bill:** I am assuming that you pay for each service that you are provided by a vendor or carrier. I say that somewhat facetiously—of course you are. In fact, if I needed to understand your telecom infrastructure and had to choose between a telecom manager's best understanding and the phone company's billing records, I would trust the bill first. Phone companies are notoriously bad at many things: answering the customer service line in a timely manner with trained personnel who follow up to see that your problem is taken care of, for instance.

    One thing they do excel at, though, is accounting and charging for every service they provide. Oh, they may overcharge you, or include things in your bill that you either don't have or never asked for, but they will get everything you owe them. I'll even go so far as to say that in all my years in telecom, I can't remember one encounter in which I saw a telephone company bill that did not include an item the customer was using. Not to say it never happens, but I haven't seen one.

    The point is, if a client asked me, "How do I begin to get a grip on all the services (telephone lines, long-distance service, Internet connectivity and other Internet products, data circuits), where do I start?" I tell them make friends with accounting. The stewards of company money will be able to tell you who bills you for telecom services.

From there, it is a matter of understanding the bill, finding out what you've been charged for, and then finding that service or product in your business to verify it exists and is being used.

Make a list in this section of your telecom book of every carrier who provides you service. List beneath that each invoice you expect to receive and its frequency (monthly, quarterly, annually). Summarize the services included in the invoice and their component costs. List the total bottom-line cost this bill should be. If the bill is for a fixed, monthly service, the billing should be practically identical each cycle.

For example: my home phone bill is about fifty-four dollars every month. I have two lines, a couple of convenience features, and taxes. Most months, the bill is right at $54.00. I write a check and mail it, never paying more attention to the bill than that. If I suddenly saw a bill for eighty-five dollars, I would go searching through the detail for the reason why and fix any mistake or overbilling with the carrier before I write the check.

Not all invoices will be the same. We pay for some services in proportion to how much of it we use. My long-distance bill is approximately fifty dollars. When I received one a few months ago that was ninety dollars, I had to figure out why. In this case, the extra expense was justified by some calling we had to do that month. It's not that variable charges like these will always be the same month to month, but a statistical change, an unexpected rise or fall in a bill like that, is a red flag to look for more. You will use all billing for the same purpose.

Review invoices before the accounting department pays. Create a grid of the months of the next couple of years so you can check off the invoices as you review them. Use this method and you will likely head off trouble before it can persist and cost you substantial money.

■ **Contact information:** For each carrier and vendor that you do business with, create a contact database. List all the relevant information, business name, address for mailing, account numbers and any PINs, security codes, or logins that you hold with them. List the telephone numbers you call to receive service or to talk about your billing and any specific contact names, if relevant.

Ask for an escalation list so that, when you do not receive a timely response by calling into the main customer service telephone number, you have some other names to call to get results. If relevant, include notes with information about your original relationship with the vendor or carrier: what you bought, what contract terms were included, and the names of the original salespeople. Also, include a copy of original contracts here to have on hand during later discussions about price and terms.

- **Communications logs:** It is simple to keep a short record of telephone calls between you and your vendors. For each company you speak with on any telecom-related business issue, jot the date, time, who you spoke to, and content of the call. There's no need to be laborious about it, any record you have to refer to will be a thousand-percent better clarification and ammunition for those adversarial calls to carriers when something promised did not get done.

  Have you ever made a report of a billing mistake or trouble with your service, to be told it would be repaired or you would receive some form of credit, only to have the credit not show up on your bill? The calls you have to make can be frustrating. Having a record helps you be clear and arms you with facts. Or better yet, use email to communicate with your vendor and carrier contacts as much as possible—the automatically created paper trail accomplishes the same thing without your needing to take extra time to make a record.

- **Trouble reports:** Keep copies of the trouble reports your employees give you. When time permits, it may make sense to sit with them and analyze whether there are consistent patterns. If you handled four claims of a bad handset on your expensive, proprietary, fancy telephone sets, you might consider buying a few extras and stocking them to have an instant fix on hand for future failures. If there are consistent

> complaints of difficulty using your carrier-provided
> calling cards, it may be time for a new carrier.

Many of your relationships with carriers and vendors will
be amicable. The vendors will provide the service you paid
for and be responsive to your calls with questions, requests, and concerns. Many will overperform, making you
so happy they will earn (and deserve) your loyalty. For
those companies, you might even be willing to pay a small
premium, within reason, to stay where you are rather than
work through the pain of change.

Some of you may not have such a great experience. You
may find yourself doing business with a company that
needs to be replaced for a number of reasons: they fail, go
bankrupt, sell out, and so forth. They may simply fail you:
their salespeople will sing a song that doesn't ring true and
promise what cannot ultimately be delivered. Their customer service will forget who you are every time you call.
They could promise you relief and credits and fixes that
will not materialize. They might harangue you for unpaid
bills when you know you have settled your obligation to
them.

These companies are the enemy of the effective telecom manager. Be prepared to go to battle to get your
problems fixed, to get out of your contract, to usurp a
credit out of their tight fists, or to fight a financial obligation that can be out of proportion to what you feel it
should be.

In a war, your best weapon is intelligence. Information.
Armed with your telecom book as both shield and weapon,
you will be better positioned than your enemy in the battles
that ensue.

In disputes over the resolution of problems, for example,
your vendor may disagree about when you first contacted
them with the nature and extent of an issue. You will have
records you can reference to show where they are wrong.
You will win the battles.

And if you are faced with the event of needing to change
carriers for positive improvement in service or products, a
more favorable financial position, or the negative circumstance of needing to ditch an ugly partner, the records you've
kept will prove meritorious. The information will be valued
like gold to the new carrier. It can ensure they will be able to

implement their relationship with you correctly the first time and as seamlessly as their process can be managed.

Exercise Audit Approval of All Telecom Carrier and Vendor Bills

To maintain your control over the financial aspects of your organization's telecom, insist that you approve all carrier and vendor bills before they're paid.

In a smaller company, this may be simple. You may already be the person who sees all the telecom-related bills before they go out. You may even be the person who writes out and signs the check to pay these bills.

In a larger organization, I urge you to invoke audit privilege over all telecom spending. Even if it means smooth talking the accounting maven or convincing the president of the merit of the extra step.

It shouldn't be a hard process to implement. When billings come in, be sure you get an opportunity to read them first. Check for obvious errors. Make sure the amounts fall within your expected ranges. Check that no additional services or charges and fees have made it into the bill that you were not expecting. Then move it on for payment.

Identify and Target Fraud Abusers

There is a difference between mistakes and fraud. Carriers make mistakes all the time by billing too much for something or charge for service not delivered. They charge fees they promised they would waive or assess penalties you did not deserve. I don't believe there is a great conspiracy to outwit the paying public out of billions of dollars through negligent practice. But the billing process and systems of these large carriers are such that these mistakes happen.

Abuse usually is an internal problem—employees spending company dollars for their personal benefit. What is acceptable use of company telecom assets can only be controlled by educating employees.

Wouldn't it make sense to have a policy governing the use of the business' telecommunications resources? In a later chapter, I'll cover the basics of a telecom use policy and give an example. This way, everyone has the same understanding of what is allowed. There's no need to be a Scrooge. Personal phone calls from work may be the only way some people hold their days together; so let's not ban them all together. But when rules are in place, you have a framework to find abuse.

In minor abuse cases, employees or people with access to your office make toll telephone calls from work. You'll see long-distance charges out of line with what you expect. If you institute calling codes for long-distance dialing, meaning everyone has to enter a code before a long-distance call can be completed and calls on your bill are then listed by the code used, certain codes will statistically stand out above the rest. Take a breezy look through the detail to verify the nature of the spending and be satisfied fraud has not happened.

Fraud is something entirely different from simple abuse. It is the systematic abuse of your telecommunications services or equipment by someone hostile to your business, who should be dealt with as adversaries.

Sudden jumps in calling card use might need to be investigated. Did the employee it was assigned to really travel that much? Could the card have been stolen?

There are different scams out there. One of the more common is for a reader to grab a calling card number from over the shoulder of a traveler. He then spreads the number around a group of cohorts and they start using your card to call back home (whatever that expensive telephone destination may be).

Enterprising entrepreneurs may stand on a street corner in an immigrant neighborhood (with its market for making expensive telephone calls and pockets of probable poverty) and sell calls to all comers at a pay phone.

Your carrier's fraud division may catch this sort of abuse soon enough. Most cards have red-flag limits built into them and carriers will kill the card and, usually, call you and ask if you really did make $3,000 of calls to Bodega from pay phones in New York City.

The point is that most fraud can be detected early and corrected only by consistent analysis of monthly telecom billing.

Measurable

Simply applied, any proven statistics on money saved through careful review and management of billing should be enough of a justification to an employer for your time and effort. If you find a mistake and fix it, report on the

For the Toolbox
FIGURE 2-1   Building Your Telecom Book

Throughout this book, you will find forms, sheets, and guidance on how to collect and keep all the relavent information about your phone equipment and phone services in your telecom book. The System Inventory Worksheet, for example, provides places for vendor contact information (names, addresses, phone numbers), a physical inventory (counts of cabinets and cards and their capacities), and lists of how your system is actually programmed (phone extensions, voice mailboxes).

With these templates in mind, I offer these two principles of organization for your telecom book.

Organize and Separate your Telecom Book into Logical Sections

However you maintain the book (three-ring binder, simple spreadsheets, some kind of database), here is what I would include:

- **System inventory:** Use the form included in this book to inventory your phone system.

- **Phone service inventory:** Use the form included in this book to inventory your local phone service accounts.

- **Wireless services inventory:** Use the form in this book to inventory all wireless phones, pagers, personal digital assistants (PDAs), and whatever else wireless you are responsible for.

- **Calling cards inventory:** List the carriers, card numbers, access codes, billing rates, who the card is assigned to, and a guide on how to use them (for those who forget and need help).

- **Data circuits and services:** List every data service and circuit you have, what it is connected to, and what protocols and connections speeds it uses.

financial benefit to your company. If you correct a slamming incident (someone switches your long-distance telephone service without your permission), reduce your long-distance cost by switching to a new carrier, lower your local phone bill by reorganizing the features the phone company provides, and let someone know the dollars involved.

- **Data equipment inventory:** What equipment is required to meet the needs of your data services? Who services it and how do you contact them should you need help? What warranties or maintenance rules apply?

- **Vendor and carrier profiles:** List all telecommunications companies who serve you. Collect business cards, from everyone, salesperson to technician. Include in your profile section original contracts or agreements, product literature, and any written pricing information.

- **Trouble and communications logs:** Use the forms included in this book to log and track trouble with your telecom services and equipment. In case of future misunderstanding, you'll be able to hold your provider accountable when they promise solutions to problems.

- **Copies of relevant internal documents:** For good measure, keep a master copy of any document you've created that you may need access to without searching the bowels of your network; telecom services policy, wireless policy, trouble logs, and any request for proposal you write.

Keep and Manage Copies

You may find that the telecom book is a tool valuable to more than just you. If your business is larger than 50 employees, you may have a financial person who could make use of such a reference. You may also have a backup—another person who can help work through telecom issues in your absence or unavailability. The boss may also, for good safekeeping, want a back up of your telecom book.

Know who needs copies and why, so when you make changes that affect the information in the book, you can update all and avoid confusion by designating one as the master copy. Consider keeping a cover page on your master copy (to make notes on when and what changes were made).

All differences between a master and a designated copy are deferred to the master. This way, truly, you have one telecom book to worry about and provide copies to other people as a convenience.

2.4 Strategic Planning

The role of strategic planning of your telecommunications infrastructure comes into play in your business at many times during its life. When you're a start-up or a new enterprise, careful thought needs to be applied to any spending on telecom equipment and services. What is appropriate?

How many lines should you bring in? Do you need voice mail? A call center? What can you actually afford? There are many questions.

Later in your business life you may need to adjust for growth. If you pursue a certain type of client in the next year, for example, you must ask, "What is the impact in employee growth and facilities? What impact will the additional business have on back office operations, the accounting department, customer service, and technical support?"

You may also, at some point, be faced with the reality of shrinking your business. This could be for survival, reaction to changing and more productive ways of doing business, or the economics of outsourcing, which all are pressures that can change your environment.

As an effective telecom manager, your role in strategic planning is to deal with how business growth and change affects the telecom services and equipment you have in place. And we're talking about forethought beyond the basic project management of adding some equipment or replacing an old system. It is upon your shoulders to understand the needs of your business and the available, usable technology well enough to guide your business on the best direction to take.

Remember the effective telecom manager mission statement: *Leverage telecommunications technology and services to the greatest possible benefit and competitive advantage of the businesss — at the lowest cost.* At times, the best idea may be to sit down and map out a plan to move you to this ideal.

Be prepared to handle the following elements of this role.

Help Craft the Big Picture of How Telecom Aids Company Strategic Plans

If your company decides on a new marketing plan or wants to look at a new venture, the questions from the effective telecom manager have to take into consideration the ramifications to the telecom side of the business.

I met recently with a company about a new business venture it was interested in. At the time of the meeting, the company owned a chain of check-cashing stores that provided a liquid cash flow. They had seen television advertising of psychic hotlines and begun preliminary research into the business. It looked profitable. They knew that, because of the "telephone-centric" nature of the business, they needed a strategic plan that involved telecommunications. So we sat and talked about the size of the business, growth, desired customer experience, and penciled out some options of what telecom technologies and services might be necessary depending how they chose to operate the business.

Without this first look at such an important element of that business, they could not begin to assign budgets to the start-up. It also made them think through what they wanted telecom to accomplish for them, much in the way a business plan forces a company to think through who their customers are and how they will succeed in capturing them.

There is a process and science to strategic planning, but the true key to successful strategic planning is to first determine need. What is being asked of the telecommunications infrastructure?

Once a clear need has been established, strategic planning requires a research of the technology that will solve the problem posed or the need established.

I like to use models in strategic planning. Most businesses have a concept of what they want their infrastructure to bring them. Many know another business that does it the way they want to, or a group of businesses, each with elements of the ideal structure they'd like to place.

In lieu of models, I like to invite experts to examine a need and respond with proposals. These experts could be your existing telecom providers, outside vendor salespeople, friends of the business with the expertise, or consultants.

Consolidate and Centralize Services, Equipment, and Billing Wherever Possible

With the economics of business unstable, and change inevitable, you may occasionally find yourself in a place of chaos in telecommunications.

Effective telecom managers that have been with companies through mergers find they now are responsible for seven different phone systems and a multitude of carriers with vendors far and wide. To be able to execute the roles of the telecom manager, it is usually more effective to consolidate these operations than allow them to exist separately. Put similar phone systems in every branch office of your company. Use the same long-distance carrier on all your lines.

The obvious problem with this ideal, of course, is budget. Yours is not unlimited, I'm sure. If your company buys another system, I'm sure it would not be okay to write a check and send over a crew to install a phone system just like yours overnight to make it easier for you to manage. But when you can control it, consolidation has important benefits.

- **Purchasing power:** You will carry a bigger stick with those companies providing your phone services and equipment.

- **Support simplicity:** When you learn most of the common problems that can occur with your Lucent Difinity G3 switch in the Denver office, it will be simpler to answer questions and resolve issues with the similar switch in the Los Angeles office.

- **Inventory:** You will be able to stock spare telephone sets and cards for your phone system to minimize downtime in a failure. You can also have on hand extra pagers, cell phones, or headsets.

- **Combined service:** Consolidating providers—long distance and local, cellular and paging, equipment and services—reduces the numbers you need to dial for billing or service issues.

- **Consolidated billing:** Fewer providers means fewer bills to audit at the end of each billing cycle. It will be simpler to catch the statistical anomalies that lead you to mistakes and fraud. And those glaring problems (having been slammed, for example) will stand out like a guy in a Taekwando outfit in a catholic church during Sunday mass.

The same principle and benefits apply to single-location businesses: as much homogony as you can apply helps in exactly the same ways.

When building the telecom book, ask yourself whether services could be consolidated. Can the local and long distance come from one company? Can the Internet access be provided by your long-distance carrier? Does your PBX vendor have the capability to provide your data and networking hardware and support? Paging and cellular technology from one provider? Two-way radios and cellular?

With the nature of deregulation of much of the telecommunications business, it is more possible now than in the last twenty years to purchase multiple communications services and products from single-source providers. Seek them out if possible to make your job easier and leverage the economics of your telecom spending.

Please take this advice with a grain of salt, though. Just because your local phone company also can provide frame relay service doesn't mean they're the best solution for your business. Just because the guy who fixes broken phones on your Toshiba DK424 has taken a Cisco Certified Network Engineer course doesn't mean he is a competent network-router technician.

Each offer to consolidate must be taken in the context of how the company ranks with its competitors in *that* specific field. If McLeodUSA gives you local dial tone and long-distance service, and you now need digital subscriber line (DSL) Internet access, investigate their references and review their network claims and plans before proceeding. They must not be allowed to provide a substandard service at the cost of the convenience of having all products consolidated onto one bill.

Plan consolidation in every circumstance you can, but accept if you must, depending on the situation, end up with multiple providers.

Remain Forward-Looking Into Possibly Advantageous New Technology

The creation of computers opened up a new world for us all. Can you imagine performing the daily duties of your job with no computer there to help? Imagine processing transactions by paper, pulling information from customer files out of cabinets, or finding information on a company you'd like to do business with by actually visiting their office or mailing a request.

Indeed, if we were living during the infancy of telecommunications technology, I would have little to say. What I would say would be written longhand or on a manual typewriter. I would have to retype this manuscript for every edit change. A typesetter would laboriously place letters together on printing plates to form the words of this book. Compared with the word processor and the ability for this book to go from my computer to the printer, almost on a direct route, and be printed for you without much human effort, the precomputer way of doing things seems prehistoric.

Yet as far as we have come with computers and the software that allow us to harness their power, we have yet to explore every conceivable application of computers. There are new programs coming to market constantly. The new processors being made run faster, the memory storage is cheaper, and the whole device is smaller. Soon computers, with all the processing power of today's most expensive model, can be worn as an eyepiece that we can instruct with our voice or movement of our hands in thin air instead of keyboard and mouse; these are still-possible adaptations and growths of existing technology.

The same situation exists in the telephone world. Alexander Graham Bell is long dead, yet the developers and engineers of today are still exploring his basic principles. This investigation means innovation that may or may not bring you to one of the tenets of the effective telecom manager—the "competitive advantage of the business" slice of the mission statement pie.

Keep your eyes open for new developments; they can come any time. In fact, evidence to support this idea has come in recent memory.

The concept of a central office and a business telephone system passing information back and forth along the telephone line (as well as the voice signal itself) was not new. But the engineer who came up with direct inward dial (DID) should have been given instant, lifetime pension retirement if he chose it because of how valuable this adaptation has been to business.

It used to be that, if you had a large number of employees, routing all the incoming calls to the individuals the calls were destined for was the purveyance of the operator. In some businesses (say, more than one hundred employees), the task could be overwhelming to the operators and frustrating to the callers. Incoming callers knew who they were calling for, yet they had to wait to be processed by the front desk. To ease the burden, a company might have to employ additional help in the position.

Direct inward dialing service allows you to buy, from the phone company, a private phone number for some or all of your employees, without the cost and equipment overhead of a separate telephone line for every number.

Do you use DID service now? If your employees don't have direct relationships with customers, vendors, or suppliers, chances are DID wouldn't be for you. But so many of us would and do benefit from it. When the technology first arrived, it would have been a competitive advantage for you at the time, right?

More recently, prominent technology companies have taken their development down the avenue of merging voice and data networks. Internet protocol (IP) is the open language that computers use to communicate with each other through that great, public, worldwide network the Internet. Because it is the standard protocol, or communications language, for computers worldwide, many corporate local networks have adopted IP as their standard protocol as well.

Telecommunications companies have worked to allow telephone calls to be transmitted in this protocol language. This way, voice-over IP telephone devices and systems may use the same network infrastructure as the computers (internal-office LAN wiring, WAN circuits built for the computers between offices, or the Internet itself).

Properly applied, voice-over IP would allow you to use your multifunction business digital telephone set at home. You would plug it into your high-speed Internet connection (DSL, cable modem, dish-based broadband). The set would communicate to your business phone system via the Internet. You would work on the phone (making and receiving calls, accessing voice mail, talking via the intercom to your coworkers, etc.) as if you were in the office.

Does this and other new technology have implications for your business? If so, where can telecom managers find information on these innovations?

They have several ways.

- **Magazines:** In the appendixes to this book, you'll find a listing of magazines that speak to telecommunications. Some will be more appropriate to you than others. They are all listed here because I have subscribed to them at one time or another, or I feel they present a professional voice in one element of the industry. You'll be happy to know that many offer free annual subscriptions. I would recommend picking through the list and selecting a small handful instead of going for the gusto and getting everything—there is such a thing as too much information.

- **Organizations:** You'll also find a list of organizations that serve either the telecommunications industry or its users.

- **Events:** Many of the organizations and publications listed sponsor, or are peripherally involved in, events that might be helpful in keeping an effective telecom manager current. Some give seminars on various subjects. The annual conventions tend to focus on the high level of various hot telecom issues such as customer relationship management or computer telephone integration. Make careful choices on which to attend. If you are a telecom manager and not involved in telecom in some other way, there are plenty of opportunities to attend end-user and customer-focused shows. Don't be shy, one visit can give you more information about what the next year in telecom will bring.

- **Peers:** When someone in your rotary club buys a new phone system, ask about it. Get a tour if you can. Ask how they reached the decision they did. What alternative proposals did they have to choose from? What were the new bells and whistles the vendors were selling? What were their applications, their benefits, their costs?

- **Vendor relationships:** Your vendor salesperson will love to hear from you occasionally if he is a professional. Let your salesperson take you to lunch and tell you what's new. Ask about recent sales he or she has made and why the companies bought what they did. Ask him or her to be your resource for emerging and useful technologies. If the salesperson is competent and professional, and works in your best interest, you'll leverage a person who spends all of their working hours immersed in telecom and should be aware of the latest developments. They will also love you for the opportunity to offer you something new to buy.

Create a Master Employee Education and Fraud/Abuse Program

There is a love affair that happens when you buy a new telephone system. It starts with a courtship of a sales process. There are hundreds of small decisions and plans that need to be made. The decision to accept the proposal. Plans for the impending wedding day of the install.

Then comes the day of consummation, the day the project is finished, the system is turned on for the first time, the new service turned up.

To prepare you and your colleagues for a successful moment of consummation, the vendor should make it easier on you by giving training classes for your employees.

The class may be an hour or so for general users and longer for receptionists and the administrator. The vendor will normally go through how the phones work, what the options in voice mail are for, and answer any questions that may be making the employees nervous. All this helps the first day come off a little less hectic than it could (trust me) without the proper preparation.

But what about later, when a new employee comes along? We touched on this earlier. In most companies, an employee hired after the cutover is given no instruction on the telecommunications of the business. No information on how the technology is to be most effectively used. Nothing but casual guidance on the policies of the business for telecommunications services and systems use.

Most people are smart enough to figure out how to get by. Put a new employee in their office or cubicle on the first day and they will figure out the basics. In no time, the new employee will be making and taking calls, performing simple transfers or conferences, retrieving their voice mail, and so on.

But what about that conference bridge system you invested in? Or the other thirteen options in voice mail that cost you so much money? Or the optional features of the phone that you felt were important because of the productivity benefit, that are no more than a drain on the original investment if not used?

Take some basic steps to have an education plan and you'll solve future questions and problems from the telecom users in your company.

- **New-hire orientation:** Start with a telecom use policy. An initial document, included in the employee manual or as part of the sign-on paperwork, can clearly state how telecommunications is to be used in the interest of your business. You'll cover what's acceptable personal use of office telephones, rules covering cellular telephones, pagers, calling cards, and so on.

- **Take it a step further with an initial training session:** As a new employee comes on board, go through the basics with the person one on one. Show them how things work, what you've learned are the most efficient features, and how simple some of the seemingly more complicated features work. To help him or her be more productive and competitive in whatever it is they do for you, sell the technology you bought.

- **Tech times:** In my role as sales engineer for McLeodUSA, a competitive local telephone company and full-service telecommunications carrier, I was responsible for keeping the sales teams up to date on our advanced voice and data products and their application. They needed a well-rounded, real-world education in all aspects of telecommunications, beyond the specifics of the products we sold and serviced, to effectively serve their customers. This made them better salespeople.

    The methods McLeodUSA and our sales engineering group chose to deliver this information were manyfold. The company would develop product training. McLeodUSA hired an Internet-based training company to offer modules on telecommunications technology to our people. Salespeople were flown to one of our corporate training centers occasionally. Or a training team was sent on the road to tour the company and educate in the field.

The sales engineers also taught weekly minisessions called "tech times." Each branch office scheduled a routine time and day for consistency sake. We developed a curriculum based on hot issues of the time or what needed to be reinforced, and held an informal lesson or question-and-answer session. Because the meetings were regular and consistent, and because they gave salespeople a known place to have a dialogue with a technical person who was "on their side," the meetings were productive. You could adopt a similar idea. You could set aside a working lunch once a month to give information and field questions from the employees about the state of your telecom infrastructure. You could offer these sessions as a way for the real people of the company to let you know which services you provide them does and does not work. You could use this time as a way of learning new ideas and uses for telecommunications. It could be a viable way to hear what your customers are telling your people about their calling experience.

- **Share problems, when solved, with everyone:** Our most wasted resource is experience. Have you ever had to deal with the same issue twice? Some phone system features, such as conference calling, notoriously give "normal" human beings trouble.

  Once in a while, maybe even regularly, let everyone know about the major or common issues you've dealt with in your role as telecom manager. Give extra training on conference calling if three people come to you for help in the same week. Let everyone know there are more voice mail options keys than save and delete. If you find yourself slammed by a long-distance company and discover that the guilty carrier misrepresented itself to one of your employees, getting them to accept the switch without authority, share the experience with everyone as a way to prevent a recurrence.

Such communications could be about purely positive items as well. Use the opportunity to inform people of changes in carrier or the pending installation of new systems. Let everyone know about improvements on the menu options in voice mail that's happening next month and the transition will go smoother.

Email works great for this, as does the all-mailbox distribution feature of many voice mail systems. If no such options exist for your business, the old paper memo awaits resurrection. Either way, communicating common problems, misunderstandings, and their resolutions could solve many of your future user problems.

- **Intranet:** If your company has an internal network and uses Web-browser technology to give access to company information via an intranet, abscond a corner of it for telecom. Create a master information section with user guides and reference documents. Post your trouble-ticket email link. As you solve problems and create new solutions for the business over the years, file the information (frequently-asked-question style if that works for you) so a self-determined user might help themselves out of a jam without necessarily coming to you for every little thing.

The Purchase Process:
A Framework for
Negotiating a New Deal
No Matter the Product
or Service

3.1 The Purchase Process

During my career in telecom I have assisted companies in
the planning and purchase of both telecommunications
equipment and services. In each instance, I found myself
covering similar ground to get the job done—following a
pattern, invoking similar principles and processes to
achieve the goal of getting the best overall value.

The common elements of these purchases became so defined that I began to use an outline when asked for advice on ways to get the best deal on telecom.

Whatever the impending event that triggers your reaching out for a new product or supplier (a move, growth, dissatisfaction with a current provider, simple, bottom-line–driven growth), this outline can help you work through it.

Granted, you'll be dealing with different types of companies and different types of equipment and services depending on what telecom you're buying. But there are enough commonalities that we can begin with the outline of a global purchase process.

3.2 Defining Your Need

Later in this book, you will have your hands firmly around all aspects of telecommunications infrastructure in play on behalf of your business. It will then be time to turn your mind to the question of whether they are the right services to have in play.

The journey of effective telecom management will take you from discovery and learning through analysis to a logical conclusion: What do you need to change about your (local, long-distance, phone system, wireless service, Internet access, wide-area data network), if anything, to achieve the following: "Leverage telecommunications technology and services to the greatest possible benefit and competitive advantage of the business—at the lowest possible cost."

The motivation for our answer may be purely financial (Can I save money, now or in the long term, by making changes?). Money is the simplest of motivations to find. In fact, I don't care what your situation is today, if you've had what you've had for more than six months, you can probably reduce your ongoing telecommunications spending by at least 10%.

But we must look beyond cost as well. There are always tempting new offers to lower this or that rate. But with every new offer comes risk. The risk is that the offer is not what it seems and will not bear the financial fruit promised. The risk is that the transition will harm your business' ability to communicate for some time, which can be devastating in even the smallest increment. There is the risk of financial penalties or a protracted fight to remove the new service if it fails to serve your needs. There is, in this modern business age, the real risk that a fly-by-night carrier or vendor could have flown by the next night they begin to serve you.

When you wish to make a change, take the following steps.

Establishing Basic Service Levels

You must first make clear to your potential vendors or carriers what you wish to accomplish. You must set a bar for your vendors to reach. What services do you wish to buy? How do you want them to work? How do you expect to be serviced? You want to weave in the financial motive here: how much money saved (in hard dollars or a percentage of spending) will be enough to risk the change? How will those savings need to be presented to make you feel secure about their validity?

There are a lot of questions to ask, aren't there?

Judge possible improvements by the merit of their application. For example: a toll-free telephone number allows callers outside your local calling area to reach your business at no cost to them. It could promote long-distance customers to do business with you. Is that valuable to your business? Are long-distance customers desirable to you?

Direct inward dial (DID) telephone service would allow you to assign private inbound phone numbers to your employees. This would allow customers to call directly to the people in your company they deal with. This would foster more direct communications between your employees and those they serve. Is this application valuable to your business?

Solicit Feedback from Your Company

I have seen installation projects in larger businesses go badly because the people most affected by the change, the frontline workers who used the phones every day to do their jobs, were not involved in the decision to change. They therefore second-guessed the telecom manager. A mood was created so that, no matter what improvements came with the change, a few sour mouths made sure they talked down the project every chance they got. Every minor, inevitable installation glitch that occurred became justification for their fears and voiced oppositions.

Asking the opinion of those people actually using the services will not only provide an insight more valuable than any book can give, but also establish buy-in at every level.

This approach worked like a charm at Carpenter Publishing in Seattle, Washington. Judy hired a telecom consultant to help identify improvements that could be made in the way their company communicated with the world.

Carpenter had a book publishing division. They also published a weekly newspaper. This meant that they operated two sales divisions, two editorial departments, accounts payable and receivable, shipping and receiving, classified advertising, print buyers, as well as numerous support staff. Telecommunications services needs varied widely.

With her consultant, Judy drafted a questionnaire to issue to their 105 employees, asking what they liked about the telephone service today, what they didn't like, and what they would change if they could.

Of the 105 employees to receive the form, only 30 or so gave feedback. Some of what she heard had to be discounted as unattainable or pure complaint or a request for a service so wild it couldn't be justified financially.

The meat of the responses helped her greatly. From it, she understood that she needed to invest in DID service, simplify the long-distance codes they had instituted on the lines to help track calls back to the department responsible, and provide a way for employees to check voice mail while away from the office without going through the receptionist.

As she developed her basic service document for the carriers and vendors to propose their solutions, she was able to nail down a specific application she needed. The result would be companywide acceptance and a more successful implementation of new services.

Another way to gather raw ideas and data for your basic service document is to find a model. Is there a company you call on a regular basis that seems to have telecom in a way you would like it? Do you like what you hear when you are on hold? Are you handled well when retrieved from hold? Does the company handle its phone calls in a way you want to emulate? Do you like what the toll-free number does when you call it? Is the way the telephone calls are handled after hours by the voice mail system or answering service unique, creative, and a benefit to those who call the business?

Ask what equipment, services, or carriers that company uses. Now, of the applications you have discovered and desire, can some be taken care of with the equipment and services (albeit with some minor change or enhancement) you currently use? Maybe even more than you might think.

Here are examples: the ability to transfer calls out of the office to cell phones in the field so callers do not have to hang up and dial a second number could be valuable to your field employees. Instead of upgrading or reprogramming your entire telephone system, the application could be accomplished by adding a simple call-transfer feature on your standard telephone service.

Traveling employees want a simple way to call back to the office when on the road. Ditch the cumbersome calling cards and add a toll-free number to your long-distance service just for employees to use when traveling.

The president of your company may want to hold sales meetings by telephone with all your agents throughout the country but is limited by a telephone system that only connects to three outside lines. Use your long-distance carrier's conferencing service and solve the problem. Here's one last example: I met with the information technology (IT) and telecom manager of a homebuilder last week who was responsible for, besides the corporate headquarters, forty-three in-community sales and service offices.

The field offices wanted parity with corporate in regard to telecom—the same telephones, features, and voice mail access. After investigation, it was determined that the phone system at corporate had a solution that, when phones were connected to the main phone system via a frame-relay data network or by using a virtual-private network through high-speed Internet lines, employees could act as direct extensions. The remote users would be able to have calls transferred to them by the corporate receptionist. They would be able to dial other employees by extension number across the network. Remotes would also have full voice mail service off the corporate voice mail system.

Transfer calls, access to voice mail, simplified calling between offices. That was the application. We set about putting a price tag on it.

To make a good decision, we needed a comparative benchmark. Because the transferring of calls to a remote telephone can be handled with a three dollars per line feature from the phone company, voice mail could be accessed today through standard telephone lines, and interoffice calls would only be three-digits longer without this new system. Most of the application could be accomplished, of course not so sexily, with little change to the existing set up and relatively low cost.

So the question was this: was the ease and convenience this voice over IP system, and the fact that remotes would have fancy, PBX phones, worth $5,700 per location in upfront equipment costs and $221 per month for the frame-relay network?

The point is, that when you come up with the desired application, see if it can be accomplished with or without a major upgrade, with the existing infrastructure. Only when you understand the answer to that question is it time to ask vendors and carriers to submit proposals for the purchase of their new products and services.

3.3 The Request for Proposal

Have you ever been involved in a government purchase of anything? If you have, you'll know that, usually by legislative mandate, government purchases above a certain dollar amount must go out to public bid. To protect the public's interest, to make sure that competition is level and they get exactly what they want, government purchasing agents draw up a thick, technical, and ripely legal document called a *Request for Proposal* or *Request for Quote.*

To avoid major mistakes when buying telecom products and services, you need to communicate your needs as clearly to vendors and carriers as might a government purchasing agent. For your purposes though, create something more informal, albeit as productive. Write, in your own voice, a document that clearly outlines the following:

- **Existing environment:** Your proposers may want to understand your current environment. It will not hurt to share this information, either from your telecom book or by providing copies of bills from carriers and vendors for them to gather their own answers.

- **Applications:** Outline what you want to accomplish in the terms of how you want things to work, not what you want to buy.

  This is the same common logic that needs to be inferred when taking a vehicle to the mechanic. Too many times, we think we know what the problem is and present the mechanic with an order to fix it. Wouldn't you be upset if the problem you brought your car in to fix recurs and your mechanic says, "Well, that was something else all together."

  You want your telecom vendor to be creative. They need to apply some engineering logic to your application and figure out the smartest, most elegant, and most cost-effective way to solve the problem you are presenting. A vendor or carrier that is way off the mark will not deserve your business. One who takes the time to understand the need as you have outlined it and brings you a proposal that meets that need is a gem to be polished and saved for future days.

- **Cost expectations:** If one goal of the solicitation of proposals is to save money, be specific about it. Don't tell everyone you want to save money; instruct them that you want a 20 percent decrease in net spending on telecom. Say you need to bring your local and long-distance budgets under $1,000 per month and see how they respond. Expect your new phone system to shorten phone calls by 10 percent and your new wireless plan to reduce aggregated per-minute costs by 30 percent.

  Because, contrary to what they would like us to believe, the business of providing telecom goods and services is profitable. There is margin to dabble with. Set a low bar and you might be surprised to find a company willing to limbo down there with you.

  Beware the potential backfire though. Ask for a ridiculous goal (I want one cent per minute long distance when the market is priced at six cents) and you might chase away good proposers.

- **Format guidelines of response:** It is simpler to compare proposals if you can control their format. Ask for per-unit pricing on equipment. Ask for local and long-distance pricing separately. Ask for a breakdown of all fees and taxes so you can be sure everyone charges the same. Know what the price is to buy extra telephone sets before and immediately after your install. If current spending is formatted a certain way in your bookkeeping program or telecom book, be sure you receive a proposal broken into the same elements to make your side-by-side comparison that much faster.

- **Contact rules:** Limit or control your vendor or carrier's access to your company. This is as much about managing the project as pure control. With everyone in your business clear on the concept that all telecom issues come through one place (as stated in our four roles of the telecom manager), your vendors should understand the same. Give them the names and numbers of anyone you want them to speak with beside yourself.

  Outline how the decision is going to be made and by whom within your company with clear rules on whether or not contact with the ultimate decision maker is allowed. If this happens to be you, this becomes an easy task.

  On the subject of decision makers; if you have a president or CEO who will give a final nod based on your recommendation, get it all straight before going through the process. It can prevent a considerable waste of time and back-end pain for you.

  As a salesperson, I recall times I received an uncomfortable call from telecom managers. On one in particular, we had worked closely together on the proposal. The relationship was good. We focused on the application and worked the right solution. The telecom manager had bought into my company as the right source for his need. He liked the budget. He loved the solution and told me I had earned his recommendation.

  When he finally called, he started by saying how embarrassed he was to make this call, but the owner of the company had decided on someone else. "Was it something I did?" I would ask not-so-naively. "No," he would explain. "Turns out Bob (the owner) golfs with a guy from AT&T every Saturday and he said your company is bad and we're to go with them no matter the cost difference." Ouch!

You sometimes don't have the control you would like. If the ultimate choice is not to be yours, let your bidders know. But be clear on whether they may contact him or her directly.

- **Time frames:** Does a natural time element to your request for proposal exist? For example, is the new phone system necessary to facilitate a move of the business or a renovation of the office? Do you need a new wireless plan to accommodate the eleven new employees coming on board over the next three months?

    If there is an impending event on the horizon, pay close attention to time frames and give guidelines on when you want responses and deliverables from your vendors. For example, if a term contract with a local phone service carrier is to expire in October, you need to have chosen to renew or replace by September to coordinate properly; be sure to allow for installation and setup times for new services if necessary and time to renegotiate rates with the old carrier if simply renewing. That means you should see proposals the second week in August. Which, in turn, means your request must go out at the beginning of August. Needs analysis and preparation of this document in July. Full audit of services (if you're not yet current with a telecom book) in late June, early July.

    If there is no imminent, natural deadline, impose one so the process doesn't drag on forever and bind the resource that is your valuable time.

- **Reserve the right to not accept any of the proposals:** Salespeople are under constant questioning from their bosses on what is the likelihood of signing you and when and so on. If it is clear from moment one that you are only taking ideas and suggestions, not obligating yourself to any one company for any service or system, you should head off any misunderstanding. Thwart that with clear and early expectations that a decision will be made at your convenience and in your best interest.

 ## Selecting a Provider

Let's now take your Request for Proposals to the marketplace.

The Relationships with Your Vendor or Carrier

When purchasing telecom, there are two basic stages of relationship with your proposers that are important to your decision. Both are vital for different reasons.

First, you have a relationship with a salesperson. You have to trust that your salesperson is competent in his products and experienced with the type of technology you're looking to purchase. In deciding to propose to satisfy your need, the salesperson may be faced with making numerous, subjective decisions on your behalf. The salesperson must also be able to put himself into your business, with you in mind, and make the right choices of what to propose.

Salespeople only lead the charge, though. No matter how good they are, unless they own the business, they are merely representatives for the company that will be serving this critical component of your business. Interview salespeople as you would a prospective employee. Find out their history, their experience. Ask for personal sales references—customers who were happy specifically with the salesperson who served them.

Second, you will have an ongoing service relationship with the carrier. These are the folks who deliver and support the service sold. Technicians and order writers. Data entry and billing associates. Customer support agents.

Is there a way to know how this company performs on the back end? How does the customer service group respond to calls with problems? What are the time intervals for turn-up of new services? What about the time intervals for changes to your new phone system programming down the line?

All that's left is to quantify the claims uncovered in your investigation. Can these promises be demonstrated or guaranteed? Is there a customer-satisfaction report available on the dealer? How about reference letters? Can you speak with some of their older customers? Can you preview the service agreement and the company's policies on response times and rates for business change orders or technician time?

Let's take a look inside the world of the telecom salesperson, a world that will seem extremely familiar to those of you who have ever been in outside sales. As an exercise, I hope this allows you to identify the process you are going through with the salespeople you are working with and maybe use some of these situations to your business' advantage.

Prospecting

Primarily, in my role as a salesperson, on any given day, my job is to find new opportunities to sell telecommunications equipment or services. Sometimes, these opportunities come to me in the form of referrals: customers told someone they knew about me or my company, the woman I bought my house from told her brother, who is starting a new business, to call me to help set up his lines. Sometimes existing customers call for help in working up a move or expansion. It could also be that I find a listing in the newspaper for an expansion of a business, or call on an old lead for a company I knew was moving to see if I could help plan their move from a telecom perspective.

Most of the time though, the new opportunity comes from cold-calling; walking into a business I've never seen before and asking to speak with a decision maker for telecom. It is mostly a fishing trip. I sometimes do the same thing over the phone.

I know that 95 percent of the people I approach are not going to be interested in a proposal from me. My job isn't to make the 95 percent buy something they don't need; it is to find the 5 percent that are interested.

Knowing telecommunications salespeople find opportunity this way means you have probably had a knock or two on your door from one of us. The unannounced visit can be an imposition. But I hope you held onto their business card in a file. It will save you time when you need to find companies to propose to you.

Qualification

After confronted with an opportunity, defined as a prospect, my job is to then figure out how likely or legitimate it is.

Qualification means that a salesperson, as delicately as he can, is attempting to determine if you have a need, are qualified to make the decision, and have the money to buy what he sells.

Qualification means determining the exact need. A good salesperson asks a lot of questions about what you want to accomplish. What are your goals? What improvements are you looking to make? What kind of management reporting are you expecting? The salesperson will also want you to quantify the savings you need so he has a target to reach before coming back to you with a proposal.

A good salesperson does a lot of listening in a qualification, or needs-analysis meeting. A bad salesperson does a lot of telling you what they and their company can do for you.

Presentation

If the salesperson has listened well to your needs and has a deep understanding of the technology and products they represent, you should see a presentation that shows exactly what you should consider buying. If you asked for enhanced toll-free service and get a proposal for calling cards, the salesperson did not do a good job.

Presentation meetings allow you to gain visceral understanding if the salesperson is comfortable with what they are proposing. In my opinion, confidence is a big seller. A salesperson who claims he is the greatest salesperson ever is one who should be investigated for substance abuse. A salesperson that looks you squarely in the eye and tells you that he believes he is presenting the absolute right product to serve the needs of your business and has no doubts about his company's ability to deliver could inspire you to decide his way.

The presentation process is overly emphasized by some salespeople, meaning too much time and energy is spent on this part alone. A good presentation is vital to success in sales, but if your entire relationship with a salesperson is in a presentation meeting, then many important steps are being missed on the way to making a wise and informed decision.

Overcoming Objections

This is where the hard-core selling occurs. You have given the salesperson all the application and technical information needed to design a solution for you. They have gone over it with their manager and technical staff and whoever else to be sure they are doing the absolutely right thing for you. You have seen a spectacular "dog and pony" show. And now it's time for yes or no. But you say you have to look at one more competitor. Maybe you're finding that the price seems high or you're not sure you need this or that piece of the overall proposal. It could be that you need your partner to look at it with you. Or you're concerned about a negative reference one of the carrier's customers gave you. Or, in keeping with today's world, you're concerned that the carrier seems headed for bankruptcy.

The salesperson is now looking for reasons why you cannot commit to the proposal and buy right now. Some of the reasons are objections, and every one the salesperson hears must be answered satisfactorily to move the sale forward.

Sometimes, the answer the salesperson gives will not be enough to overcome the objection, and your sale goes to a competitor. I can never begrudge a customer for that. If I have done my job and educated the customer to my proposal, my company, and my own capabilities, and they find something within the package that they are not as comfortable with as with another vendor, who can be mad at that? Salespeople know they cannot win every opportunity.

Sometimes, a salesperson will hit a *condition* that halts the sale. A condition is an objection out of the hands of both parties. Usually, this means that the customer has a previously undisclosed financial penalty from an old carrier or a punitive contract to honor. Occasionally, this means the customer, not the final decision maker they appeared to be, has received a no from above.

Closing

Closing is such a battered word. In sales talk, closing has traditionally meant the point at which you fight a yes out of the customer. Salespeople have been told to pull out the 500-page sales books on closing techniques and keep at it until the customer said no twenty times or thrown them off the property. This antiquated approach to sales is so recognizable and amateur that it shouldn't be given the dignity of playing along. If a customer is not ready to say yes, it is because they have a question still unanswered, a point not fully understood, or a true objection yet to be resolved.

If the previous steps in the selling process are done professionally, closing is nothing more than the natural conclusion of things: signing the service agreement, establishing the turn-up date, and completing the customer information form.

Thus the selling process is an understandable system of flowing from initial contact through closing of the sale, with definable milestones in between.

Let's take this to the next step; put yourself back on the telecom manager side of the desk, and recommend a course of action that deflates the advantages the science of selling gives salespeople. Doing so will give you checks to measure the qualifications of the proposing carriers, and tips to maximize the experience of purchasing telecommunications to your company's advantage.

Prospecting

Just as a salesperson goes on a fishing expedition for prospective customers who may be ripe to purchase what they sell, you should look to assemble a pool of potential vendors to propose solutions to your need. Don't reach out to more than five to ten; we're looking to eventually narrow the field to three or four real potential vendors, to create a competitive environment, and be assured we are seeing the best the open market has to offer.

Start with your current carrier or vendor if you're happy with them but let the carrier know you are going to solicit a couple of competitive proposals.

Remember when we said to find an example, in another business, of how you want your system to work? If you are using a model, call in that company's vendor as well. Then go to the open market using referrals from friends or, because you've been saving them, the business cards from salespeople who came calling during the past year.

Qualification/Needs Analysis

Interview candidate salespeople just as you would prospective new employees. Ask for their "resume" of experience (knowing that the most experienced in terms of years are not always the reps who have the deepest understanding of the technology they sell). Learn a little about the company they work for. How long have they been in business? How many customers do they serve? How deep is their product line?

Bring the candidates you feel best about into your office. Inform them that this is an exploratory session only. During the meeting, be open with their questions. Show them your existing telephone system. Share with them your history with your current carrier, your list of current services and long distance spending and what you like and don't like about the service you get. Ask for their preliminary opinions on your requirements.

Look for the salesperson who asks good questions, who seems to grasp the technology, and who demonstrates experience and confidence in their ability to provide you with the solution you're after.

Invite the top three or four back to present you with their solution.

Presentation

The sales presentation is when you begin crafting those questions you will need to have answered before you are sure this is the right system or service for you. Is the price what you expected? Does it include everything on the proposal or are there other service charges, taxes, or fees you need to understand to make a good decision? Is this a company you're comfortable having a long-term business relationship with?

After each presentation, even the last, say that you will get back to the salesperson because you have a couple more proposals to look at.

Objections

It's now time to get serious about just two of the proposals (if you have that many that are right for you). Cover all the outstanding issues from your presentation meetings. Ask each vendor or carrier to match attractive features and services proposed to you by others. Ask if there are any additional promotions that you could take advantage of. Ask to see an installed, working system at a customer's site.

When you have two solid proposals, even if you have settled on one as the more perfect or more affordable of the two, you might consider telling the vendor that you have a competitive offer that you are also considering and ask for him to come back with the absolute best price and package. Although your best choice may already be cheaper, this will usually force the salesperson to go to a manager and come up with some kind of concession for you.

Close

At the closing, go through the paperwork carefully. Ask to have everything explained so you are satisfied with it. Confirm that the price includes everything. Confirm the terms. Confirm the timeline of the proposed turn up. Verify that you both agree on the follow-up schedule for any post-installation work—routine maintenance of prescheduled upgrades and so on. Confirm what your responsibilities are in the turn up. Leave no detail unanswered.

In fact, require this checklist in writing. It will be a valuable tool to ensure completion of the proposed system.

When you have made a final choice, do me a personal favor, please. It takes a special quality to be a successful salesperson of telecommunications systems and services. If a salesperson has listened well to your application, has designed the right solution using the technology that will best serve you and your business; if the salesperson has justified the expense to you and fought for the best possible price and terms from his company, and put your needs before his or hers at every step, reward that salesperson for his effort. Send a thank you letter to his boss. Refer the salesperson to someone else that he may help.

3.5 Managing Change Successfully

Cutover is the term for that moment when your old way of doing things ends and your new system or service is fired up for the first time. Cutovers need to happen in a way that does not disrupt the course of a business day.

In equipment-related projects, cutover is the last step of the installation and comes only after the system is mounted and powered up, after the programming has been keyed in, after your people are prepared for the change through training, and after the phones (if this is a phone-system install) are unpacked and set out on everyone's desks. The term literally refers to *cut*ting the telephone lines from the old system and moving them *over* to the new.

In the carrier world, the same project management dynamics apply; controlled move from one service to another, predictable timeline, and minor impact on the day-to-day operation of the business.

Small cutovers can be completed during the business day. More complicated installations take time and are best done after hours.

Properly organized, installs cutover smoothly. This should be the goal of any vendor or carrier; to prepare and preplan the change so well as to have the cutover be a mere formality. And though most are sensitive to the business reality that work cannot be completely halted for the installation of equipment, there are some things you can do to ensure that your cutover will run as smoothly as time and experience will allow.

Do Your Part

Leave no possible blame on you for not having completed some task you were responsible for. If you were supposed to have an extra electrical outlet installed for the new system, be sure it gets done early. If you were supposed to come up with a call flow for the interactive voice-response (IVR) systems, finish it. If you were supposed to call the local exchange carrier (LEC) and order the removal of your PICC Freeze, do so. If the vendor needs an employee list to program your telephone extensions, get it to him sooner than he expects.

Set the tone under which you want the project to go and you will avoid problems later. Be the customer that's easy to work with, that's involved, and you'll get the better end of your new supplier's attention.

Keep the Timeline

It's okay to stay in constant communication with the carrier or vendor about how they're progressing along the installation checklist. (You took the time to get a project timeline from the vendor, right—the list of items that need to be accomplished, their order relevant to each other, and the approximate date for the completion of each?)

If you have a diplomatic way of approaching it, stay on top of the timeline with the installers and, if they're slipping, ask if there's any way to help move it along faster.

The things that typically make projects late are either avoidable (laziness, procrastination, or technicians pulled away from your install because of another customer) or unavoidable (parts that haven't been delivered to the vendor yet). You want to know about these things as they are happening, not on the day you expect the system to be up and running.

Be Serious About Training

Training on the system or technology you have bought is an obligation the vendor has in fulfilling the purchase and a responsibility that too many vendors allow to slip. It is vital to have some end-user training. It will be tough to take full advantage of your new investment if, on the day of cutover, your people are just learning it; dropping calls, upsetting customers, and losing business. See that you schedule your people to attend training (including and especially yourself).

Being serious about training also can mean watching the installers and talking to them about the work they are doing. Maybe some of the phone system programming is simple enough that, with support documentation, you can learn to be self-sufficient. Setting up new employees in your voice mail system or being able to move a telephone extension yourself can save your company $100 or more per call in service charges. If it doesn't take a degree to learn, wouldn't it be great to build your own voice mail trees, program a new call accounting report, add email accounts with an online management tool, or reroute a DID extension so that calls to an employee who has left the company can ring to someone else's desk?

Know When to Cry Wolf

I call this tactic strategic whining. And, in fear of sounding braggadocio, I am somewhat of a master at this.

I'll give you the biggest tip you'll need in dealing with the postsales relationships with your vendor and carrier: they are a completely reactive business enterprise. Salespeople do their best to schedule their resources, but, on any given day, it is the real or *perceived* emergency that gets the most attention.

Use this knowledge without abuse to ensure your cutover goes as planned. Knowing when to go above the head of the person you are dealing with and how to state your case dramatically is an art. You cannot use anger and intimidation. You shouldn't allow your business to be assumed, either. It must be earned. If your timeline is slipping unreasonably, if your training class has been cancelled without being rescheduled, if you receive an invoice for work that should have been included as part of the installation, run your concern up the chain of command. Be reasonable, but be unrelenting. Tell them, "I expected it to happen this way and no one has told me anything is different so I expect your people here today." Be angry in a calm way. Use expressed disappointment as a tool. You have taken great pains to make the right choice and to set the groundwork of what you should and do expect from your vendor. Hold them to their proposal.

Tell Your Customers

Have you ever called a place of business, asked for the party you are calling only to be told something such as, "I'm going to try and transfer you but if I disconnect you, call back at the following number" or "We just installed a new system so bear with me . . ."

Your customers have a preconception on how their call will be handled. Anything that strays from that preconception is going to arouse in them an impression; one that could be good or bad.

If there is any chance your callers could be affected negatively by the change, send your biggest callers a postcard saying that you've invested in upgrades to help serve them better and they should soon see a change. Describe for them, simply, what the change may be, how they may be affected, and how their experience may be affected. Include the notice with your billing statements or record a notice into the preamble on your Automated Attendant. Or simply mention the changes to them when they call you.

Just say something.

4

Local and Long-Distance Telephone Service

 Why Are There so Many Sales Calls from Telecom Companies?

The most common daily task for the salesperson, regardless of the differences in market, product sold, or status as a junior or senior representative is the need to cold call. Many times this means walking into a business salespeople have no prior relationship with and attempting to start one.

Some salespeople take to cold calling like seven-year-old boys to Pokemon on the Nintendo Gameboy. For others, it can be the single most intimidating aspect of the job.

When time is of the essence or a prospect database is geographically dispersed, cold calling becomes a purveyance of the telephone. You have thirty seconds to make an introduction, appeal to the prospect with a major business benefit, and try to secure the next stop in the sales process, the appointment.

You may cold call in your line of work. There are businesses whose sole means of soliciting and handling business is by telephone. Some have even elevated the science of telemarketing to a fine art through the use of enterprise and technology.

Yet, every art has a dark application. There are some who have applied it in ways that enrage the average prospect. An example of this is calls from automated systems telling you to hold on for some sweet offer or prize you have won. Most times, the script the representative is reading doesn't give her a breath pause and therefore prevents the listener from chiming in with a rejection until she has made it through the first fifty-five seconds. (To speak without breathing for a minute at a time must take special breath training.)

The script is not the same month to month. Sometimes it is "We'd like to offer you our great cellular service." The next month it may be "When you sign up for our service we'll send you two phones."

For example, I get cold-called by Qwest Cellular once a month. The latest call from Qwest Cellular started out with, "Sir, we will be sending you in the mail a cellular telephone and . . . ." All without giving me the dignity of actually saying yes to anything.

It almost breaks my spirit to have to end the call from Qwest the same way every time. Usually, I wait until they're finished. Sometimes, if I don't have time to wait, I have to burst in and put a stop to the call. "I am already a customer of yours. I've had a Qwest cellular phone for more than two years and I'm very happy with it."

"Oh. Well, thank you for your time, sir."

"Until next month," is all I can say because, although I've asked time and again to be removed from the call list, I still receive calls.

Sometimes telemarketing calls are frustrating but they can also be effective. Telemarketing is one of the most cost-effective and productive ways to sell. Properly used, the concept and the technology created to execute it have been a productivity boon for credit card companies, mortgage brokers, fund raisers, collection agencies, and—an industry the practice is almost synonymous with—telecommunications companies.

This brings up the question: Why are there so many choices of local and long-distance telephone companies? To answer requires a bit of a history lesson.

The deluge of offers for new and cheap telephone services is the benefit of government interventions that have freed the telecommunications market over the past two decades. The telecommunications business used to be a heavily regulated government monopoly. Today, any company with resource and will is allowed to fish for your business. I would argue with anyone that the result has been positive, regardless of the headaches and hassles open competition seems to have brought with it.

The public telephone network, with spiderlike runs of wires and cables that interconnect almost every home and business in the country, began as the Bell Telephone network, a public utility and a regulated monopoly. The thought was, with a guarantee of monopoly status, this enterprise would surely provide access to all. If you lived in a hard-to-wire location miles away from the center of town, with a tough road up to your residence, the cost to bring wires to you would be offset, within this one enterprise, by the cheap-to-equip, high-density locations such as business districts and city centers.

The government would regulate pricing of the services purchased to be sure this monopoly could balance its profit against the public good of the services provided.

The phone company then, as now, had two major and one minor business that produced revenue. You paid for your connection to the public network—the monthly phone bill for your line. You then paid a metered (per minute) rate for calls that were connected for you along interstate telephone lines for local and long-distance service. As a more minor enterprise, Bell also provided the telephone equipment you needed to take advantage of the network.

By the 1970s, the network itself was nearly finished. There weren't many areas in the country not reached by telephone.

Then an innovation happened. By taking advantage of their rights of way, railroad and oil pipeline companies began to lay fiber-optic telephone lines in the ground to create networks that could be used to carry long-distance telephone and computer network traffic. The availability of non–Bell-owned networks allowed competitors to begin showing up.

As early as 1969, an upstart company built microwave radio towers to transmit telephone calls between cities. Microwave Communi-cations, Inc. (MCI), competed directly against the Bell system for its long-distance business.

But the Bell Telephone company used some creative and apparently illegal methods to prevent competitors from taking away business. In some cases they told customers that a telephone connection from anyone but the Bell company to any equipment a business had from the phone company would cause the whole public telephone network to crash.

Access between customers and these competitors was the wall erected to stifle competition. The phone company could use its ownership and control of the local telephone networks to block competitors from the long-distance business.

This became the foundational argument for the Divestiture Act of 1983. In it, an antitrust judge, based on the Sherman antitrust laws, ruled that the Bell Telephone network had to be broken into separate companies. Regional boundaries (called *local access transport areas* or *LATAs*) were drawn. The local side of the telephone company's business was broken into 12 pieces and became the *Baby Bells* (*regional Bell operating companies* [RBOCs]— Southwestern Bell, Bell Atlantic, Pacific Bell). They were still granted public utility status and maintained the privilege of limited monopolies on their markets. But they could provide services and operate only within the borders of the LATAs they were assigned by the Federal Communications Commission (FCC).

Calls placed between LATAs became the province of the last portion of the original Bell system—American Telephone and Telegraph (AT&T). It was then ruled that the Baby Bells had to give equal access between their customers and long-distance companies, including AT&T.

The floodgates opened for competitors in the long-distance market and brought overwhelming choices; more than 300 companies directly providing access to a long-distance telephone network.

Not coincidentally, a typical long-distance telephone call today costs a mere fraction of what it cost businesses and private individuals before the divestiture.

In 1996, Congress sat down again and drafted the Telecom Reform Act. Its goal was to remove the barriers to competitors who wanted in on the local telephone business. There are businesses and individuals who think there is money to be made by taking over the local telephone bill. All those billions of dollars a month spent on phone lines. And the second line for the kids. And the line that is in to get on the Internet and not have to give up the main telephone line. Whoops, almost forgot the line that feeds the pager. Even car cell phones require a physical connection from the radio cell site it's currently communicating with to the public telephone network.

Local phone companies, not desperate to share their customer base, afraid they would spend billions of dollars putting wires in the ground only to have the investment lost to competitors, blocked the road to the phones in your home.

Stop, the RBOCs said. All these "wanna-be" local phone companies were free to compete in that cash cow, the long-distance business. But the original Baby Bells were prevented because the rules of divestiture limited them to LATAs.

So, a deal was cut. If the local phone companies allowed competitors access to the local phone-wiring networks they had built to resell and reuse the existing infrastructure to provide competitive, local phone services, the FCC would allow the RBOCs to compete in the long-distance business.

The result is that you may already be seeing competitive local phone companies vying for your business.

What all this upheaval means to you is lower costs for telephone services and faster availability of new products.

In the world of the effective telecom manager, this means choice and competitive leverage in negotiating favorable pricing and results in times of trouble.

Making new choices could mean innovation and savings for your business. By reviewing your local and long-distance spending annually, you could easily reduce cost by ten percent or more. Each year.

To effectively leverage the advantages of this openly competitive local and long-distance telephone services market, you need to get down to basics. Go to your telecom book. Is there a simple picture there? One long-distance carrier? One local phone company? One type of service for all your lines? If so, you are the envy of all the others who may read this book. Many businesses accumulate services over time. You add a line here, change a feature there. The result is fractured or multiple billing.

The rest of this chapter presents a short reference and understanding of most of the basic types of local and long-distance telephone service followed by a look into the business of managing this aspect of the telecom infrastructure.

4.2 Central Office Lines

Every day a new technology term comes along that must be added to the mental library. Most come as acronyms; so many that whole dictionaries of terms have been created, hundreds of pages in length, to attempt to catalog and explain them. To complicate matters, the telecommunications industry cannot even agree on a single term for the same technology region to region, specialty to specialty.

For example, the basic building block of the telephone company's network is the single copper wire telephone line. In essence, it is identical to the line that provides service to your home. Most businesses use single copper telephone lines, albeit in greater quantities, to run into their business telephone systems.

But there's also these lines called *CO* (central office) lines, named for the switching facility in neighborhoods that is the point of connection from one line to the rest of the network. They're also called *1FBs*—one flat-rate business line. Or *1MB* for one measured business line. Also, *POTS* (plain old telephone service) lines.

Confusing? It doesn't need to be. To understand, each circuit is a single pair of copper wires; a pair to make a complete loop of wire through which electrical current flows. One wire for current in. One wire for current out.

It was Alexander Graham Bell that figured how, when he ran a low-voltage electrical current through a circuit of copper wire, he could vary the frequency of the current to transmit and reproduce a signal from a microphone through a speaker.

The best way to understand the CO line is to think of your home phone. For electrical current to flow, the circuit must be closed. In an idle telephone, the circuit is broken so no current can flow. When you lift your receiver, a switch hook comes up and closes the circuit. The current that begins to flow is called a loop current. The CO switch recognizes this closing of the circuit and sends dial tone along the line, an indication that it is waiting for instructions.

Instructions come, of course, in the form of touch tones called *dual tone multifrequency* (DTMF).

Why does a nine and six on a telephone keypad sound the same when pressed? Because the tone is actually the product of two different frequencies sounding in harmony. Varying dual-tone combinations make up the recognizable 12 characters of the telephone keypad, even when the combination, the harmony, representing a different key on the pad, produces a sound similar to others.

All the tones heard through a telephone—busy signal, call waiting, dial tone—are just variations of currency frequency.

As with the rules of English, there are always exceptions. Remember the loop-current signal that starts a phone call? Not to confuse, but there is another type of CO line called a *ground start trunk*. It functions essentially the same as a regular CO line but instead of signaling the CO loop current, this line is initiated by grounding the circuit. Certain types of telephone systems can only reliably make positive connection and disconnection from the public telephone network using grounding as its start-signal method.

So at its most basic, telephone service from the local telephone company is provided on CO lines.

4.3   T1

When the number of lines needed to support call volume of a business grows, the choices for telephone services become more complicated. With that complication, though, also comes sophistication.

A *T1* (also known as *T-Span* or *DS1*) is a digital telephone line; a data signal. It is a computer line that uses a specific protocol that only phone equipment and the telephone company switching equipment can understand.

Think of when you dial up to the Internet using a modem. Your computer grabs the modem and you hear a dial tone on the line. Then comes a series of unintelligible squeals and howls that sound like static. With all the time in the world to listen, most people could never decipher what is being said between the two computers. The important thing is that *they* understand each other; the result is being able to get online after the squeals are interpreted by the computer.

A T1 is a live, high-quality telephone circuit, running twenty-four hours a day between the phone company and your business. A T1 carries twenty-four telephone calls along the one connection by dividing the connection time into tiny, even, perfectly synchronized to the millisecond, slices. Imagine standing in front of a children's playground, looking at a merry-go-round filled with twenty-four children. Your eyes face straight ahead. As this piece of child's playground equipment spins around before your eyes, each child would come into view for a fraction of the time of a revolution.

In a T1, the devices on each end, synchronized to each other to the millisecond use the narrow window of each time slice to pass a stream of digital information. All the bits that come up in one of the twenty-four time slices constitutes one channel of the T1; one full telephone lines worth of information.

What Is Digital Signaling?

A T1 is a digital signal. That's computer talk, right? We all understand that stuff; ones and zeros? Not exactly. I had a tough time verbalizing the concept when a client would ask me, "Why does it matter if this or that is digital?" It's more useful to define it in results: no static, cleaner lines. Herb Rosen, the owner of Trans-West Telephone Company in Phoenix, Arizona, has the best explanation of what digital signaling means.

Visualize that you have baked a cake in a California kitchen. It just may be the greatest cake ever made. A beauty to look at and a pleasure to eat. If you put it in the back seat of your car and drove it to your Aunt Ruth's in Cleveland, Ohio, what would arrive would be the cake, somewhat damaged by the trip. The cake is your telephone signal. The car is the carrier wires. The damage is static.

In a digital world you would bake the cake, your perfect creation. Then you would document an exact recipe for the cake; stick the recipe in the back of your car and drive it to Cleveland. Even if you spilled coffee on the recipe, even if you sat on it the whole time, or you used it to wipe rain off your side view mirrors, from it could be reconstructed a perfect copy of your cake. (The cake is the signal, the recipe the digital representation of the signal, the reconstruction of the signal remaking the cake.)

Bulk Local Phone Lines and Inexpensive Long Distance

When provided by your local telephone company, one T1 becomes a path for you to receive up to twenty-four local phone connections. The economies of scale mean that the carrier can provide enhanced phone services for businesses or will usually make price concessions; a per-line savings for renting the whole pipe. T1 has a greater effect on costs for your long-distance service, though (more on this in Chapter 6).

ANI/DNIS

The digital commands necessary to reproduce a telephone call occupy only a portion of the time slice given for each channel—only 9k to 16k of digital data per second are needed to produce telephone quality voice. Because 56k to 64k of bandwidth is available per channel on a T1, a long-distance telephone company can use a T1 as a launching pad to provide more services than just the connections of your telephone calls.

The method of embedding information within the telephone signal itself is call in-band signaling.

On inbound calls to a toll-free number, the carrier has the ability to pass information about the caller along with the signal itself. Automatic number identification (ANI) is, in essence, caller identification on a long-distance T1.

Number only. And if your phone system is intelligent enough to interpret ANI signaling, the phone number of the caller can be captured and displayed on telephones or stored for reporting.

Dialed number identification service (DNIS) is another signaling product that allows the carrier to provide multiple toll-free numbers on one T1. For example, you could order ten numbers and publish them for different products in a marketing campaign, or assign them internally to different departments in your business. You might publish one toll-free number for customer service calls and another as your main business line. The separation allows you to track your callers by whatever categories you choose.

In a scenario without this technology, the calls would have to arrive on separate lines, so that 800-555-1234 rings on line one through five and 888-555-6789 rings on lines six through ten. With DNIS, the carrier sends a signal embedded within the call that repeats, usually, the last four digits of the number dialed so the phone system knows it, regardless of which of the T1 channels the call came in on. A system that takes advantage of DNIS can interpret the information and route calls to different extensions or departments based on the number called or display on a telephone which toll free number is ringing so you may answer it differently from others. And do it sharing a common set of lines for efficiency.

You could, if needed, have dozens, even hundreds of different toll-free numbers on one T1 if it served your purposes. For example, using DNIS and a T1, a national answering service could sort out its client's calls from another. A customer service center responsible for multiple products could answer different numbers for different products using different scripts.

4.4 ISDN

Phone companies began to realize that human voices were not the only traffic being shuffled down their telephone lines and reacted with new products and services to sell. To make the best use of the carrier's existing infrastructure, integrated services digital networking (ISDN) was developed to provide data-certified telephone service on traditional copper telephone wiring.

At the foundation of this more modern service is the digital signaling that allows a line to be broken into channels. Splitting the line into channels allows the ISDN protocol to strip all the control and signaling information to a separate channel instead of embedding information into the phone call itself. The concept is called *out-of-band signaling*. The effect is that the carrier channels are free to carry only content.

ISDN has two distinct flavors.

Basic Rate Interface (BRI)

BRI is the home variety of ISDN. Across one copper telephone circuit, a digital signal, time-sliced, is divided into one digital carrier (signaling) channel and two bearer channels. Carrier as in carrier of all information and bearer as in bearer of the call itself. With an ISDN modem or telephone at your house, you can use one ISDN BRI line to make two phone calls at one time. The bearer channels have a guaranteed data capacity of 64 kilobytes per second (kbps), which means your Internet call or laptop dial up to the office network will operate much faster than your regular modem call.

But here's where ISDN gets interesting. Because the two devices on each end of the call (CO and ISDN modem) are smart and are controlling the bearer channels from outside the signal itself, both bearer channels can be bonded together to make one 124 kbps channel for a data call. Dynamic allocation of bandwidth—therein lies the greatest strength of ISDN.

Primary Rate Interface

The big brother of BRI, primary rate interface (PRI) uses a T1 as its telephone connection, giving more bandwidth to dispense. Therefore, on an ISDN PRI connection, the devices on each end have one carrier channel and twenty-three 64 kbps bearer channels to allocate, which would make for a "fat" data call. Or, not to malign voice, twenty-three quality voice calls.

Mostly, ISDN PRI is sold as an advanced T1. Because the signaling channel can be used in conjunction with voice on the bearer channels, you can receive local caller ID on an ISDN PRI as well as ANI. If you have videoconferencing equipment, you can bond channels and dedicate them to a data call when you need your bandwidth-intense video conference, only to disband the channels at the call's completion and open the channels for voice connections when you need them.

Though more of an advanced, premium service, ISDN PRI does not always cost more than a channelized T1. There seems to be no hard or fast rule on pricing. In some markets, ISDN is priced below standard T1 pricing for local service. In others, significantly above. It will depend on what your market will bear, on who your local carriers are, or on the dynamics of competition in your area.

For the carrier, ISDN is inexpensive to deliver after it equips its network to provide it (not all do), but can be more complicated to set up and install. The decision to use ISDN, therefore, should come from the merit of the application itself.

BRI, in comparison, can be sold one of two ways: either as a flat monthly rate service or as a metered service (where you pay a monthly connection fee plus a per-minute or per-hour usage charge). If, in your market, BRI lines can be bought either way, the choice of which to use depends on how much time you plan to use on ISDN calls.

4.5 Direct Inward Dial

Direct inward dial (DID) gives you private telephone numbers for any and all telephone extensions within your business and is a service that can be delivered on analog, copper telephone circuits, or as channels on T1s. How DID achieves what it does is essentially the same.

Many companies have a private telephone number for each employee. To give every person in an office a private telephone line could get expensive. If you employ fifty people, that would mean fifty lines at around fifty dollars per month. That may be money better spent on a company game room. Or free caffeinated beverages for employees for life.

The advantage of private numbers is that employees get to have direct connections with their customers. With the ability for phone systems to provide back-up services such as voice mail boxes and call forwarding to operators, letting a customer call directly is a great way to establish the relationship you need for your business to be better than the thirteen (or 200) competitors scrambling over each other for the customer.

Direct inward dial allows you to pool a number of circuits (lines) into your building, but stack an almost unlimited number of telephone numbers through those circuits to achieve private numbers at an effective cost. The concept works because not everybody who is issued a number would be receiving a call at exactly the same time. For example, a telephone system vendor in Seattle had seventeen employees, each with private numbers stacked behind four DID lines. The vendor never did receive a complaint from a customer that, when calling a private line, he or she was not able to get through, meaning four lines provided enough pathways for twenty private numbers to provide consistent, open service.

Okay, pop quiz. Who remembers DNIS? It's where the long-distance phone company identifies the toll-free number your customer dialed by sending your phone system a few extra digits after the phone call rings in. DID is the same technology, just applied to a local telephone service. Those are the basics, but a few more specifics are required.

Your caller dials one of your assigned DID numbers. The number is assigned to Gregory, the extremely successful manager of your customer service department. The telephone company CO that serves you, upon seeing the telephone call bound for one of your numbers, grabs any of the available DID trunks to you. You have four. Two are in use. The third is free. The CO signals your phone system on the third line, with a ring, that it has a telephone call to deliver. Immediately after the first ring, the CO pulses the last four digits in Gregory's phone number. The phone system hears the four digits, knows the call is for Gregory's number, and begins ringing the phone associated with the number (Gregory's).

4.6 The Future of Telephone Lines

Earlier sections of this chapter have covered the types of telephone lines and services you are ninety-five percent most likely to use. There are more. And although not even the following list is conclusive, for our purposes it's adequate. Here are some of the ways engineers at telephone companies have come up with to move telephone calls for customers.

Ear and Mouth

An *ear and mouth* (E&M) circuit is an analog telephone line that is actually two pairs of telephone wires instead of one. One pair is used to carry the signal. The second is used to pass control information between the two connected devices about the signal on the first. Its most common purpose is as the bearer line for analog DID service and the tie lines discussed later.

Foreign Exchange

A telephone call between Phoenix and Tucson bears long-distance telephone toll charges. Companies from Phoenix are constantly attempting to penetrate the Tucson market, so many that doing business in Tucson as a Phoenix-based business can carry somewhat of a stigma. It is sometimes called *poaching*. It's as if a big brother is coming into a little brother's room and taking CDs without permission. Customers are not always warm to the outside company, generally preferring to keep business in Tucson hands if possible. Maybe you have a similar business dynamic between two communities in your area.

One clear signal to a Tucsonian that a business is a poacher is a Phoenix telephone number. And, although a natural option, a toll-free number would still be a dead give away.

To avoid the problem, a Phoenix business can install a Tucson foreign exchange line and muddy the waters at least long enough to earn a chance to do business in Tucson. Basically, a local Tucson number is assigned by the local phone company, then routed up state to Phoenix. Tucsonians calling the local number would ring long distance at no charge to them. As far as they are concerned, they have made a local call.

From the Phoenix office, calls can be made into Tucson across this local line with no toll charge as well.

Tie Lines

Run a length of string between two cups across the yard between your house and your neighbor's and you have created a *tie line,* a direct telephone connection between two points. In business, of course, string is an impractical medium on which to communicate between two points. Businesses need to talk across their connections to have their computer systems talk. If the conversations are always happening between the same two offices, why not just run a dedicated telephone line (string) between the two? Then the conversation could happen any time, at any or all of the twenty-four hours in a day. Two computer systems could be chattering away in the background without interruption. Two phone systems could be linked in such a way as to act as one; a person in the first office could dial through to the second as one telephone extension in his office might be used to dial another.

Tie lines are leased from telephone carriers to meet such a need. Generally, for voice traffic, they are single channel lines leased alone or in bundles. When the need is data (such as the digital interconnection of two telephone systems a data need), there are usually one of two configurations: the single line (56k worth of data) or point-to-point T1 (for 1.54 megabytes).

Off-Premises Extension

A single voice tie line, not carried as an E&M signal, meaning it is not a live, open circuit twenty-four hours per day, is called an *off-premise extension (OPX).*

Southern Aluminum Framing in Chandler, Arizona, has a remote warehouse a couple of miles down the street from its main building, and supervisors have daily questions regarding warehouse inventories, so they had Qwest (formerly U.S. West) install an OPX line. The line is connected to the phone system at the main office. The warehouse phone simply became an extension that can be called only from within the main office.

The Future Telephone Line

Data has taken over our world. The data world is such a reality that most people have almost become numbly comfortable with it. This has kept the network engineers busy thinking of new and better ways to move all this data around the world.

Even though it almost doesn't make sense to call them telephone lines because their only purpose is to carry data traffic, there has spawned a new breed of circuit. Have you heard of frame relay? Digital subscriber line? Asynchronous transfer mode? For large companies, the thirst for special types of telephone lines has prompted all kinds of new developments. They can be summarized in the following way: when anything is converted to data, it is changed from its original electronic form (sound waves of a voice, a scanned fax document, the keystrokes of a keyboard that make up a file) to a series of ones and zeros. These data can be transmitted in bursts (packets) across data telephone lines to be delivered to another computer and reassembled for use on the far end. The method by which the data is moved is called *packet-based switching.*

Think of having to move the contents of your bedroom to a new house you just bought on a beach in Malibu, California. First you take the bed apart, empty the drawers, take down the pictures, and then you break the room down to it elements. You then pack the elements in a set of boxes. Mark each box with what's inside. Put it on the truck. On the far end, you reverse the process.

In packet-based switching, groups of data are assembled in a packet. The packet is labeled with what it is, where it came from, and where it's going. The packets are transmitted across the telephone network and delivered to their destination to be unpacked and reassembled. Because data is malleable and can be copied and stored easily, these networks use ultra-effective methods of moving traffic that, as a by-product, cause problems when they are used for voice telephone traffic.

Problems first arose in the process of unpacking and re-assembling voice telephone calls at the delivery end of the transmission. For computer files, data can be compressed. When transferring a data file across an open circuit, it is conceivable that some data packets can be lost and a computer file can still be assembled from 90 percent of the original parts. If the data network is congested with a lot of traffic, packets can be held up and made to wait until the path becomes free, then delivered without the effect of delayed delivery being noticed in the final reconstruction. The effect on voice data is that calls being delivered with missing information will have holes in the conversation. It will sound like the clipping that can happen with digital cellular telephone calls. Compressed and decompressed telephone calls also lose quality.

Equipment manufacturers (such as Cisco and Bay Networks) who develop the gateways onto these data highways are solving the problems of carrying voice data along their data telephone networks and, soon the problem will have been solved. This new breed of telephone circuit, one originally created as a way to use the Internet at high speed or connect the servers at two offices, will be open to talk across.

4.7 Making Outgoing Long-Distance Calls

The vast public switched telephone network is a wonder. All the various owners of local and long-distance networks routinely pass millions of calls back and forth to each other on their way to their final destinations. At each junction a call encounters, carriers have responsibilities. Billing for the call must be accounted for. Quality must be measured and maintained. The health of the network must be constantly kept in check. It's amazing that it all works.

Local telephone companies create networks within local geographic coverage areas. Put simply, they place switching offices throughout a city—each covering an area so that their furthest subscriber can be reached within the voltage tolerances of the wire they put in the ground. Wire from the switching office run out to neighborhood cabinets. A street (or streets) may have several hundred pairs of copper wires running down them, pairs branching off to the businesses and residences on the street. These wires are collected at local wires centers (also called *pedestals*) and are then connected to the live lines that feed back to the central office.

Inside the CO, the line is then connected to the switch that gives the dial tone that allows people to make calls. From there, trunk tie lines (high-capacity, switch-to-switch circuits) interconnect the COs.

The interconnections are built in such a way that a call from one neighborhood to another can be routed to any other CO in the city; sometimes directly, sometimes through an intermediary point.

A long-distance carrier places a *point of presence (POP)* in a city it wants to directly serve. The POP may contain a switch or it may just be a wiring point for traffic that "backhauls" to a switch in another city. Either way, it is the on-ramp to the long-distance network for its customers.

The carrier's job is to haul calls between cities so its network comprises POPs joined together with interstate trunk tie lines. The medium of choice for moving calls between cities is fiber-optic cable, special glass wire that carries signals in the form of light. These have several convenient characteristics: fiber can be immersed in oil or water so it can be run underground and even share pipe pathways with other material.

Fiber can be less expensive to run, per foot, than copper because of carrying capacity. A single strand of fiber-optic cable may be only as wide as the width of a human hair. Under cross-section, you would see a thin outer sheath, then a layer of insulation, then a speck of clear glass in the center. The fiber core in its insulation looks a little like the yolk in a fried egg. This 6-mm fiber-optic cable is currently capable of carrying 40,000 simultaneous telephone calls. It would take a bundle of copper wire as large as the trunk of a mature pine tree to accomplish the same thing.

The networks of local and long-distance carriers communicate with each other using common signaling languages, or *protocols*. In much the same way the Internet protocol (IP) allows disparate computer systems the world over to speak a common language. Signaling system seven, synchronous optical network, and in-band multifrequency signaling allow telecom carrier networks to successfully move billions of minutes of calls throughout the world — most of the time perfectly.

Understanding the process of switching has relevance to the life of an effective telecom manager. The first benefit occurs in the inevitable trouble-shooting process that immediately follows a trouble report. For example, Mary in the customer service department says that every time she tries to call a customer in the state of Maine, she gets a fast-busy signal instead.

Understanding how a call might be routed through your carrier's network allows you to ask questions to narrow down the problem: Are other states affected or only Maine? Does the problem only occur to that particular phone number or to any call to the affected area? How exactly did she dial the number? Could she tell which telephone line she used? What specifically happens when she calls — is there a recording of some kind, a busy signal, a fast-busy signal?

Understanding where in the process that call is in making it from your office to its destination can help you identify the problem or be a conscientious reporter when you speak with your carrier about the issue should it need to go that far.

The other major benefit of understanding the switching of telephone calls is to educate you on the costs of the services you buy from carriers. To that end, there are two types of long-distance calling. The distinction lies in how the call is routed.

Switched Long Distance

A long-distance telephone call has three elements of cost for the carrier. There is, of course, the cost of moving your call along the carrier's network of wholly owned, leased, or subleased telephone lines. The long-distance carrier also pays the local company on each end of the call a per-minute fee to originate and terminate the call for them.

For example, I am a Qwest customer in Phoenix. McLeodUSA is my long-distance carrier. My mother lives north of Seattle and GTE is her local phone company. For McLeodUSA to provide a long-distance telephone connection for me, they have to pay Qwest to carry the call from my house to their switch in downtown Phoenix (about one and one-half to three cents per minute). McLeodUSA also pays GTE to terminate the call from their Seattle-based switch across GTE's line to my mother's house (about the same cost). Add in that raw network expense and McLeodUSA's costs end up at about six or seven cents. They mark it up, charge me, and voila—profit.

A call placed for you by a long-distance carrier using your CO lines as the point of origination is called a *switched call.*

Dedicated Long Distance

When a long-distance carrier installs a T1 directly between your office and their switch, they are bypassing the local phone company, creating a direct, dedicated connection. Because it's T1, up to twenty-four calls at a time can come across the connection. You pay a flat monthly fee for the entire circuit (instead of a line-by-line charge) and can use it only for long-distance calls. But, because the carrier has eliminated one third of the cost of every call (origination fees), your charges for long distance are reduced.

4.8   Toll-Free Services

It's an elemental leap from understanding outgoing long-distance service to understanding incoming toll-free service.

The basic difference is that, with inbound service, you enter into an arrangement with a long-distance company to allow callers, who would normally be paying a toll for a call to you, to dial your number free of charge to them. There are a couple of technological leaps that had to happen to allow such a service.

The first would be the billing issue. How does the call happen to be billed back to you? This only happens because each and every time someone dials your toll-free number, the carrier who provides the service to you must be the carrier to transmit the call through the toll (long-distance) realm and deliver it to you. To make that happen, long-distance carriers work in conjunction with the local phone company at each end of the call (as in the example of switched calling), albeit in a slightly different fashion.

With outbound calls, the local phone company knows which long-distance carrier to pass your calls to because of its internal *PICC (presubscribed interexchange carrier code)* database.

The local phone company (in a switched world) through whom your customer is making the call has to know which long-distance carrier to pass a toll-free call to. This is handled through a centralized database system.

All toll-free numbers bear one of a series of prefixes established in the Numbering Plan of America (NPA). To date, the NPAs are 800, 888, 877, 866, and 855. More will be issued as capacity demands. This allows the original *LEC (local exchange carrier)* to know to request from the System Management Server (SMS) database the name of the responsible *IXC (interexchange carrier)*. After the number has been identified as belonging to a specific carrier, it is switched through tie trunks to that IXC. From there, the IXC moves the call to its destination city and completes it through the local phone company.

As with outgoing calls, the IXC incurs cost from the originating and terminating LEC, and you and its own network are charged accordingly.

There is a design and cost advantage to your being a dedicated (T1) customer for toll-free service as well—not in making toll-free calls, but in receiving them. If a long-distance carrier can deliver toll-free calls directly to you via a T1 between you and them, and bypass the LEC, they again reduce cost by a third and can charge you less.

Originated Toll-Free

Toll-free service can mean more than just switched or dedicated inbound calls. The local phone company that allows you to use its network to make a toll-free call recovers the cost of the use of its network by charging the long-distance provider responsible for the toll-free number (origination). This collection of pennies-per-minute can be lucrative income for the LEC.

If the LEC provides local telephone service to an organization that makes a lot of toll-free calls, the dollars charged back to IXCs can really add up.

An example of this type of organization is a university or college campus. Students are high toll-free number users, simply because there is a concentrated population making calls out of a controllable phone system network and long-distance service is generally not available to students through university phones. A mid-size university campus may process hundreds of thousands of minutes per month of toll-free calls. So it is not a stretch to see why this origination revenue may be a target for a competitor.

If a competitive local telephone company can handle these toll-free calls instead of the incumbent LEC, it can charge back to the IXCs for these toll-free originations. And because competitors are not subject to the same corporation commission or public utility entity rules that govern the incumbent LECs, they may be able to charge a penny or two more than LECs. The cost of network is not higher, but the company's profit margin will be greater.

As an incentive to organizations that make a lot of outbound toll-free calls, alternative and competitive LECs will approach them about installing circuits to the university's phone network for the express purpose of processing toll-free calls. As an inducement, these carriers may offer a commission back to the institution: a split in the profit. An institution with enough traffic may earn back a penny or a half-penny on every minute of toll-free calling.

Carriers may apply the commission to offset any services they provide that *do* carry a charge (in case you're a customer of theirs for other products) or cut you a check at the end of the month.

Enhancing Toll-Free

Toll-free numbers can be enhanced to allow business's customization. On the simple side, you are able to instruct your carrier to restrict the coverage of your toll-free number geographically. You may not want someone in your city to be able to call a number that costs you money. You may have a regional business and want to allow customers in the surrounding three states to call you but have the number not work from the rest of the state. You may wish to receive calls from Canada.

Maybe you wish callers to be allowed to dial your number from more than the usual contiguous United States. With some carriers who have made the necessary arrangements with the telephone companies and governments of certain foreign countries, you can establish toll-free service to allow callers to come in from other countries as well.

Enhancing toll-free service can grow in complexity from there, limited more by your imagination than by the technology. Some carriers have made investments in sophisticated, computer-based toll-free routing and switching systems. Using the software language of these servers, a carrier can create a custom application to apply to your toll-free calls.

The server, upon receiving one of your calls for processing, applies a preprogrammed protocol to the call before delivering it to its intended destination. The information the switching network has at hand to make a decision is the number the caller is dialing from; from there, it can extract where the customer is located, the toll-free number he dialed, the date, and time of day.

With all this information, it is simple to create programs such as modifying the way calls are routed based on the time of day or day of week. You may prefer to route all early-morning calls to an East coast office and evening calls to a West coast office, without having callers dial different numbers morning and night. You may want callers automatically routed to a specific location based on where they are calling from.

Here are two brief examples: A company that distributes vitamin supplements through a network of manufacturer agents throughout the country wants to use a single toll-free number in its national advertising. When leads come in, they want the calls to flow to the rep who "owned" that sales territory for the state the caller was in.

In another example, a discount tire store chain based in Arizona has hundreds of retail locations throughout the West. When you dial the company's main toll-free number, its carrier's enhanced toll-free server figures out where you're calling from and presents the customer with the nearest three stores for them to chose from.

All very sophisticated.

But there's plenty more. These systems are voice capable, meaning they can, instead of only routing on time of day and geographic information, prompt the caller with a menu. Or ask customers to enter a personal identification number (PIN), which the carrier can validate through a link it may establish to a database.

The programs can be developed to provide you with an automated call center, processing calls using an interactive voice response system.

Businesses that incur huge, short-term spikes in calls may use a carrier's enhanced toll-free platform to help them handle the volume—a carrier's network is built to handle thousands of calls simultaneously, whereas your business has, because of financial practicality, a more limited capability. A good example would be a pay-per-view provider. If you've ever ordered a movie or other program through the phone, you know it's done mostly through an automated system. Most subscriptions for pay-per-view are requested in the minutes leading up to the program itself, creating a huge spike in calls. Such a company would use the capability of a carrier's network to handle the load and process calls on their own system, which is more cost-effective, when demand is reduced to manageable levels.

The point is, just because you have or need a toll-free number doesn't mean the questions stop there. There are robust and productive options available to your business. You will, of course, pay a premium for enhancing the basic toll-free service.

4.9 Telephone Calling Options for the Traveler

Hotels have unique needs in a phone system. They need a high-capacity console for the front desk, inexpensive but multifunction telephones with two or more lines wired to each room for guests, and highly functional telephones for staff and departments so there is effective communication between guests and staff. In an uncomplicated fashion, hotels need to be able to control guests' ability to make long-distance telephone calls (turn on or off long-distance to a room, for example). Any voice mail system should be simple enough for a guest to use with no more training than a tent card on his nightstand table. Mailboxes must be emptied almost daily when guests depart, with enough ease to be managed by nontelecom, front-desk staff.

In fact, many times, it is better for all involved if the phone system somehow communicates electronically with the front desk check-in computers. Staff only need check a guest into her room, then the phone can be activated for long distance, the voice mailbox freshly created for the new guest. If possible, the guest's name should be automatically programmed into the phone system. This way, when the guest calls downstairs for clean towels and an ironing board at 3:15 a.m., the tired front-desk staff knows who she is by looking at the display on the phone without having to reference a room number chart.

With all these sophisticated needs, the most critical element of a hotel phone system may be a small peripheral device called a call-accounting system. This little computer allows hotels to charge their guests for long-distance telephone calls.

Think about that a moment. From a hotel room, you directly dial a long-distance telephone number and the next morning the call and related charges are sitting on your bill, waiting for you to pay up. How does that happen? There's a little technical magic at work.

The phone system has the ability to output a record of every call made on the system. The moment you said, "I love you" to your nine-year-old and hung up the call, the phone system generated a line of information about your call. This record stated the date and time of your call, its duration, and the number you dialed.

The call accounting system, connected to the *station message detail reporting (SMDR)* port on the phone system, looks at the phone number to figure out how much to charge you for the call. It figures, mathematically, your long-distance rate per minute for the call, adds any surcharge the hotel has added and factors the hotels percentage markup, and sends a bill record to a printer (in smaller properties) or to the property management system to wait for you the next day.

The markups and surcharges are determined, to some degree, by the hotel. If a hotel pays six cents per minute, you may be charged forty-four. The logic is that forty-four may be, for example, AT&T's highest tariffed long-distance rate and therefore is a fair market price for the service. Of course, for the privilege of using their telephone line to make the call, the hotel may also ask you to pay a per-call surcharge each time you pick up the phone.

Everything that a hotel does for you, from having a business center to providing certain room options, has its value to the hotel weighed against whether it can produce income or not. Telephones are one of many profit streams a hotel develops. For telephone calls, the discussion may begin with "How do we recover the cost of the expensive phone system and pay for all the lines and services through telephone calls?" A hotel will then see the potential for healthy profit at the end of the month. A hundred-room hotel may net a couple thousand dollars a month in profit!

This means two things: one, if you use the hotel for long-distance calls while traveling, chances are you're paying a much higher price for the privilege than you have to, and two, you have no control over how much employees spend when they are traveling.

Zero-Plus Dialing

So how do you beat the hotel's system, as outlined previously? The easiest way would be not to direct-dial the call, right? That is, not to pick up the phone, dial "1" plus the long-distance number (called *1-plus*) and use the long-distance operator to make the call. You'd think dialing "0" (called *0-plus*) would allow you to avoid high charges. You know you'll be able to charge the call to a credit card, bill it against your home phone, place the call collect to whoever you're trying to reach. Simple right?

The hotel would actually love it if you did this.

When you access a line and just dial 0, the hotel's phone system routes you to a specific carrier. The carrier then is extremely helpful in processing your call.

The carrier pays the hotel a percentage of all revenue it generates from your 0-plus calls. The rate you pay for the call (first-minute rate, following per-minute rates, any per-call surcharges and fees) is set by the carrier in cooperation with the hotel. Together, they pick what to charge based on how much of a commission the hotel wants to receive back from the carrier on such calls. The more the hotel wants to receive in percentage, the higher the carrier needs to charge to cover it.

The same 100-room hotel that may make a couple thousand dollars a month in profit of direct-dial calls may also make a thousand bucks in commission from their zero-plus provider.

All this is one of the major reasons calling cards are such a good service for your business and why you may be faced with managing them as part of your role as telecom manager.

Calling Cards

With a calling card, you dial a toll-free access number that bypasses the hotel's two traps for your call (1-plus and 0-plus). But it still can feel like it costs so much (relative to spending on calls directly from your office) to use a carrier-supplied calling card. It's less expensive to go into the Sip 'N Shop and buy a card that gives 100 hours of calling at five cents per minute rather than using the AT&T calling card and being stung for a surcharge of fifty cents or more.

It's important to understand that there are two different types of card and two different underlying cost structures. There are technical similarities, but enough difference to warrant explanation.

Prepaid Calling Cards Throw-away prepaid calling cards are provided by a company that buys these minutes from wholesale long-distance providers. Sometimes the maker of the card is the carrier themselves, but this is rare. Small companies who make and sell prepaid calling cards can get away with a few rule-bends that cut their cost to provide minutes on cards that an MCI would never be able to get away with.

With the card, you call into either a local or toll-free telephone number to access the debit card platform of your provider. You are prompted to enter the card PIN from the front of the card, then are given access to dial through to whatever number you choose. Your card is debited in value based on a schedule of points that correlate to the face dollar value of the card.

By printing a local call-in number on the front of the card, the debit card company avoids using a toll-free number access and escaped paying the LEC an origination charge. The provider incurs a long-distance charge through whoever provides its debit-card servers with long-distance service. If you are not in a local area served by the card provider, and you therefore need to dial a toll-free access number to reach the debit card platform, you are usually charged a higher rate for the call.

This system works like those VISA debit cards you can buy where you load the card with a cash deposit of some kind, then use it anywhere VISA is accepted until the dollar value is exhausted.

After your prepaid calling card is exhausted (that is, you've used all your minutes), it will no longer be accepted for calls by the automated system. You simply throw the card away at this point or, with some, you can use a credit card to charge the minutes up again.

Your card's value is expressed in carrier math. For example, a ten dollar card would be worth 200 points. Because one point would equal one minute of calling, you'd effectively be paying five cents per minute, right? Well, that only counts for domestic U.S. terminating calls. For Canada, Hawaii, Alaska, and the U.S. Territories, the calculation may be three points per minute. There may also be a connection surcharge of three points. A pay-phone surcharge of six points. A toll-free call-in charge of an extra point per minute. International termination, if allowed by the provider, is scored based on how the per-minute cost of calls to that country equals value in points. Read the back of the card carefully to understand the true cost.

Carrier-issued Calling Card Financially, a carrier-issued calling card works more like an American Express charge card. The cost for each transaction is applied to the card. At the end of the month, you receive a statement asking you to settle the balance.

Functionally, the card works the same way as a debit card. You call into the calling-card platform, are prompted to enter your code numbers, then asked to enter the number you wish connected. Some cards offer features such as "#" (that is, the pound sign) after a call, which lets you make another call without needing to reenter your codes.

If your card is issued by your current long-distance carrier, the billing appears with the rest of your long-distance spending. You get to see what calls are made and who is making them on your statement at the end of the month.

Enhancements to billing are also available. You may, for instance, have a name assigned to the card so on billing, you do not have to cross-reference a number to name just to figure out who incurred what charges.

You pay for calling-card usage on a per-minute scale. Carriers make up the additional cost of providing card-based traffic by charging a premium (ten cents on the card vs. six cents for calls from your office), and some will assess a flat, up-front surcharge for each call.

The bottom line, with the additional reporting and understandable pricing, carrier-based calling cards—so long as you understand the math and there are no "gotcha's"— should be as good or a better financial deal than prepaid cards.

4.10 The Companies You Will Be Doing Business With

As you organize your telecom life, especially local and long-distance telephone services, it is important to understand the structure of the supply side of the telecom industry. How are carriers built? How do they organize themselves? What does it take to provide services? And, the most important question: What does that all mean to you?

With the deregulation of the local phone business in 1996, competing in the local and long-distance telephone business became an attractive proposition that got a lot of attention. This opportunity, and the fact that capital was freely available because of the technology stock boom, saw the creation of hundreds of competitors. Some of the new carriers' business plans were based on sound business principles. Others were not. Yet most of the new companies grew.

With stock at inflated prices, and favorable tax laws that encouraged mergers of publicly traded companies through stock swaps, many incumbent and new carriers consolidated.

Then technology stocks swooned and fainted. Business had to fall back on their plans. Those who had leveraged on returning to the capital markets to fuel continued growth found their doors closed with the subsequent contraction of the economy and drying up of the capital market. Scores of these businesses simply failed.

The ones that survived had either grown to an independent inertia in size or had access to operating cash reserves and somewhat healthy revenues.

Incumbent Local Exchange Carriers

Remember the first FCC-mandated deregulation of the telecom business? In 1984, the Bell system was broken up. Left behind were twelve RBOCs and AT&T. The LECs saw local deregulation coming years in advance and took steps to prepare for the open, competitive market they knew would be imposed upon them. Not to say they haven't resisted. Remember, these are wealthy, protected businesses with a huge stake in keeping things as status quo as possible.

One of the first approaches LECs took to defend their turf was to invest millions in the lobby system; that is, they attempted to be part of the deregulation conversation so that it did not treat them too unfavorably.

Another early tactic was LECs introducing term contracts. LECs went to the customer base and gave favorable pricing or feature packages in exchange for multiyear (typically five) commitments. These contracts included penalties if customers left.

After, we began to see LECs sell services through outside agents. Before deregulation, LECs sold directly to business. Agents gave the incumbents a greatly expanded field sales force and gave them secure future income that was less likely to find its way to a competitor. There was also some small resistance from LECs in working with competitors—in violation of the rules of engagement under deregulation.

In more recent years, as competitors have emerged and been successful against the LECs, there has been consolidation. Of the twelve original incumbent LECs, only four now exist. And none of the four carry their original names. GTE and NINEX are now Verizon. Southwestern Bell, Southern Bell, Ameritech, and others are part of SBC Corp. U.S. West was purchased by a long-distance and data company called Qwest.

What this means to you today is that your local phone company is alive and well, even if its name has changed. It is still most likely one of the richest companies in the local phone service business. By now, pending FCC approval, it may be able to offer you long-distance and data services to complement its local offering.

Local phone companies' biggest advantage is size. There is an inertia built into having been the only game in town. Even if they do a poor job of servicing customers and competing head to head with a more nimble, more technologically current competitor, it would take years to burn away all the customers they have. Which gives them the advantage of wealth. The revenue streams already in place are somewhat protected. The profits earned on all the stable, old business they have will still be rolling years after competitors have chipped away at the customer base (even if they whine and beg for rate increases a couple of times a year).

And because (although they are public companies) they are primarily cash-based, they will be more able to grow than a highly in-debt or leveraged new business. They will be able to buy up failed competitors for pennies on the dollar, taking another business plan and set of network assets out of the way. They will be able to expand the wireless and data markets because, right now, they are practically the only companies who can afford to.

So if your LEC plays it smart, sits back, and invests its cash wisely, it will see much of its competition simply die. Which means, to you, the effective telecom manager, the incumbent LEC can be the most stable, secure place to keep your business.

The Big Three

Ah, long-distance companies . . . but who is just a long-distance company today? AT&T, MCI Worldcom, and Sprint were the three major long-distance phone companies to make it through the last two decades. I single them out, not because they are better than other long-distance voice and data companies, but because they have similarities among themselves that no other companies have.

The first similarity is that they have constructed wholly owned networks through which they carry traffic. This is a distinction that some other companies can claim, but these three have taken the concept to a tier one level. Tier one level means a backbone carrier, a carrier that owns or controls its own physical telecommunications network and therefore provides service with the most direct accountability. Tier one carriers often act as wholesalers to tier two and three carriers, who either own no network assets and completely depend on resale or own regional or partial networks and fill in their holes with resale of other carriers.

Tier one carriers also are full-service companies. Typically, all the long-distance services discussed in previous pages can be provided by these companies. If a product available through a long-distance company is marketable and useful, chances are that MCI, AT&T, and Sprint will be one of your choices.

Another distinction these companies have is relative wealth—the wealth of having been in existence longer than most competitors. They may be leveraged and have structured some substantial debt to stay ahead of their markets, but generally speaking, it is unlikely you will see these three names completely fail or be purchased by someone else.

A third distinction about these companies compared with competitors is that they have the ability to expand services on the back of existing, long-term, and highly profitable old business. Which allows them to spend cash to grow in a poor capital market. And expand they have. You'll see these three names popping up and offering every telecom service from wireless paging and telephones to Internet access and Web hosting.

MCI and AT&T have entered the local phone business, although the jury is still out (both inside the companies themselves and their investment community) on whether these were financially sustainable decisions. What this means for you is that, for long-distance and related services, the big three may be the more stable, solid choice.

The Competition

So who else is out there? You probably receive scores of communications from other names all asking for a chance to serve your telecommunications needs. Who are they? How are they structured? What are the advantages and pitfalls to doing business with them?

Again, the three forces that created an environment in which there is competition to the LECs and IXCs are in a state of flux. But the models for how to create a competitor are pretty straightforward.

As a new company, you either build a telephone-switching network and then sell services off it to customers, enter into an arrangement with existing companies as a wholesale customer and resell their products in your own name, or some hybrid of both.

Facility-Based Carriers

The model of building a switching network and selling customer access to it is an oversimplified description of a complex business problem. Two examples follow.

Company A went into business at the end of 1996, just after deregulation. It received readily available investment money. It installed switches in three states and made arrangements to interconnect with the LEC (to reach customers) in each and wired a network to connect the switches.

The company invested in the latest CO switches from Northern Telecom, which would give them a wide array of local phone service products to sell to business. They interconnected to a tier one Internet backbone provider as well.

Company A spent and built and ended up with a solid, regional network, which it wholly owned and controlled, with which to go to market. It also ended up with quite a bit of red ink on the books. But investment money was freely available (so the company could get more cash if needed, whenever needed) and besides, the business plan called for profitability in seven years. It had plenty of time.

The plan was to offer what is known as an integrated T1 service to customers. They would use T1 circuits from the LEC to connect with customers. The twenty-four available channels would be divided in the company's network between local phone lines and bandwidth for Internet access. To be profitable, this approach needed customers with twelve or more lines of service, so they focused on larger accounts.

This approach was typical of many early competitors. The majority of early competitors thought that customers with the largest phone bills would be the quickest and most efficient road to profitability. Conversely though, this approach created inflated competitive pressure over the smallest category of customer.

Then the economy turned. Businesses could no longer expand assets without new investment. With immature revenue streams, compressed to paper-thin profitability by unexpectedly fierce competition and expensive networks to maintain and grow, many companies grew desperate. For a time, there was a glut of super-cheap services being pushed to market in an attempt by competitors to bring in quick cash or shore up its growth numbers to presumably inflate its sale price.

Many of these types of companies simply folded—closed their doors or were sold for assets and a pittance to the original investors. Some made it through, albeit crippled by circumstance.

The second example, Company B, is a competitor that saw deregulation coming early and began its business plan in 1994. It quickly assembled the capability to sell long-distance telephone service by wholesaling it through one of the big three, thus creating a revenue base of customers to grow on. It solicited investments and, in smaller metropolitan markets (instead of in one of the major, ultracompetitive areas such as Dallas or Los Angeles), Company B began to build a local telephone network upon deregulation. It began reselling the incumbent LEC product, adding a new service layer and field representation as a differentiator.

Company B used the profitable revenue model of selling local and long-distance service to small and medium-size businesses to attract more investment. Its stock value increased. Stock could then be used as currency to continue growth through merger and acquisition. This expanded the company into smaller and smaller markets.

Company B leveraged this growth and investment to purchase a nationwide data network and began an aggressive growth plan to take its local, long distance, and now Internet access into new markets.

Approaching a new area, it first entered into an arrangement with the local phone company. By reselling the LEC, although not as profitable as selling services off its own switch, Company B was able to gain market share and build a revenue stream for that market. Reselling also allowed the company to focus on the customers other businesses were ignoring: three- and five-line business accounts with an average of $100 per month in long-distance spending. That not many competitors were after this business, and that it took little or no physical investment to bring a customer on board, justified the expense of building a network in that market.

Once the network was built, the plan was to migrate all the resold customers over onto the more profitable, wholly owned switching facility where the product could be better controlled. With deeper up-front revenue and delayed investment in network, this type of company had a profitability date of three years instead of seven.

Then came an economic movement that froze new investment. The stock tanked and took away the ability to merge or purchase through stock swaps.

But with already invested cash and profitable revenue flowing into the company, the economy did not run them out of business, but did cause cessation of new spending. If managed properly, companies structured this way will continue and will be able to survive with cash on hand and current revenue growth through to stand-alone profitability but will stop growing the way it did. It effectively will be frozen to what it has built to date.

Resellers

Some companies went the total resale route. These will usually be smaller, more regionally or locally based companies that provide you with much the same services and products you get from the incumbents. They may be able to bring you the advantage of better customer service and more of a field sales and support approach than the LEC itself. A disadvantage would be that, because the company does not own the network that provides services, you may suffer delays in getting problems resolved or new orders processed.

Agents

You may also be approached by a different type of business that, as with a reseller, has no direct ownership of the product. These businesses are agents. They enter into marketing agreements with carriers and sell their products for commissions.

One advantage to this approach is agents may represent multiple carriers. If one carrier has great local phone service but weak long distance, the agent may be able to package two carriers together to create the most beneficial offering for you.

Agents will also do some of the complicated leg work involved in managing local and long distance. They may offer support service, meaning you call them with problems instead of the carrier directly. This could be a huge benefit if your underlying provider is bad at proactive customer support. And agents do not cost extra to do business with because they receive payment not from you, but from the carrier in the form of a commission plan.

A disadvantage to agents is that they don't own the product they sell. They do not make ultimate decisions on how that product is installed or serviced. They do not have direct influence on the employees from the carrier servicing your account. They generally cannot get anything done with their carriers faster than you could do yourself if you know what you're talking about when you call.

Another disadvantage may be the nature of the arrangement they have with carriers. Agents are not employees of the carrier; therefore, they receive a different kind of training and support and have a different accountability. Training for the field sales force usually consists of classes, support staff, and direct managers all making sure the reps know what they're doing when they are working on your behalf. Carriers only really have a quota as their tool to control the actions of agents. They sign contracts that make agents work under a certain conduct, but the accountability is not so direct. The training is looser. Management can control agents only through the money arrangement, not through threat of losing a job. You may find agents who don't completely understand the technology of what they're selling or the necessary details of their carrier's product offerings.

Another disadvantage of agents may be that because they are independent from the carrier and driven by commission, if another carrier comes along and cuts a much better deal with the agent, the agent may drop the carrier it sold you on. You may find yourself switching (or being switched) to services not so much based on your need, but based on the financial situation of the agents themselves.

Who are agents? Agents can be completely independent businesses. All they do is represent local, long distance, and Internet carriers. They sit down with clients, understand their need, then come back with three options for them to choose from. It's a good business.

An agent could also be in another business, but who has added the agency to bring added products and services to their customers. Your telephone system vendor may be an agent for the LEC, an IXC, or a competitor. Your data equipment provider may talk to you one day about telephone service. And putting your telecom business in their hands may be a positive thing for you—especially if you have a good relationship and they understand how to service your account.

But beware: One trend in the agent game is companies that call themselves straight consultants. Usually, a consultant is a person you hire to perform certain tasks for you for a fee. Maybe you need help with an installation project or need to hire expertise in an area new to you. You may pay a consultant by the hour or by the project. In telecommunications, a consultant may help you audit your telecom infrastructure, selecting new vendors or carriers or helping you write a Request for Proposal for a new telephone system.

Some agents approach customers as consultants. They will offer to evaluate your telecom environment, then recommend specific changes. This "consulting" service may obscure the fact that they have an interest in the outcome. When they return to you, some of the options will involve switching carriers—at which point, they will be making a commission.

If there is any bias whatsoever, if the person will collect a dime or has any specific interest in where you place your business, they shouldn't be able to call themselves consultants. If you hire a consultant, you expect absolute loyalty to the customer first and a total lack of bias toward any specific solution. They must truly operate with only your interest in mind when evaluating and recommending.

The Future Telecommunications Carrier

It is conceivable that all this positioning, consolidation, expansion, and failure in the local and long-distance arena could have a huge positive side effect for some companies. With weaker, smaller competitors that are either prime targets to take off the market through purchase or by standing by and watching them fail, a company that can weather the storm may stand alone at the end of the day.

The dream of being a supercarrier, a company that can provide all telecommunications services and take on customers in every profitable market, is keeping many a telecom company CEO awake at night. The incumbent LECs have the financial power and the expertise to pick up an infrastructure from failed competitive local exchange carriers (CLECs) in other regions and expand their reach nationwide. The big three, if they can pull off entry into the local phone business, could easily be in such a position. The handful of CLECs that have the business plans, leadership, and finances to see the economy into better times could also continue an expansion that should ultimately take them national.

Some companies will get there by merger, some will grow organically. But in the next ten years, consumers may be faced with a choice of only a handful of supercarriers, all of which can provide facility-based local, long distance, and probably a slew of other telecom products.

But because these companies will be huge, the process challenges to them in successfully implementing and servicing accounts will allow local or regional carriers to spring up again after the investment market allows them to generate new funding. These competitors will be different than in the past, though. They will be dominated by the supercarriers and unable to effectively compete.

Unless one of the technologies that could allow this to happen is *wireless local loops*. Today, getting phone service depends upon being reached with wiring of some kind. With wireless, the cost to bring lines to you is no more than a $100 dish on your roof pointed at the nearest mountain tower. When the technology to connect you (and a thousand of your closest neighbors) is cheap and stable, carriers will be able to swarm into incumbent areas without depending on incumbent LECs. Today's competitive landscape for local and long-distance services is full of choices. By asking careful questions of the proposing company, you can quickly determine how they provide the services they offer. From there, it's a matter of making an educated choice: is there a compromise being made by doing business with Company A over Company B? Is that a compromise you can live with?

4.11 Evaluating Your Current Services

What telecom services do you use today? How many telephone lines are hooked to your phone system and what type are they? What features are active on those lines? Who is (or are) your long-distance carrier(s)?

To give a fair evaluation of how effective your current telecommunications environment is in satisfying the needs of your business, it is imperative to begin with a full accounting of all services in place.

Billing

The first place to start when accounting for all services is with the billing you receive from your telephone companies. Compile your local and long-distance bills for a full month. In your telecom book, make a list of each account, the carrier, and the contact telephone number for billing inquiries or service.

If the long-distance charges appear within your local phone bill (even if you receive service from a carrier different from your local provider)—meaning it was billed to you by your local phone company on behalf of the long-distance carrier—list these amounts off your local bill as separate accounts.

If you see a local telephone bill with multiple long-distance charges on it, chances are there is a fixable problem with your long-distance service. You would most likely prefer to do business with one long-distance company. You may have negotiated a specific rate with this carrier and even be billed separately for the calls you make.

If multiple carriers are showing up on your local bill, some of your lines may be *picked* (the term used for being pointed at a certain long-distance carrier) to the wrong carrier. It could also mean that someone in your office is using one of those 10-10 codes to make long-distance calls.

Both situations take long-distance service and pricing out of your control and should be corrected and can be fixed by calling your local carrier and arranging a correction to the programming of your lines.

You need to sit with each account and figure out exactly what you are paying for. There are several ways to find out, depending on the service.

Local Exchange Carrier Records

The protocol for various company's bills will be different but it's safe to say the first page on any local phone company bill will comprise a summary of your charges, outstanding balance, new balance, taxes, and fees. Somewhere beyond that will be line items that represent services and features. The line items may list individual services (eleven lines at $29.99 per line, for example) but these items usually are more vague than that (monthly service at $299.45, for example).

Billed items may represent telephone lines themselves or charges for features and various fees for services. Talk to your phone company about what each line item means. In your telecom book, list the telephone lines you are paying for, the voice mail service, and the feature under each line. Understand what each item is, what it does for you, and how much it costs individually. Make a complete accounting for each dollar on the bill.

As a help to your cause, understand that local phone companies keep huge and sophisticated databases for every customer on record. If you request, you can be shown a complete record of the services under each account. What you will see is something like that shown in Figures 4-1a and b. The universal service operating codes (USOCs) you see listed beside the line numbers tell the phone company everything it needs to know about how to provide service to you on those lines. Some USOCs represent billable items such as lines and features. Some USOCs are just for programming (they may tell the system in which order to hunt). They may also represent features and tax categories to be applied to the lines on your account.

Taking the step of requesting an LEC record and getting definitions of the USOCs could be the most thorough way to account for every item that appears on your bills.

One thing about your local phone bill not to worry about is any metered service rates you may be charged if you live in local toll-calling areas. In Chicago, for example, your local line is something unfamiliar to other parts of the country—a metered business line. It means that you pay per minute for local calls. The per-minute charge is calculated based on mileage bands determined by the phone company.

You need only be concerned with fixed, recurring monthly charges at this point. Set aside any bills for any telecom service (data, wireless, or Internet) other than voice telephone line accounts.

Long-Distance Billing

Looking through your long-distance bill will show you line items for services rendered, that service summary between page one and where the detail begins. It may show your total long-distance spending broken down by interstate and intrastate, domestic and international, and inbound and outbound calling. Each category will have a summary of minutes. (These numbers will be used in Chapter 5, when we concern ourselves with the cost per minute you pay for metered service.)

Do you have any? Are there line items on your bill for monthly service fees, T1s, charges for billing formatting, or special features? Have the carrier's rep go through these with you so that you are satisfied you know the physical services and associated costs of all the carrier does for you.

Verify the Local Services

Now comes the fun part. You only want to pay for services you actually use. Just because the carrier bills you for it doesn't mean you actually use it. Make sure that every line and feature you pay for is present.

Billing Breakdown

FIGURE 4-1a **Reading LEC Customer Service Records**

As a customer, one of the most valuable ways to find out exactly what services a carrier provides to you and how much it charges, is to request to review your customer service records. These are the database records LECs use to keep track of your account.

To be useful to the switches that run your phone lines and the billing systems that produce your monthly invoices, each element of service on your account is encoded in the LEC database using universal service operating codes (USOCs).

Carriers don't all use the same software programs. This sample is but one instance from one carrier. With this single-customer, Qwest LEC record, you can gain a better understanding of the concept of LEC records and USOCs.

1. **The billing telephone number (BTN):** One of the telephone numbers on your account (usually the main working phone number) is assigned as the master account number. This aids the phone company relating your service and billing to your company.

2. The official, legal billing name for your business.

3. Carriers make separate accommodations for the name and address that will be listed in their white and yellow pages directory in case it's different from the billing information.

4. Where the phone service is physically connected may also be different from your billing or listed addresses.

The easiest way to verify the actual existence of telephone lines is to get on the lines, one by one, and check what numbers they are. But you can't tell just by looking. Some lines may be labeled, either at the point of demarcation (where the phone company actually delivers service to your business) or on the phone system itself. This information cannot be totally trusted. On the d-marc (the point of demarcation between the carrier's network and your service location), labeling is the responsibility of the telephone company technician. There's usually no accountability of technicians to their employer to do it by the standards, so some may take a lazy approach.

5. On this LEC record, there is a note here of a contract this customer has with Qwest. Listed is a contract number and an expiration date.

6. From here, USOCs provide all the corresponding detail necessary for the carrier to provide service and bill your account correctly. In this example, RSX is a code for a type of 1FB phone sevice that includes special pricing (probably relative to the pricing and features packaged under the contract). All relevant programming is included with the USOC reference. Under the RSX USOC, the PIC line shows the code representing this customer's long-distance carriers (in-state and state-to-state), ZCN means that this phone line is included under the contract, CTX classifies the line as a Centrex service (relative to contract), and TGID tags the line with a trunk group ID (relates lines together on rollover or hunting groups).

7. The separate USOC, N13, tells the technicians to include caller ID on the service and relates its pricing again to Centrex contract pricing.

8. USP1X is a simple example of a USOC that has no programming relevance. It simply tells the billing system to charge $5.75 per month for a wire-care insurance product Qwest offers on their 1FB-type lines.

9. Some USOCs refer only to taxes, causing the billing system to add federally or state-mandated taxes to your phone bill for each line of service you have. For example, the USOC's PORXX (universal service fund) and 9PZLX (line number portability) both refer to taxes.

10. A notation has been made here to ensure the hunting order of the lines on this account are correct.

The labels on your phones themselves, if written in by the vendor or by you, could be more accurate. But don't just trust written information. Access the lines individually. Call a telephone that has caller ID, perhaps a cell phone. For stand-alone devices such as fax machines or modems, this is as simple as using the telephone handset of the device or connecting a basic, analog-style telephone to the device's telephone jack and checking the line directly.

On key-style telephone systems, where every phone has buttons to allow access to each of the telephone lines, you can select lines one by one for the check.

Some lines may be blocked to providing caller ID information. There are telephone numbers you can call, set up

For the Toolbox

FIGURE 4–1b Customer Service Record Response

Customer BTN :4805550220

```
480 555 0220 111    SEP 25 02 *CSR  LIVE  P    1    21    *APVL  PNX  C21XX
ABC PROCESSING

XSBN 1 480 555-0220  /CS C21XX
---LIST
    LN     ABC PROCESSING
    LA     555 W 5 STREET, TEMPE
---BILL
    MCN    XXXAS1AXXZZ
    SS
    CBR    480 555-0220
    BN1    ABC PROCESSING
    BA1    555 W 5 STREET
    PO     85284 TEMPE AZ    /TAR BC
    ZCN    C5555555, EXP 12-20-02
---S&E
    ORIG SERV ESTAB 9-17-97                       PBX EQUIPMENT

123097 3968               C21XX/MTN                          .00    .00
21600 2091 555-0220       PORXX/MTN/TN 480 555-0220          .43    .43
                          /CTX IDP2100
21600 2091 555-0222       PORXX/MTN/TN 480 555-0222          .43    .43
                          /CTX IDP2100
```

(1) (2) (3) (4) (5)

```
21600 2091 555-0222    USP1X/MTN/TN 480 555-0222                        5.75      5.75
                            /CTX IDP2100

7 100 0034 555-0220    9PZLX/MTN/TN 480 555-0220                         .56       .56
21600 3232 555-0220    RSX /MTN/TN 480 555-0220                        28.65     28.65
                            /PIC 0333/LPIC 0333
                            /ZCN C55555/NMC /CAT 1
                            /CTX IDP2100 /IDP ID2100
                            /LCC NC9 /LPS /RNR
                            /TGID 2100 /TGS *TGUUA

123097 3968 555-0220   N13 /MTN/TN 480 555-0220                          .00       .00
                            /CTX IDP2100

123097 3968 555-0220   9ZR /MTN/RAX 1B/TN 480 555-0220                  7.39      7.39
                            /CTX IDP2100

7 100 0035 555-0220    9PZLX/MTN/TN 480 555-0220                         .56       .56
7 100 0034 555-0220    9PZLX/MTN/TN 480 555-0220                         .56       .56
21600 3232 555-0222    RSX /MTN/TN 480 555-0222                        28.65     28.65
                            /PIC 0333/LPIC 0333
                            /ZCN C55555/NMC /CAT 1
                            /CTX IDP2100 /IDP ID2100
                            /LCC NC9 /LPS /RNR
                            /TGID 2100 /TGS *TGUUA

123097 3968 555-0222   N13 /MTN/TN 480 555-0222                          .00       .00
                            /CTX IDP2100

123097 3968 555-0222   9ZR /MTN/RAX 1B/TN 480 555-0222                  7.39      7.39
                            /CTX IDP2100

7 100 0035 555-0222    9PZLX/MTN/TN 480 555-0222                         .56       .56
```

⑧ ⑨ ⑥ ⑦ ⑩

HTG A1 - 555-0220, 0222

RMKR   ZCN C55555, 60 MOS EXP
        12-30-2002

by the telephone companies for the use of their own technicians, that connect to a system that reads back the number they called from. Your phone-system vendor may know this number, and so might your phone company (if it is willing to say).

On PBX and hybrid-style telephone systems, where you dial a "9" or press an outside line access key to make calls or where the system selects an available line for you from a pool of lines connected to the telephone system, verifying individual lines becomes harder. This creates a possible complication in verifying several types of lines.

- **Ground-start trunks:** To verify standard, loop-start telephone lines, you connect any standard telephone device, dial, and go. To initiate a call on a ground-start trunk, the circuit must be grounded to signal the LEC switch for dial tone, requiring special equipment and technique.

- **T1:** The individual channels of a T1 are not accessible without special equipment.

- **ISDN:** Because of its BRI or PRI format, you will not be able to access the individual lines without going through an ISDN interface (ISDN modem or ISDN-capable phone system).

Not to fret, though. Most types of phone systems that support these lines will have a feature that allows you to access individual, even digital or ground-start, trunks.

In phone-system programming, the lines are assigned an identifying trunk or line number. The *direct access* or *line access* feature allows you to dial a code or press a line access button, enter the trunk you wish to access, and, when you receive a direct dial tone from the line, proceed with your check of the number of that line as usual.

There are also line types that do not fit either category. DID trunks, for example, may allow in-only service. You therefore will not be able to access a dial tone through them and verify the call. To be sure all the numbers you're paying for work, call and note where the call comes in on your phone system.

Verifying Features

If your phone company is billing you for a feature, make sure that it is working on your lines. Different features require varying approaches before you can check them off your list.

Hunting, the technology that allows a caller to dial one number and have his call automatically roll to an open line if the number dialed is busy, can be an expensive feature. Check it by making the main number busy then dialing it. Did your second call make it through? Did it make it to the next open line? Make that one busy and call again. Keep going until you can verify that every number in the group of hunted lines rolls to the next.

Verify what happens to a call after the last line is reached (the seventh call into a group of six busy lines). Do callers hear a busy signal? Are they routed to voice mail? Are they routed to another group of lines or a totally different phone number in another office?

If there are forwarding features on your lines, follow the instructions of your carrier and check that forwarding works as promised.

Three-way calling, call transfer, caller ID—does it all work?

After you have verified every feature, it may be a good time to ask, "Why?" If you pay for caller ID but only two of the twenty-seven phones in your office can display the information, why continue the service? If you have a group of seven lines that hunt off your main number, why are you paying for call forwarding on the second line and the main line? Would anyone be calling that second number? Would you ever need, to protect anyone calling it, to forward that specific telephone number to an alternate destination?

If your phone system has a conference-calling feature, why pay for three-way calling as a service from your local telephone company?

Verifying Long-Distance Services

Making sure your long-distance house is in order is a simpler job.

Outbound First, while you have access to all your telephone lines, check that the outbound long-distance telephone calls are routed correctly. On a standard CO line, this job falls onto the shoulders of your local phone company. Through the PICC system, the local phone company programs in its switching network which long-distance carrier you have chosen and routes calls for you. From each of your telephone lines, dial 1-700-555-4141. You will hear a recording telling you which long-distance carrier is programmed to that line.

The PICC system is not infallible, of course. The incredible rates where all you have to do to use the service is dial a code that begins with 10–10, for example, is actually a PICC. If a PICC is manually dialed on the line right before a long-distance call, the call is forced to the carrier who the new code belongs to, overriding your preprogrammed default PICC.

Therefore, well-intentioned (or not) members of your company could be forcing long-distance telephone calls away from the carrier (commonly called dialing around) you have negotiated favorable rates with. Checking the PICC is only a test to make sure the lines are set up correctly; educating your employees to only use the company-selected carrier is a second step.

If this becomes a problem in your business and you can't get people to stop dialing around, some phone systems have the ability to deny any telephone call that is dialed beginning with a PICC.

The preprogrammed PICC set on the line by your LEC is not infallible either. A carrier using deceptive business and sales practices could cause the programmed PICC on your lines to be changed without your permission (a practice most often called *slamming*).

Here's an example: You're watching your favorite television show when you get a call from a telemarketer.

"Hi, this is (whoever) from MCI and I'm just calling to let you know that we're going to take your current $7.95 per month service fee and 10 cents per minute to just $3.95 and 10 cents. How does that sound to you?"

By the speech, the rep was implying that you're already a customer of MCI's. She'd have you believe she's just a friendly rep on a bored Thursday night who decided to do you, the one and only super special MCI customer a grand favor by calling out of the blue and dropping your long-distance rates. But what if you're not an MCI customer?

It sounds like a company trying to confuse people who are not a customer into saying yes to a seemingly innocuous and friendly question as a pretense for signing them up as new customers. If you weren't fully sure of who your carrier was and said yes to the question, by FCC rule, you would be giving approval to this rep to switch your service to MCI. That is one major way slamming gets done.

Some phone systems can protect you from slamming by forcing your carrier's PICC down the line when sending long-distance calls out.

Inbound

Because toll-free numbers are managed directly by your long-distance carrier and not through the LEC, it is easier to account for each service a carrier may bill you for. The first thing to do would be to verify your list of toll-free numbers from billing to make sure what each is for. Dial each one and be sure it rings through to its intended destination.

It is the effective telecom manager's role to question why a business has the toll-free numbers it does. To manage the services properly and exercise your fiduciary responsibility, you need justification. With some carriers, just the possession of a toll-free number on your account incurs a monthly service fee.

Account Codes This service, provided by long-distance carriers, allows you to protect yourself from unaccounted long-distance calling. Understand if yours are verified or unverified.

The verified version means the carrier maintains a list of account code numbers for you, and callers will only be permitted to complete their long-distance telephone calls when entering a valid code. A caller attempting to use a code not on the list will receive a recording from your carrier politely rejecting the attempt to make a call.

Call the carrier and get a complete list of open codes. Check that against your internal list. Then ask—to whom or what purpose were they assigned? Is this purpose or person still valid? When the list of desired codes is accurate, make a test call with each.

In an unverified account code environment, you will be allowed to dial any code of a certain digit length (three digits, for example) to complete calls. Unverified codes are easier to check. Do they work? Try a handful of possible codes to be sure.

Account codes are a line-by-line service. Your carrier must apply the feature on only the telephone lines you specify. You may not want the service on all lines—it can be a hassle to have to dial an account code to complete a long-distance fax or modem telephone call.

Beyond toll protection, your carrier can provide billing reports to you with calling expense sorted by code. Businesses use account codes so the expense of long distance can be allocated: by the employee who made the call (for example, John Houston is code 444, Mary Partridge is code 442), by the purpose (calls on behalf of the hotel side of the business use code 645, calls for the time share side of the business use code 655), or to categorize calls by client (use the last three digits of the client number as the account code).

Calling Cards Are all the calling card codes your carrier has on your account valid? Can you account for them? Who has them? If you have cards or codes on file, check that they work by making a test call.

Hire a Vendor

If all this is a little complicated, you might enlist the help of your telephone system vendor or a qualified telecom consultant. Having a technician verify all the services that show up on your bills is completely worth the investment.

See Figures 4-2 and 4-3 for what you can watch for on your local and long-distance phone bills.

Billing Breakdown
FIGURE 4-2 **What to Look For on Your Local Phone Billing**

After you have completed a thorough review of your local phone services (reviewed LEC records, eliminated unnecessary items, renegotiated your pricing plans), the monthly audit becomes a short and simple process.

Although there are 100 variations on what phone bills look like, when performing a regular monthly scan, it is useful to follow the checklist below. These are the things that *should* be checked every time a local phone bill comes in. Then, if no obvious anomalies are present, the bill can be paid with good conscience.

Items to review include:

1. Is the total amount due in line with expectations, based on an understanding of all charges for lines, features, taxes, and expected variable costs such as long distance?

2. Were you credited correctly for your last payment made?

3. Is the monthly service, the section of your bill charging for basic line costs, correct? Some carriers are kind enough to break this section into usable detail; many are not. The costs listed here, though, should be predictable enough to use as a check that this bill is fundamentally correct.

4. Is the number of lines of service (if shown) correct?

5. If the bill shows charges for features separate from line costs, are they correct?

6. If any installation, one-time, or nonrecurring fees appear on the bill, did you expect them? Are they correct?

7. Review the taxes to be sure the quantities, categories, and amounts are correct.

8. Look for detail on variable charges:
   - Are there any LEC long-distance charges? Are they correct and within norms? (You might also look to the long-distance bill audit checklist provided in this book to be sure you're billed correctly for any toll charges).
   - Are there other long-distance carriers listed on the bill? If so, do you know who they are, what service they provided, and why? Again, check the pricing.
   - Are there any pay-per-use features or rental line items listed on the bill? If so, are they expected and correct?

9. If you were expecting credits from previous bills, be sure they're included?

10. Is there anything left on the bill, any line-item, charge, or notice that you do not yet understand from your complete audit of telecom services? If so, call the carrier and ask for an explanation before paying the bill. (It's easier to have amounts taken off what you owe than fight for and track credits promised to be given you at some later date).

You should be able to pass through these ten questions in just a few minutes. Only if a glaring anomaly stands out would you need to spend any more time on the bill.

Billing Breakdown

FIGURE 4-3   What to Look For on Your Long-Distance Billing

Performing a regular monthly scan of your long-distance phone bills is as short and simple a process as the scan of your local phone bills. It can happen easily once you have completed a thorough review of your long-distance accounts (reviewed your bills and identified all services, eliminated unnecessary items, renegotiated your pricing plans).

This simple checklist lists the items that *should* be checked every time a long-distance bill comes in. And just like your local billing scan, if no obvious anomalies are present, the bill can be paid with good conscience.

1. Is the total amount due in line with expectations based on an understanding of what this carrier provides to you in services, charges for all call types, fixed monthly charges, features, and taxes?

2. Were you credited correctly for your last payment made?

3. If any installation, one-time, or nonrecurring fees appear on the bill, did you expect them? Are they correct?

4. Review the taxes to be sure the quantities, categories, and amounts are correct.

5. Look now to the detailed summary, the section of the bill (assuming this carrier provides such detail) that breaks down the total new charges into its elements. There should be both variable and fixed costs listed. For variable costs, determine that the per-minute rates are correct. Divide the cost (after discounts but before taxes, by the total minutes for that category—for example, if your state-to-state line item shows 472 calls for 1,950 minutes at $150.72 before taxes, our cost-per-minute is 7.7 cents).

   Nonvariable charges are easier to audit. If the carrier agreed to provide account codes for ten dollars per month, make sure you see ten dollars on the bill.

   Reviewing the summary details. Look for the following categories:
   - State-to-state (variable)
   - Intrastate (variable)
   - IntraLATA (variable)

- Extended area (variable)—calls to Alaska, Hawaii, or Puerto Rico that are neither domestic nor truly international
- International (variable)
- Calling cards (variable with some possible fixed charges)
- Monthly recurring (fixed)

    —T1 or other circuit costs

    —Port connections

    —Billing summary charges

    —Feature fees (account codes)

6. Is the number of lines of service (if shown) correct? Does this quantity correspond to the quantities of per-line charges and taxes?

7. Are the quantities of toll-free numbers, calling cards, account codes, and separate locations correct?

8. Does the total of all the detail line items add up to the total new usage charges on the front of the bill?

9. Spot check a few detailed phone calls for per-minute price and minimum call length.

10. Look quickly for any extremely long or extremely expensive calls and decide whether they're worth extra investigation.

11. Are there any pay-per-use features or rental line items listed on the bill? If so, are they expected and correct?

12. If you were expecting credits from previous bills, be sure they're included?

13. Is there anything left on the bill, any line item, charge, or notice that you do not yet understand from your complete audit of telecom services? If so, call the carrier and ask for an explanation before paying the bill. (As with your local bill, it's easier to have amounts taken off what you owe than to fight for and track credits promised to be given you at some later date.)

You should be able to pass through these twelve questions in ten minutes or so. Do this every month and you'll never be taken by surprise by your long-distance bills again.

4.12 Possible Improvements That Can Be Made

Now that you have audited your current services, it's time to think about the services you have and their usefulness to your business. Consider the following possible reasons for making changes or improvements to your basic telephone service. This is not a complete list of all there is to think about when buying local or long-distance service, but valid information to consider.

Cost-saving measures include the following.

- **Consolidation of lines:** Has your business accumulated telephone lines over time? In the beginning, were there only a handful connected to the phone system? Then someone added a modem and a line was ordered for it. Then the shipping and receiving computer needed to communicate electronically with a freight service and a line was ordered. Then someone wanted a private line, which was ordered. Then the president bought a new laptop with fax capability and a new line was ordered.

  Many different types of devices can make use of dial tone: fax machines, modems, terminals for credit cards, and so on. Most of these rarely need a dial tone or only just for a few moments at a time. (Companies I've known have found themselves with two lines for every employee.) All these lines can add up to a significant bottom-line item.

  There is a less expensive way to provide a dial tone for all these devices: assign analog extensions off your phone system. As an extension, the device can access one of the phone system's available lines from the pool. Inbound calls can make it to their destination as well. An incoming call for a fax modem, for example, can be routed directly to the device through the phone system.

  By consolidating lines and devices through the phone system, you could save your business a great deal of money over time.

- **Conversion to DID:** DID service would allow you to consolidate the number of telephone lines you need to handle all your traffic. The routing of calls is handled as a software feature of the service. You can put all your numbers across one pool or a group of circuits. The issue of traffic capacity is now one of total calls at one time, regardless of the number the calls come in to. For example, a business with a ten-line main hunt group, two fax machines, two modems, and three private lines may get by with only ten to twelve DID trunks compared with seventeen standard lines. Because numbers usually cost pennies per month, you could also consider assigning everyone in the company a private phone number and cut the receptionist's load.

- **Sharing devices:** Consider line-sharing devices. These boxes, usually the size of a large can of sardines, allows you to share one telephone line, therefore one telephone number, with several devices.

  For example, a small motel needs its fax machine to share the fourth line on the phone system. They rarely receive faxes, for themselves or their guests. The hotel bought and connected a line-sharing device. It connects on one side to the telephone line and on the other to the fax machine. Whenever a call comes in on line four, the device answers. The caller is not yet aware his call has been answered because the device plays him the sound of a ringing telephone. It does this to buy a little time to listen to the line, which is listening, of course, for either the *carrier-negotiation* (CNG) tone that a fax machine puts out or the squeal of a modem. If it hears either of these special sounds, it connects the call to the appropriate device. If it hears neither of these telltale tones, it passes the call on to the telephone system. This is an elegant solution to the expensive small-business problem of paying for more telephone lines than are needed.

- **Centrex packages:** In many cities the incumbent local telephone company offers package pricing for local telephone service. It comes under many names: Centrex 21, Customer Choice, Centronet, or Centron. The premise is that, for one flat price on a term agreement, you receive basic telephone service bundled with a variety of possible features. Compared with the individual pricing of these features, Centrex pencils out nicely.

Centrex is more relative as a pricing tool than as a way to get your hands on hot phone company features. Generally speaking, the features offered are relative only to smaller customers. If you have a company of more than ten employees, chances are you've invested in a telephone system that allows you to place calls on hold, make conference calls, transfer off-site, or take more than one call at a time on your phone. These features, therefore, as functions of your telephone service, are overkill.

But not always. The ability to forward your main line to an answering service after hours, see caller ID on your phone system, or transfer calls to cell phones without tying up two lines per call could be a bonus.

Features may include the following.

- **Voice mail:** How are your telephone calls answered at night? What if all of your lines are busy? Does your caller receive a busy signal?

  As a telephone company–provided service, voice mail can be used to improve the experience callers have in attempting to reach you at times when it's not exactly convenient for you to get the call.

  LECs offer a variety of options besides basic voice mail as well. At a minimum, your callers will be able to leave you a message so you don't lose the opportunity to speak with them. At a higher level, LEC voice mail could allow you to build menu trees and give callers options, such as the choice of which of your employees to speak with or an option to transfer to a backup location if you wanted.

  Voice mail is a relatively inexpensive add-on that can offer immediate benefits, but beware the cost. At seven dollars to fifteen dollars per month per box, you may be able to justify the expense of buying an in-house voice mail system to add to your phone system for the price of about five LEC mailboxes. (See Chapter 5 for more information about permanent voice mail systems.)

- **Call forwarding:** Using call-forwarding options allows a business telephone number to be answered from anywhere without callers having to change what they do to reach you. Not all call forwarding is the same. Be careful in what form you're buying it. It can be set up to work in a variety of conditions (line busy, no answer after a certain number of rings) and can be pointed at any destination that can be reached by a telephone call (answering service, employees home, cellular phone).

- **Call transfer:** If you need to stay connected with your business and your clients but need to roam, a phone company–provided call transfer feature may be an option to help you. A call coming into your office, answering service, or voice mail system can be transferred back out, through the phone company network, to your cell phone. Callers don't have to hang up and dial a new number hoping to reach you. On transfer, the original line becomes free for a new call.

- **Caller ID:** At home and on a cell phone, caller ID is helpful. It helps identify who is calling. This information can be used to either screen the call (it can go to voice mail because of who it is) or alter the way you answer (personal vs. business call). This is also helpful to a business because you could alter the way you handle that call.

    There are technologies that allow your phone system and computer to work together to this end. Your phone system interprets the caller ID, sends the information to capable programs in your computer (such as contact-management software) and activates the customer record on your computer screen as the call comes to your desk.

    Many phone systems are also capable of changing the routing of an incoming call based on who's calling if you choose. How nice would it be to be able to block a nuisance caller from getting through? Or to have bad-debt customers routed straight to collections when they call? Or your best caller put straight through to your desk?

    But there are three significant challenges to this "killer application." First, many of the calls received are blocked; a phone's display shows "unavailable" or "private."

Second, many phone systems are capable of displaying only either the name or number on your display, not both. Can you decipher who of your customers is ringing in just by their phone number? A private person, with a more limited list of contacts, might have no problem with this, but in business I have customers I don't talk to for six months.

Third, think about the telephone lines of your business. When you make an outgoing telephone call, which line do you use? If you're a larger business, it could be any one of a number of lines from a pool. You dial 9 and the phone system provides you an available line. The phone company will display the telephone number of the exact line you dialed out on. So who you call, to correctly identify you, must maintain a database of every phone number on your phone system. Not practical, right? (And to be fair to the technology, this last problem is solved through something called a screening ANI on T1 service where, no matter which channel of a T1 you use to make an outgoing call, the same telephone number is displayed to the network for caller ID and billing purposes, but we're a long way from having a standard way of handling caller ID. So, caveat emptor.)

- **Speed dial:** This may or may not be beneficial. If, in your business, you maintain frequent communication with a select list of customers, vendors, employees, and others, a convenient speed-dialing list could be helpful. The phone company can provide several options for how many numbers to store and save. But look to your phone system's capabilities first — you may be able, at no monthly cost, to store and retrieve a much larger list than you think with the equipment you already own. A Toshiba telephone system bought in the late 1990s, for example, allows you a system list of 100 numbers and a phone-based list of forty speed-dials.

- **Conference calling:** Another convenient feature that can be added to your local service. With it, you'll be able to connect to multiple parties (the number is dependent upon the capabilities of the LEC's switch in your area). The switch's software is designed to keep the volume of each line at full strength while it is joined to others.

LEC-based conference calling usually is billed as a flat monthly service. Long-distance carriers often have conference services that allow you to set up a toll-free call-in number that everyone dials in to join at the same time.

With a smaller business, however, your need may be to connect two or three outside lines at a time. Again, look to the capabilities of your telephone equipment. Most competent telephone systems allow conferencing up to five or six parties without special equipment.

Long-Distance Services and Applications

Some telecom managers feel that telecommunications sales is a second-class profession. There are many salespeople who've used slimy, pushy, and sometimes illegal practices to shift money from you and your business to them and their businesses. You may be offered pricing that sometimes doesn't pencil out on the back end. You may be asked to sign agreements that carry huge financial penalties if you move to another competitor. You have been promised world-class service only to spend hours on the phone later working through a problem with a briefly trained nineteen-year-old new hire in your carrier's call center three states away.

Almost every business has at least one telecom-related horror story. So you see the challenge in long-distance sales, or "slinging long distance." Just as the legal profession is made up of more good guys than bad ones, many telecom salespeople go about it in a truly professional way. They understand that what they sell is often reduced by customers to commodity status. They are placed into bidding wars in which the value of their offering is calculated in price only.

In fact, the majority of companies (that have an office in your city and are willing to sit across a table from you and make a proposal) are competent and professional and know how to create a proposal that has deeper value than just price. If you are a volume user of long-distance service, what more could you look for besides price? What more is there to basic local and long-distance service? Here are some ideas to consider.

- **Outbound rates by area:** It is simpler to manage long-distance spending and audit billing later by letting you pay a simple, flat, per-minute rate for all long-distance calls. And this should be the standard offering although some carriers want to charge a higher rate for calls within your own state, or to the extended calling areas that can include Alaska, Hawaii, the U.S. Virgin Islands, and Guam. If you will be making international calls frequently, it may pay to ask for the rates to the countries you're most likely to call.

- **Rounding and the minimum:** In long distance, there is profit in the math. At the basic level, the application of a minimum calling length matters. According to Active Voice Corporation, a voice mail system manufacturer based in Seattle, Washington, thirty-five percent of all business calls are not completed the first time you get voice mail or speak for a brief moment with a receptionist. These are extremely short calls. If you are faced with the choice between a long-distance plan that imposes a thirty-second minimum charge to your calls and another only six seconds, the cost for short calls can be affected. Let's assume you pay ten cents per minute for long distance. A fifteen-second call with a six-second minimum costs three cents. With a thirty-second minimum, you pay five cents for the same call. Averaged out over a month, you're paying more than a fifty percent mark-up.

  Think about the rounding calculation as well. A company rounding in full-minute increments is inferior than one rounding to the nearest tenth of a second.

- **Another rounding feature:** Telemarketers have unique long-distance spending needs. They make a disproportionate amount of short outbound calls compared with a normal business. Picture a room of fifteen telemarketers, each with a printed list of leads on the desk in front of them, pounding out call after call for eight straight hours a day. What do you think are their odds of connecting with each lead they dial? And, of the leads they successfully reach, what percentage of those calls do you think are terminated in the first moments of the call?

In some telemarketing companies, the outbound calls are actually placed by machines, computers that can dial dozens of calls simultaneously, detect if the call goes unanswered or hits an answering machine, then disconnect and initiate a new call in the fraction of a second.

Because telemarketers are high-volume users of long distance, they negotiate great rates. But are they so great? Say 3.5 cents per minute is their rate. If eighty percent of the calls end within eighteen seconds (on average), how much would each call cost? Fifteen cents. A hair over one penny. But wait, calls are rounded to the nearest cent. So now the call costs two cents. That's a ninety percent mark-up on the call if you're looking at a true cost per minute. So the wonderful 3.5 cent rate doesn't look so good (it's effectively 6.6 cents per minute!).

Savvy telemarketers convince their carriers to bill them in fractions of a penny for calls. The product is usually called something like *four-digit rounding*, meaning that the price is calculated to four digits beyond the decimal. The same eighteen-second call would cost $0.0105 on the bill instead of $0.0200. Does this have any relevance to your business?

■ **Inbound tied to outbound:** Don't let carriers convince you that there is some intrinsically higher cost for them to provide inbound, toll-free traffic for you than standard outbound long distance. There isn't. Therefore, the rate you pay for your toll-free calls should equal the per-minute price for outbound long distance. The minimum increments and rounding should be identical as well.

■ **Inbound calls:** There are options available, with practically every carrier, when ordering toll-free service, such as regional allow/deny routing. You don't have to let anyone who wants to make a call at your expense get through. Using a basic allow or deny logic, you can restrict your toll-free number to work only from where your customers might call. If yours is a statewide business, only allow in-state calls. If it's a national business and you don't have many customers in your own state, deny calls so people down the street can't cost you money when they call. Allow or disallow Canada, and so on.

- **Enhanced toll-free:** Review the section in this chapter that discussed advanced toll-free service options. Read back over the many enhanced options available when you ask your carrier to apply some programming logic to the routing of your incoming toll-free calls.

- **Calling card surcharges and features:** Often overlooked as a "they're all the same" service when setting up a long-distance or local account, the pricing for your calling cards need particular attention.

    Pay special attention to surcharges and minimum call lengths. As is justified by the carrier's underlying cost, the base domestic rate will normally be higher than your direct-dial rate, but ask to look at the international rates. They should be more in line with your direct-dial plan, because there's not much of a cost differentiator for the carrier to complete an international call for you whether through a calling card platform or directly off a local line.

    While you're looking at the calling card plan closely, go through the carrier's offered feature list. There may be some great improvements hidden there. For example, a small feature such as # (that is, the pound sign) after dial that allows you to make a new call after completing the first in the same call without reentering the calling card PIN, could be a huge time saver for a traveler who makes a lot of calls.

Billing Considerations

There are hundreds of different ways that carriers represent billing information. Some bills are quite good, meaning that individual items of service (features, lines, calls, taxes, fees, surcharges, etc.) are listed individually and priced in such a way that you know exactly what you pay for what. In the long-distance side of things, it means a bill that lays out the numbers so you can figure out what you paid per minute for the different types of calls.

Some bills are bad. One globally respected long-distance carrier has a billing format that is so complex and confusing that the basic cost per minute is nearly impossible to correctly calculate. Maybe this is the point. Maybe it's possible this huge, multinational corporation had a team of lawyers and accountants conspire to create a bill so difficult to interpret that the mere mortal customer will just give up on trying to understand it and write the check. More than likely though, this company's billing software program, in a attempt to meet the various needs of millions of customers, grew too complicated over time.

Pay attention to your proposer's billing. Many companies offer all manner of options to customize the information you see.

- **Paper billing:** To properly find problems and effectively figure out what you're paying for services, you need to do some math to your bill. To save time, look at the summary report options from the carrier and have your billing presented to you in shorthand. The company should, for example, provide a toll-free calls report summarized by the state of origination, which could help you see if your marketing efforts in certain geographic regions are having the desired effect of driving calls. Can they also show you a summary of call by line used, which, if it showed that certain lines were not used for long distance whereas others were, could point to problems with the lines themselves? Can they calculate the cost per minute for all call types for you?

- **Locations:** Ideally, if your business has more than one location, you would like to write one check but be able to interpret information separately about telecom for each location. If each location is a separate cost center according to your accounting methods, maybe each should have their own phone bills and pay for their telecom separately.

If you wish to control spending centrally and consolidate volumes for price advantages, most companies give you options in billing. Most long-distance carriers, CLECs, and LECs offer consolidated billing—a master bill that collects the total amount for all your separate bills. Each location's detail billing itemized within one master bill for the whole account.

If you're a multilocation business, pay close attention to the location options and choose the one that will best help you meet your mission. Know that some options will carry a charge.

- **Account codes:** As described earlier in this section, account codes are a handy tool of carrier technology that allows you to organize calls into groups for billing purposes. If you adopt them, ask to receive summary or detailed billing information about your long-distance spending organized by code.

- **Electronic billing:** Some carriers will be able to offer versions of bills on diskette or CD-ROM. Make sure electronic versions of traditional billing offer information in a format as easy to access and analyze as its paper counterpart.

To accomplish this, some carriers offer a nice front-end program, bill viewing software with which to look into the detail of the billing itself. Many times, the viewer software includes summary reports you can view or print. To know if their program will work for you, be sure you can sort or arrange the billing to research specific questions that have come up on your bills in the past.

Some carriers' electronic bills are nothing more than a flat text file, a stream of raw information, and only useful after being imported into a database program of your own. To make use of it, you must be somewhat of an expert in manipulating computer data.

Some carriers now allow you to view electronic billing online by logging into special websites. Ask to review a sample; this may be the ideal way for you to receive your bill.

Even though you may receive an electronic version of the bill, ask for paper copies of any summary reports and a payment coupon to keep things in order.

More Math Games

The cost for long-distance telephone service is easy to understand. But at its base level, what are you buying? Nothing more than air. Time on a long-distance network. Access to the carrier's wires and lines and the service of connecting your telephone to another some great distance away.

Long-distance pricing plans are based on simple cost per minute. Because time is the denominator for the math of what you pay, your charge for a call should equal the length of the call multiplied by the rate per minute—simple. Or is it?

At the beginning of this section, some of the lopsided math games carriers play when calculating charges for calls were discussed. Besides the basic rounding and increment math, avoid stepping in the following pits of quicksand.

- **1010:** "All calls under twenty minutes for only ninety-nine cents and only seven cents per minute after that." Sound familiar?

  Look at that more closely: ninety-nine cents divided by twenty minutes. That's a mere five cents per minute. A great deal, right? Only if the call actually lasts twenty minutes. Do you remember the statistic I attributed to Active Voice Corporation that only thirty-five percent of business calls are completed on the first attempt? The rest end up in some form of messaging environment. So now how does your ninety-nine cent call figure? That's ninety-nine cents divided into 1½ minutes. That's sixty-seven cents per minute! No longer such a deal.

  Because of the true math of long-distance calling, the fantastic rates you see displayed on television are rarely worth the trouble of dialing the code—the carrier is banking on it.

- **Other good rates for long distance:** There are some absolutes in the long-distance business. One of them is underlying cost. Because what LECs charge to long-distance companies for origination and termination of long-distance calls is federally mandated, every facility-based legitimate carrier pays similar cost. Then why can some no-name company based in Florida offer you rates half what your MCI rep says is the best, most competitive rate he has available?

There are numerous mathematical ways a carrier can compensate for a below-cost face rate per minute. One, the rarest of all, is just to lie. Sign you up at one rate but give you another.

A second way would be to charge you a higher call minimum, such as starting to bill all calls at three minutes.

A third would be to charge you a monthly access fee—real, fixed monthly dollars that, when averaged back into your call charges, raise your effective cost per minute.

You could also be charged a higher rate for the first few minutes. Or a higher cost per minute after the first three minutes. Or a higher rate for the last eighteen months of the twenty-four month agreement you had to sign to get the good, introductory rate. Or an inflated rate for calls to Alaska, Hawaii, Guam, Canada, or international destinations.

Another good trick is to give you a rate that's based upon a discount of a "tariff" rate. The tariff is the legal document a long-distance carrier files with the FCC stating its pricing practices. Here's an example of how one company uses an off-tariff discount to get the super-low face rate per minute they sell on up front.

You sign a two-year deal to get a three cent per minute domestic long-distance rate. Your rate is determined by giving you a 50 percent discount from the six cents per minute standard rate.

Three months after you become a customer, the carrier refiles the tariff for a 25 percent increase in rate to nine cents. What happens to your price? It goes to 4½ cents—a 50 percent increase. The carrier can refile and redefine the pricing for a tariff plan as often, by how much, whenever, and without warning as it chooses.

All these additional charges and math games, when aggregated back into the amount of time you actually make calls on the carrier's network, bring the true price up, allowing the carrier to show you a sexy up-front cost.

If a long-distance deal is too good to be true, be skeptical. It makes more sense to negotiate a clear, competitive arrangement with a legitimate national carrier instead.

- **TCUs:** Total cost units (TCUs) (and similar billing schemes used under other names) are a category of long-distance company mathematical brilliance that deserves its own explanation.

Time is the basic increment of calculation for long-distance calls. On your bill, you see calls listed with their time and equivalent cost. A TCU is a billing increment that, when used on a long-distance bill, looks just like time, but is, in fact, a measurement of something else altogether. It is a special number used to represent a formula the carrier has applied to calculate the cost of your call. A carrier, wishing to obscure the fact that the true cost per minute for its service has no relation to the rate you signed up for, uses a complex formula to alter its pricing. Instead of inflating the rate, the carrier inflates the number that normally represents the length of the call and makes this new number look like it represents time.

In one example (used by a now-defunct carrier), this confusing formula, if translated into English, would read something like this: The total TCUs for a call will be calculated as 1 TCU per every minute of a call plus 1.5 TCUs per call for administrative overhead plus .2 TCUs per minute for marketing expense. The net result is that a one minute, thirty second call would be calculated as 3.3 TCUs. If your rate for long-distance calls was ten cents per TCU, the call would cost thirty-three cents. That's a twenty-two cents per minute rate, carefully hidden.

And because the formula is disclosed in the FCC tariff filing (which is a public document you can view; you look at the many-hundred page tariff filed by your current carrier all the time, right?), the practice is perfectly legal.

Most customers with TCU-based bills don't understand that TCUs do not represent time. They would just assume the call was actually 3.3 minutes and that thirty-three cents was the right amount to be charged for the call. The call should have, in fact, only cost fifteen cents.

There is no legitimate business reason to apply TCU math to long-distance calling plans. Avoid them in your LD spending.

■ **Equipment considerations:** Some new local and long-distance services necessitate new phone system equipment. A long-distance T1, for example, may reduce your monthly long- distance bill from $3,000 to $1,270 per month, but using it on an older telephone system could require several thousand dollars' worth of upgrades and add-ons.

Some telephone-service salespeople get customers to sign up for service when their phone system is in no way capable of taking the new service. For example, a CLEC salesperson signs the customer up for an ISDN local T1 with full DID and caller ID capability. The only problem is that the customer's antiquated Intertel Premier telephone system has no such capability. Nor will it ever because the manufacturer supports it only for replacement parts. To accommodate the ISDN service, the customer would need to invest somewhere in the neighborhood of $50,000 for a completely new telephone system. The couple of hundred dollars in monthly savings on the phone service itself wasn't going to cover that expense any time soon.

Always be sure of the exact implications of proposals that local and long-distance telephone service have on equipment. Be sure that you can "dollarize" the benefit; that is, you can pay for the improvement with savings from the new services in the form of hard (cash) or soft (labor savings, customer experience improvements) dollars.

Meaning, for the LD-T1 example, if the cost of equipment is $6,000, the buy-back from savings ($1,730 per month in long-distance spending by installing a T1) is 3.4 months, which is worth pursuing. But if the savings were a mere $100 per month, the sixty-month spread on the cost of equipment should cause you to wait.

■ **Growth considerations:** A change you make in local or long-distance service should carry a shelf life of at least one year. To leverage pricing benefits, carriers will ask you to sign three- or even five-year agreements. Is the technology or service you're buying now going to carry you that far into your future?

- **Pricing:** Will the price you pay today still be competitive in the future? How can that be guaranteed? Some carriers have clauses in their agreements that allow you to go back and renegotiate more favorable pricing if you can show competitive bids.

  Ask questions of your carrier that will give you the security that the decision you make today will carry into the future.

- **Contract minimums:** Beware of minimum-usage requirements that say you must use a certain amount of service each month to be eligible for discounted pricing or you will have to pay a penalty to the carrier. The minimums always seem reasonable when you're signing the paperwork but many forces can drive usage below the threshold. Besides, you never know how you'll change the way you communicate in the future.

  If a carrier insists on volume-based pricing or has minimums with penalties, ask for the right (in writing and without penalty) to modify your usage levels in the future should business changes require it.

Billing Breakdown

FIGURE 4-4   **What to Do If You're Slammed or Crammed**

Slamming is an insidious, deceptive practice. Switching you away from your chosen long-distance carrier, then (usually) charging you abusive rates for service, is virtually theft. Should you take complete control of all your telecom billing, you will undoubtedly encounter this beast during your reign.

At its worst, the switch is made completely without your consent; the offending carrier simply places an order with your local phone company to redirect your PICC. Some IXCs take advantage of the fact that it is not the LECs responsibility to police your choice of PICC to any great

(continued on next page)

(continued from previous page)

degree. The telecom industry runs mostly on an honor system (with some checks and balances) when dealing with IXC-initiated changes to customer accounts.

A carrier may use deception to gain your consent. This deception usually takes the form of a document you sign (a sweepstakes entry, a check made out to you, a survey of some kind) that contains fine print authorizing your switch. The deception could take the form of a phone call in which a telemarketer elicits a yes from you for a seemingly innocuous question (is this Mr. Johnson?), captures the "yes" response in a recording, and uses that "verbal authorization" to enable the switch.

Cramming is more rare but just as insidious. Cramming is the improper billing practice in which companies insert additional or erroneous billing onto your telephone bill. To catch cramming, watch for call charges, service fees, promotional fees, any line item on a phone bill that doesn't make complete sense; call the carrier and ask for an explanation.

When you find evidence of slamming or cramming on your phone bills, follow this simple list of actions to protect yourself and, hopefully, reverse the charges.

1. **Document everything:** Start a new page in your telecom book and keep notes of all correspondence and phone calls. When straightening out a slamming issue, no matter how small, you may find yourself repeating information and reasserting previously covered ground.

2. **Call your local phone company:** Most unauthorized long-distance billing shows up on your local phone bill. The local phone company is usually acting only as a third-party collector of long-distance charges and not as the actual provider of service. You have the right to ask that the carrier remove any disputed charges from your bill. This way, the LEC won't hold you accountable for outstanding long-distance charges and threaten to cut off your service when you don't pay the disputed amounts. While you have the local phone company on the phone, be sure to switch all your service back to your original carrier.

3. **Call your old long-distance carrier:** Let them know you were taken away without authorization and ask for help in getting you switched back. Place accountability for sorting your account out into both the LECs and the IXC's hands.

4. **Call the offending IXC:** Contact the offending carrier and tell them you feel you were switched to its service without permission and do not owe any charges it is attempting to collect.

   Here's when things start to turn gray. Most likely, this type of carrier, which may have been willing to "bamboozle" you into switching service, may not yield so easily and forgive all. Some, you may be surprised to know, immediately yield and reverse all charges. They probably make enough money off the people that don't catch the slam or don't care enough to complain to put up a fight for your dollars. But you have rights when the company won't immediately relent. To give an order to a LEC, a carrier must have your express written or verbal approval.

5. **Ask for written verification (or recorded) proof of the authorization:** If the company says you did authorize the switch, ask it to prove it. A copy of any signature should be easy enough to produce and compare against your own. A legitimate carrier may capture a recording of your approval (or use a third-party verification service to do it for them). Demand to hear it. If the company cannot produce such proof, it should not try to collect anything from you.

   If it can provide the proof, even if it is not your authorization (the company got a minor employee to agree to something on the phone, it got written authorization in one of the less-than-upfront ways described earlier, you remember a weird phone call you didn't quite understand at the time but now seems relevant), you may choose to still assert that, though technically legal, the authorization was obtained under false pretenses.

6. **Get all credit promises in writing.**

7. **Resist, resist, resist:** Refuse to pay if you feel strongly enough that you have been wronged. Or, consider asking for the balance you owe to be adjusted to the rates you would have paid had you been with your original, and chosen, carrier.

8. **File a complaint:** If neither reasoning nor logical resistance works, you still have legal recourse. You can file a complaint against the carrier with both the FCC and the public utility or corporation commission in your state. These organizations, driven by the attractive politics of being hard on the worst offenders in the slamming scam, have

(continued on next page)

(continued from pevious page)

created painful penalties for offending carriers. Sometimes, just the mere mention of this type of complaint, if valid, will cause a carrier to walk away from the headache.

Of course, your best defense in all of this is a good offense. Educate your employees about your policy on telecommunications and the nature of slamming and cramming fraud. Tell them that, whenever questioned about anything related to telecom, either over the phone, through the mail, or in person, to bring you into the picture instead of acting on their own.

4.13 Ten Things to Do Before Signing any Local or Long-Distance Phone Service Deal

When you have made a decision of what products and services you wish to purchase, and just before you apply the purchase program outlined in this book, to going out and finding a supplier, here's another list for you to consider. This may help you avoid many of the miscommunications and hidden expenses that can accompany the sale and implementation of telecommunications services.

1. **Get a schedule of all costs:** The attraction to a new carrier may be pricing. Domestic long distance will now cost you four cents and 1FBs are twenty-three dollars per, but what about everything else? How good is the outbound long-distance rate if it comes with an inbound rate of double? What's the advantage of low local-line rates if your voice mail charges are escalating through the roof?

    Be sure that, as part of your service agreement, you receive a full schedule of all applicable pricing. It should cover all possible cost categories so there can be no expensive surprises later such as calls to Canada, Alaska, or Hawaii or features such as voice mail or call forwarding. Even if rare, include any category of calls you think you'll ever use.

2. **Are the taxes and fees the same:** Tax and fee categories for long distance and local service are regulated by the FCC and your state's public utility or corporation commission. The guidelines to carriers on what to charge in taxes and fees are calculations of both fixed (.028% state telecommunications utility tax) and variable (no more than five dollars per line for presubscribed interexchange carrier charge) formulas. As part of due diligence in pricing, ask for a breakdown of taxes and fees.

3. **Credit issues in writing:** There are several circumstances in which you might find yourself incurring an extraordinary cost to make a switch to a new carrier. You might incur a penalty of some kind with your incumbent carrier to settle a term obligation you had with them. There may be costly new equipment required to support the new service. There may be installation fees. These charges can be significant.

   To avoid having these situations stop customers from coming on board, your new carrier may offer to help cover some or all of the real expense of switching. Usually, you will be offered credits against upcoming future billing with the new carrier—which means you may have to cover the costs out of your own pocket up front and recover them from the new carrier as you incur new bills.

   To assure no confusion or miscommunication on as important an issue as real money, have these credits spelled out on your service agreement. Never take someone's word that you will be taken care of after you come on board in lieu of getting the details in writing.

   Here's an example of how important this is. A heavy construction machinery rental company was facing a $28,000 termination penalty on its old contract if it chose to do business with a competitive carrier offering service. The salesperson for the new carrier assured he would take care of the credits on the back end. The customer signed up. When the rep left the carrier's employment two weeks later it took the threat of legal action by the customer to get the credits—not a great way to begin a five-year customer/carrier relationship.

4. **Rollover policy:** Rollover is the term in a service agreement that states what happens at the end of a term. Here's an example: Imagine you sign a one-year agreement with a new long-distance carrier. In some contracts, there will be language stating that if you do not give notice in writing in a certain format to a certain group at the carrier's corporate office, your term could be automatically renewed for another term.

5. **Always have an exit strategy:** In telecom, service agreement terms there are three kinds of out. The first deals with you wanting to walk away from the agreement for whatever reason. Getting out of an agreement usually comes with a penalty. You may be asked to pay a per centage of the remaining value of the agreement in whole or in part. You might be asked to pay back any discounts or waived installation and set-up charges you had been granted up front. Either way, know the rules ahead of time so if that unfortunate day comes, you can predict and build in the financial consequence.

Another out should cover carrier errors. Somewhere in the agreement should be language describing your remedy for holding your carrier accountable to the services it provides. It cannot fail to provide you service as agreed without repercussion. Read your deal and be sure it is clear.

Usually, the deal will spell out your notification responsibility and will ask you to make service-related complaints in writing, then wait a prescribed period of time before the contract is nullified. Should the issue be resolved, the carrier, if you follow its rules and it fails to remedy your legitimate complaint, should release you from any further financial obligation.

The third way out of a service agreement is usually listed as a trial period or initial probationary period during which you can cancel your agreement with little or no penalty.

Some carriers give you thirty days or more to kick the tires and see if they are providing the level of service you expect. However long it is, note it on your service agreement and mark it on your calendar. And note the exact language of when this trial period starts. There's a clear distinction from "starts the date of the agreement" and "starts the date of initial service." Because some services may take a couple of months to deliver, any trick to shorten the effective length of an initial trial should be uncovered early.

6. **Don't worry which state the jury's in:** There will be a ton of small print in the service agreement. You can't read or be bothered by all of it. Don't worry about minor issues such as what is force majeure or in which state will legal battles between you and the carrier be arbitrated. Focus on the things that affect your service, most of which are listed in these ten tips.

    Pay close attention to the service order paperwork—especially on advanced services. The paperwork a salesperson completes to sign you up usually has two flavors. There is the service agreement, which is the contract that has been discussed in such depth. The other paperwork is how the company spells out how to deliver your service. Ask to review its order forms. If purchasing a T1 or other complex services, review it with your telephone system vendor to be sure it conforms with your equipment.

7. **Really, really call references:** If you would like an objective third-party opinion and really will take the effort to reach out to these references, call someone you know and trust who is a customer. Better yet, ask your salesperson if he will give you the name and number of one of his more recent sales. Or the first company that bought from him. Or someone he knows within a mile or two from your office. Then, with the salesperson there, ask to call the reference immediately. How the salesperson reacts to this simple request will tell you more than you need to know about how comfortable he is with what he sells.

8. **Escalation list:** Wouldn't it be great to get an immediate response to your problem when you call your carrier? The challenge is that most carriers are structured so that customer contact is centralized and generalized as much as possible. You are given

a toll-free customer service number. It rings to a large facility staffed with a constantly revolving array of people with all levels of skill and ways of dealing with customer issues. It is a clearing house for problems, mostly just taking information, opening trouble reports, service dispatch requests, or billing tickets. The people there do not solve problems, they just initiate the machine that solves problems.

To differentiate themselves, some carriers offer you local account managers. The local manager offers hands-on support if necessary, wedging himself between you, the hard place, and the rock that is the company he works for.

You may also be told there is a local technical staff of some kind, that this or that person is your liaison. If offered these names, compile a list of the best and most appropriate people to call for the different possible issues you may need to work on. Make sure they're available to you. Ask for a backup name and number for each of the people on the list. Best of all, get the names of managers.

9. **Insist on a first billing visit:** The best time to fix a problem with your bill is the moment you first see it. Ask your rep to hand-deliver the first bill from his company. If billing is mailed automatically to you, ask him to come to your office the day after it arrives. Go through all items by line item. Do you understand everything? Are the charges correct? Has everything you bought been delivered? If mistakes occur, fix them now.

10. **If you don't understand it, walk away:** Take these ten ideas how they were intended—as suggestions and thoughts on signing smart agreements with carriers. Not all points will be relative to you.

The installation and provisioning of telecommunications services is not a minor feat. Just because the incumbent has been able to provide you with a telephone at your home for seventeen years without unexplained interruption doesn't mean they'd be great at doing that ISDN T1 at the office. There are way too many variables and opportunities for miscommunication and failure—on both sides of the agreement.

And with even newly formed carriers scaling back operations daily and a labor pool of qualified technical personnel stretched because of the number of competitors, too often an imperfect system and undertrained staff is what you get with your order.

You cannot risk as vital a business tool as telephone service. Don't let the details slip. If a carrier is vague or slow to respond to your requests for clarification, walk away from the table.

See Figures 4-5a, b, and c for data sheets for your telecom book.

Billing Breakdown
FIGURE 4-5a **Local Telephone Account Audit Form**

Accumulating a proper inventory of your telephone lines arms you to make better decisions about what services to change when looking for improvements to make in your telecommunications infrastructure. Use this form to break down your local telephone accounts.

The columns are intended to be used as follows.

1. **Location:** List the physical location of the account being audited.

2. **Account:** List the actual billing account number, the carrier, and any contract status.

3. **Lines:** List each of the telephone lines or circuits billed under the account.

4. **Designation:** Where do the lines go? Is the line your main number, one of the rollover lines in your phone system, a fax machine, a modem, or a frame-relay circuit? List a description for each line.

5. **Hunting:** In what order do your lines rollover (1, 2, 3, etc.). If there is more than one rollover sequence in the group of lines listed on the account, show the first as A1, A2, A3 and the second as B1, B2, B3.

6. **Features:** Briefly note any features being billed against the line (call forwarding, voice mailbox, hunting, caller ID).

7. **PICC:** Note the carrier who is programmed to serve you for state-to-state long distance.

8. **LPIC (local presubscribed interexchange carrier):** Note the carrier who is programmed to serve you for in-state or local toll long distance.

Billing Breakdown

FIGURE 4-5b   Local Telephone Account Audit Form

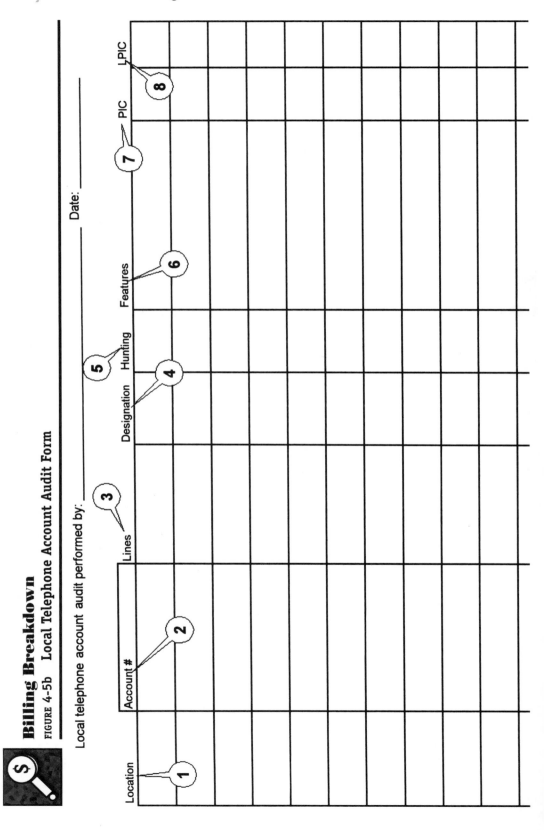

Billing Breakdown

FIGURE 4-5c   Local Telephone Account Audit Form (example)

Local telephone account audit performed by: _____   Date: _____

Location	Account #	Lines	Designation	Hunting	Features	PIC	LPIC
3101 Main	602-555-1100-2	602-555-1100	Main	A1	CF Variable	0288	0288
	Contract to 04	602-555-1101		A2		0288	0288
		602-555-1102		A3		0288	0288
		602-555-1103		A4		0288	0288
		602-555-1104		A5		0288	0288
		602-555-1105	fax		CFNA to 1106	0288	0288
		602-555-1106	fax			0288	0288
		602-555-1107	fax			0288	0288
		602-555-1108	alarm			0288	0288

Business Telephone Systems

5.1 The Different Types of Telephone Systems

Most businesses with more than a couple of employees or a couple of telephone lines use a business telephone system of some kind. There are models of all vintages and all designs, made by scores of different manufacturers. No matter how different they look, they all perform the same role, which is to share the telecommunications resources of the business (e.g., local telephone lines, long-distance service, voice mail system or service, access to public and private interoffice networks) with the users of those services via connected access terminals (telephone set, analog station port, etc.).

You may have a four-phone, seventeen-year-old AT&T Merlin system or you may own a sophisticated, 300-station Avaya Definity PBX.

Phone systems can be simple. There are still 1A2 systems in use—the kind with large, beige plastic telephone sets and a row of oversized clear buttons that light white when a line is in use. You may have seen this type of phone in an old government office or in the detective bull pen of any nostalgic police-based drama television show, such as *NYPD Blue.*

Phone systems can be complex. Some manufacturers have even taken the phone system virtual, allowing you to connect telephones to your computer and use software to make and take telephone calls.

Most systems fall somewhere in the middle of the two examples in sophistication.

In this modern, high-tech age, business telephone systems are usually based on a digital architecture (much like the personal computer), are reliable, and offer software than can drive dozens, maybe hundreds, of features and options.

As a telecom manager, you have three responsibilities to the telephone system.

1. To evaluate the system you currently have, understand its capabilities and features, and its current application to your business.

2. To manage the day-to-day operation of the system, which could mean administrative programming (adding a mailbox to the voice mail system for a new employee or ordering new telephones for new offices) or coordination with a vendor for service, repair, and adds, moves, or changes.

3. To improve the system whenever practical and financially justifiable.

The first step in travelling this path of responsibility is to understand some basic concepts about telephone systems. In a hazy way, telephone systems can be classified by three definitions: *key system, private branch exchange (PBX),* and *hybrid.*

Key Telephone Systems

Key system usually refers to a smaller system, say, thirty-two phones or less. "Key" comes from the term *key-line appearance*, meaning that, on small systems, a button for every phone line appears on every telephone that is connected to the system.

I have a customer who is the U.S. representative for an Italian sandal manufacturer. The company has eight main telephone lines. On each phone throughout the office, there is a button to represent each of the eight lines. This way, everyone in the office shares responsibility for answering calls when the receptionist can't get to them.

Although generally more limited than their big brothers, key systems may have features only once seen on bigger systems (because of the flexibility of digital architecture and that most phone systems are just proprietary computers running phone system software), such as voice mail. Key systems give small offices the benefits of a big-office phone system at a relatively low entry price.

PBX Telephone Systems

When phones were a relatively new and rare technology (yes, there was such a time!), connections between telephones were made manually by branch-exchange operators.

The copper wire to a telephone would wind its way through a neighborhood back to an operator board somewhere. There, it would have been wired into a panel at which an operator would sit. On her board, the operator could see a light representing every connection she was responsible for and had plug-in patch cables (cords—hence the name cord board) with which to make cross-connections between lines.

An electrical signal was driven down the line with a hand crank that signaled the operator to come on the line. She would then manually patch the call to the line going to, for example, John's house down the street. Or to another operator board (across interoffice lines called *trunk lines*) if the call were out of its own exchange. A single-operator cord board would handle a hundred or so lines.

If a company had telephones at its place of business and had enough telephones to fill its own board, it would get its own operator, making it a private branch exchange. (Neat the way that all comes together, isn't it?)

Too expensive to maintain as a manual process, the switching of telephone calls between lines, making telephone circuit connections, became automated with the invention of automated central office switching systems. This automated central office concept is still the way the public telephone network works today.

Soon, private companies could buy these PBX systems to cut down on costs. Instead of paying the phone company for a separate line to every desk, employee phones were now an internal extension of a private system. So a company could share a smaller number of connections to the outside world (because not everyone in the company needed an outside line at the same time) and pay for all the internal lines only once. Now a private, commercial enterprise, PBX telephone systems grew in features and capacities exponentially.

Thanks to the economies of scale and the huge price tags of these monster, private systems, most of the development of telephone technology was made on PBX systems. Any application that is possible with business telephone systems is usually first developed into a manufacturer's PBX system.

Hybrid Telephone Systems

Because of the rapid improvement of the semiconductor processor and the ability of a digital-based system to emulate, through software, features developed on the PBX, along came the hybrid.

In today's market, a hybrid is either a scaled down version of a manufacturer's PBX, usually with most of the same capabilities (such as the ability to handle digital T1 or direct inward dial [DID] trunking) and features, but with a more limited maximum size and processing capability. Or, a key system where the manufacturer has been able to develop a small system to a bigger scale, taking advantage of a larger processor. Hybrids, unlike key systems, can also usually accommodate the digital trunking (DID lines, T1s) that used to be the province of only PBXs.

Hybrids cover the market from thirty or so phones to sometimes two hundred or more. Overlap occurs with key systems in small line sizes and with PBXs in larger, more complicated applications.

5.2 Voice Processing Systems

This section of the chapter discusses voice mail; alternatively considered the most wonderful or the most hated development in business messaging today.

Active Voice is one of the companies in the voice mail business. In the early 1980s, the company consisted of three men who were involved with the base technology that allowed voice mail to happen. What they saw developed in a lab at the Massachusetts Institute of Technology was the ability for a computer to listen to an audio signal, interpret it, and turn it into a digitized computer representation: a file. This was a different concept from the current technology of answering machines, which made actual recordings, usually on cassette tapes, of voice messages.

For voice mail, specifically, a telephone-style connection had been created for a computer that allowed the human voice to be converted to the ones and zeroes that computers thrive on and recorded into a file. After this recording became just another file on a computer, all the rules of how computers can manipulate files followed. Now you could copy this recording with ease, store it, and sort lists of these files in databases. Therefore, at its core, a voice mail system is no more than a database that manages files that are recordings of messages, all packaged behind a nice program that provides users an interface they can deal with.

This new capability of computer technology was seen as a natural expansion of the telephone system and adopted rapidly by the big telephone equipment manufacturers of the time (AT&T, Northern Telecom, Rolm, etc.). Huge, specially designed computers were made by or for these manufactures to add voice mail capability to their PBX phone systems. These systems were built to be somewhat reliable and brought voice mail quickly into the public realm.

The early manufacturers bragged about reliability and insisted on manufacturing their own hardware, even though voice mail was no more than a database. Software companies, Active Voice one of them, not wanting to be hardware manufacturers, decided that they would take the computers they could buy off the shelf at the local computer store (IBM PCs and clones) and build voice mail systems.

In response, the big manufacturers said they could make a better voice mail computer if they made it themselves, that the PC was unreliable. And they were right, at first. But computers grew faster and more powerful in loping strides that took everyone but the most prescient by surprise. Soon, the big proprietary manufacturers still building their own machines were sitting on overpriced, outdated technology with problems such as—because they were not as available as standard, off-the-shelf PC hardware—hard drives that cost $10,000 to replace.

Along with inexpensive hardware, the PC-based manufacturers of voice mail systems also had the advantage of being able to focus strictly on the program itself, on perfecting the voice mail software. They completely took over from the large manufacturers in practically all but the absolute largest firms.

To be fair, most of these proprietary manufacturers have since adopted the standard PC hardware as their own so that today it would be extremely rare if a vendor proposing a voice mail system to you would be offering one that is not built on a standard PC. What this means is that over the past fifteen years, voice mail has become a mature application.

With the speed of development, there are two types of messaging server today. The first is a voice mail system. The second is what is generally called a *unified messaging server*.

Voice Mail

A standard voice mail system handles voice telephone calls for your business and, although, this may vary by manufacturer, performs three specific functions for you.

First, your voice mail system is an answering machine for every employee in your business. Remember, it's an answering machine that allows you to save and delete messages, to forward them to others in the business, and to have one or more personal greetings for your callers depending on either the type of call or your current availability. It should be able to notify you of messages by flashing a light on your telephone, paging you, or even calling you at home at night. When listening to your messages you may be able to speed them up or slow them down, skip on to the next without listening all the way through. It may be able to tell you when the message was sent and, using caller identification (ID), the number of the person who left the message.

For your caller, voice mail is an answering machine that allows him, usually, to review the message before committing to it, to dial zero and get out to an operator instead of leaving a message if that's what he prefers, to mark the message urgent, and to have options besides just beep, talk, and hope that the message was received.

Individual mailboxes don't have to belong to specific individuals. Human resources may have a departmental box that anyone can grab messages out of. Sales staff may have one for taking leads after hours or when they are out of the office. Technical support may have an emergency mailbox that pages whoever is on call to deal with emergencies that week.

The second application of a voice mail system may be that it can act as an automated attendant or receptionist. It should answer incoming telephone calls and present an opportunity for callers to dial through to a destination. It may give numeric options for callers to route themselves (press 1 for sales, 2 for accounting, 3 for our business hours and address, etc.). It may allow callers to dial a specific extension and be transferred. It may offer a directory so callers can spell a name through their telephone keypad and be directed through to an extension.

The third application of voice mail is that it may give you the ability to provide information through messages that normally would have to be distributed on paper or told over the phone. *Listen-only mailboxes* and menus allow your callers to get directions to your office, rules on submission of work to you, the show times of your latest production, or the bid date for your latest construction project. Any general information that could be more easily and conveniently disseminated through a recording and costs you in employee time to relay it live could be handled by listen-only mailboxes.

Unified Messaging

Welcome to the future. Do you use e-mail? For business or personal use? Does your company have a Web site? Do you ever travel and need access to faxes or voice mails or e-mails when you are on the road?

There are so many ways for people to communicate with each other that a problem one voice mail manufacturer in marketing material called *infoglut* has developed.

Unified messaging proffers to bring these disparate messaging technologies together under one roof.

The world has become computer-centric. Unified messaging gathers voice mail and fax messages and puts them into your e-mail inbox.

The idea is that all message types can be managed through a single interface. By gathering different message types together, the manufacturers of unified messaging systems (usually voice mail manufacturers who have expanded their systems with this new talent) create an incredible efficiency of task when communicating. If your work involves constant communication with customers, giving the choice of multiple methods of communications (telephone, e-mail), and being able to manage them in one place is an advantage you may have over a competitor.

Because of the link between messaging types and that the link is managed by your voice mail system, the other upside of unified messaging kicks in when you're not in your office. Have you ever been in an airport, waiting for the call for your flight to begin and remember that you need to check your messages for the day? The only option used to be to listen to voice mail using the nearest pay phone. You could connect the PC to one of those traveler business work stations and dial in for e-mail, or have your office send your faxes to the hotel. Are these choices ever convenient? There are e-mail systems that could send messages to a pager on your belt, but what about faxes or voice mail? Can't send those to a pager on your belt. All these different places to go for messages, these differing interfaces to deal with, are just too much.

One of the easiest interfaces to deal with is voice mail; just dial in and listen. So what if, when you called into voice mail, you had three new voice messages and two e-mails? Wouldn't it be great if it could then read the text of your e-mails to you, allow you to record a response, in your own voice over the telephone, which it would, graciously, attach to an e-mail response as a computer sound recording (.wav file) and zip over the Internet to the originator? All the above are technologies available from your neighborhood unified messaging server vendor.

Ports

The telephone connections between a telephone and voice mail system are called *ports*. You buy a system based on how many ports, how many simultaneous pathways into your voice mail system you need. To gauge this, you ask how many of your employees might be checking messages at the same time, how many callers may be leaving messages at the same time, or how many callers might be being answered by the automated attendant at the same time. The total may be fewer than you think.

Here's a good guide: A rule of thumb is ten users or less to one port, more if you are using the automated attendant feature.

As you may have already concluded, the use of voice mail is vital for business today. Your callers expect it. Your competitors all use it. Whether you employ a traditional voice mail system or a unified messaging platform depends on how you answer the next question.

What About the Price?

Some vendors make and sell small voice-only voice mail systems for less than $2,000. Most often though, voice mail is sold based on either port size or features (to make voice mail inexpensive, some manufacturers will offer a reduced rate system that comes without automated attendant, for example, or the ability to have no more than one hundred user mailboxes). On the higher end of voice mail—systems with six, eight, even sixteen to twenty-four ports—voice mail runs about $1,000 per port. Spread that cost around eight to ten users per port and you could as easily justify it as you would any piece of productivity software.

5.3 Computer-Telephony Integration and Computer-Based Telephone Systems

In 1994, I was working for an interconnect company called Tri-Tec Communications. My second or third week there, the sales rep for one of the telephone systems we represented came through the territory on a training mission. He gave us an hour of his latest thoughts and theories about the state of our business and about the newest tools we had for our sales bags as far as the products his company made went.

About half way through his presentation, I remember a distinct moment where he foresaw our doom. The wave of our collective futures was a technology called *computer-telephony integration (CTI)*. It meant that the same old telephones we had been installing for fifteen years would soon be connected to a computer. It meant that computer screens would become our telephones and the device we use today, the thing with a handset and push buttons, would disappear soon after. So great and compelling was this wave that it would sweep away any who tread water with the same old mentality. "You must become a computer company," he warned. "You will be selling computers as telephones and installing software instead of phone systems. Computers are so much better than phones that as soon as the great computer-telephony integration happens, it would only be a matter of two or less short years and you would be out of business."

It is true that the integration of computers and telephones has meant a lot to companies that provide telephone technologies. In fact, many of the more sophisticated applications of telecommunications technology would not be available today if the computer and software world had not been given a hand into our business. It has happened more slowly than our manufacturer rep predicted because I think he (and most of our industry at first) overlooked the simple fact that the need for this sophistication was either slow in coming or too customized in nature to support an instant—just add customers—revolution.

Traditionally, telephone systems have always been closed proprietary systems. If you wanted to add features, lines, or telephones for your Toshiba telephone system, the only place you were going to get it was from Toshiba directly. Computers are the opposite. The hardware comprising a personal computer could have been made by any of a long list of manufacturers. Out of ten or twenty components that make the system whole, it is feasible that no two have been made by the same manufacturer. Computers are based upon open standards that allow anyone to throw his capitalistic hat into the computer business ring and to build pieces and parts.

PCs are also completely open from a software perspective. Meaning all the different software out there is written to work with the operating system loaded on your PC and if you want to add or change something, you have any of a number of places to go for it.

To make the great integration with computers happen, telephone systems had to be modified to allow computers to send commands to them across some kind of cable interface. The first incarnations of the technology came in two flavors, as discussed in the following sections.

Desktop to Desktop, Telephone to Computer

In the first flavor, you could link a single computer and a single telephone through a cable connection. Phones were adapted to a cable connection to a serial port on the PC. All you needed to take advantage of this link was software to control the telephone. For the software piece, some developers created an actual reproduction of the telephone on the screen where you clicked on the buttons to dial or access features of the phone system.

The software took control of the telephone through a Microsoft-developed standard language called *TAPI (telephony applications programming interface)*. This open-standard applications interface allowed software developers to write programs that could work (in theory) with any telephone system that was TAPI compliant (as long as the manufacturer had written the TAPI integration into its source software and could establish the required physical, cable connection).

More sophisticated applications were soon developed in which a PC user could, for example, open up his ACT! personal information manager software and click on a contact from the address book. The software would automatically dial the phone number of the selected contact. If caller ID was available for an incoming caller, the computer could read the number off the phone, check it against the personal address book and bring up the entry for the caller as the call was ringing.

The industry went wild over itself for a while about such great tools. Some users bought onto the concept. But not enough momentum was built in these desktop productivity enhancements in sales to create the revolution.

Computer Network to Telephone System

The second original flavor of CTI was pioneered first by Novell, who created a standard called *TSAPI (telephony services application programming interface)*. Novell took a slightly different approach to making one computer and one telephone work together at the desktop. The physical link was made between your Novell computer network server and the base cabinet of your phone system.

When a telephony-based software application wanted to exercise a command over the telephone, the command would be sent to the base controller for the phone system. If, for instance, you clicked on an address book entry to dial someone from a telephony PC software application in this environment, the server would tell the phone system to make extension 221 (or whatever was identified in the software of your phone system) dial the following number.

The advantage of dealing at the network level was that more sophisticated applications could be written, programs that could see the phone system as a whole instead of just the narrow view between one telephone and one PC and could deal with multiple extensions and multiple lines of traffic at once. When making routing decision or selecting features to program, developers could look at the whole network environment for resources instead of just the databases and programs accessible to the individual PC desktop.

One example would be a program that, upon an incoming call to your Automatic Call Distribution run call center, waits to see which extension the phone system is going to route a call to, then pops the screen of the matching PC at the same desktop, regardless of where on the network that PC may be.

The Next Level: PC-Based Telephone Systems

What was warned about most vehemently in the beginning of the computer telephony age was that telephone systems would be replaced by computers and phone system manufacturers would be forced off the market altogether, that a PC could be a phone system and could provide connections to telephone lines and have telephones attached. That if it could be done, it would be cheaper and run better than a phone system, that development of new features would happen faster because of the standard, off-the-shelf nature of the PC world.

The physical realities of the PC was one of the biggest original problems triggering this aspect of the CTI revolution. A standard, off-the-shelf personal computer is a machine made from several base components. One of which is the processor. Phone systems also have processors, sometimes running at much slower clock speeds than the chips that come in our home PCs. But they are not alone. In a typical telephone system, the base processor provides some horsepower for the system but there may also be a small processor (or switching matrix) to deal with the connections between incoming lines and stations. There may be a separate processor to deal with the load of a T1 line card alone. A station card, running eight telephones, may have its own processors.

Telephone system manufacturers had grown adept at building their customized computers, the telephone system, to distribute the load and process all the traffic the system is required to handle.

What is your tolerance for timely processing of telephone calls on your business phone system? What if you picked up the receiver and heard dead air instead of dial tone? Wouldn't work, would it?

The PCs single-processor approach to computing bogs down under heavy loads. A slow telephone system processor could result in delays in getting a dial tone, a hesitation or pause as a connection to a line was made, and buttons that take two or three seconds to respond when touched on digital phones. PCs may be able to multitask five or ten desktop applications at a time, but what would happen to a competitor if forty telephone conversations need to happen simultaneously? This is an event even the most basic phone system is built to handle without problems. The physical design of a PC didn't bode well for it becoming a telephone system either. A mid-range telephone system could provide expansion for anywhere from forty to some that can support five hundred or more attached telephones and lines. A tower PC clone may have six expansion slots to add peripheral devices: modem, video card. Only three of them may currently be free. With such a physical limitation, this PC wouldn't be able to support more than three device cards.

PBX and telephone system manufacturers, when selling you a telephone system, are building you a custom computer with all the physical equipment to give you the ability to connect telephones to telephone lines provided by them. All the accompanying features (the ability to place a call on hold, a button that flashes when a phone rings) are given to you through the software provided with the system; another proprietary component. A PC-telephone system, because the hardware is now the standard, off-the-shelf PC, needs an operating system before it becomes something you can run software on. In real-world language, that means that your phone system must be a software program running under, for example, Windows NT on a PC that provides the physical connections between lines and telephones. For telephone systems, it is unacceptable to not be able to pull dial tone on your phone while the system thinks about something. It is never okay to reboot the phone system in the middle of the day and have no way for callers to reach you until the reboot is complete. It is never appropriate to have your phone system "freeze up" on you while in the middle of a phone call.

If these things happened, you'd be screaming at your phone system vendor to fix it or rip it off the wall and toss it into the parking lot. And because of the hardware construction and the state of operating systems, the pure PC-based phone system has still never truly gained full market acceptance. Which is not to say that the world hasn't come close. In the mid-1990s, a company called DASH put out a respectable telephone system that resembled a tower PC and used some standard, off-the-shelf PC architecture. It was used mostly in smaller offices, the largest being a development company using about fifty phones.

There are scores of NT-based systems on the market now as well, some with a robust feature set and ever-growing capacities. They have partially solved the physical limitation by establishing communications between the telephone handsets and the server via the network Internet protocol (IP) (eliminating the need for a physical station port for every telephone). Yet they still seem to struggle to find a market. They are still more expensive than traditional phone systems line by line, and some do not yet offer the types of telephone-based features business users have grown to depend upon and have severe limitation to their growth.

The limitations to the PC's ability to be a good phone system will undoubtedly work themselves out. And these types of systems will succeed—if the market is patient enough to see them through the learning curve. But—and that's a big but—the predicted future that the traditional, proprietary phone system is doomed may still come, albeit in a different way than the telecom industry may have foreseen, or may want.

Is it possible that manufacturer's rep in 1994 had the right idea but was looking at the wrong device to take over for the phone system? There is a piece of standard hardware in many businesses that have computer networks: somewhat similar to a telephone system, it was designed and built to accommodate physical connections between stations (PCs) and lines (network segments). It has the processing power to run software to add features on top of its core responsibility. That equipment is a *network router, switch,* and *hub.*

Think about that: A router-based telephone system. Cisco has one. So does Nortel. Bay Networks has one. Avaya (formerly part of Lucent) has one. They have enhanced their products to the point where they integrate voice calls into their traffic between network points.

This base platform was built for the kind of processing and expansion that is demanded by telephony applications. They are ahead of the telephone system manufacturers because they are in the best position to leverage the standard architecture argument and the combination of the computer and telephony worlds and taking telephone system sales away. A router is a switch, right? So is a telephone system. So yes, maybe, five or ten years later than he thought, that rep was right after all.

Examples of CTI in Today's Business

What does all this industry-insider activity mean to you? Of course, time has marched on and computer telephony has evolved. Microsoft's server-level, network-based telephony Applications Programming Interface based on its Windows NT operating system has become a standard platform for CTI servers. Which means if you are a Windows NT environment on the computer side, there may be many telecommunications, especially call center, applications and programs for you to use.

Interactive voice response (IVR) systems are one. These are the servers that allow you to do things such as call into your bank and balance your checkbook through a telephone interface. Other IVRs allow you to check flight times and upcoming schedules.

Multimedia call centers that are equipped to handle your e-mails, Web chats, faxes, and your voice telephone calls are another example. Messaging systems that integrate voice mail, e-mail, and faxes into a single in box on your desktop is another use.

All these applications are products available to run on Windows NT servers. Whatever your opinions of Microsoft as a company, its operating system has become the one most written to for computer-telephony integration.

When judging CTI and PC-based telephony, it is important to know the difference between proprietary and open computer telephony solutions. A good litmus test for whether the server you are looking at is an open or proprietary platform (be it a predictive dialer, an IVR, or voice mail server) is will it work with phone systems other than the one you currently own? Can the hardware the server runs on be purchased through your standard PC hardware channel?

Ease of administration issues are another huge benefit of open systems. Because of the nature of Windows NT, CTI applications are traditionally administered the same way as any Windows-based program running on NT. You add your users in directory services. You use properties tabs and profiles and all the same organization and application tools you are used to with other server-based applications. See Figure 5-1 for a look at voice-over Internet protocol as a service and as it relates to telephone systems.

For the Toolbox
FIGURE 5-1 A Look at Voice-Over IP

Voice-over Internet protocol (VOIP) is a technology that allows telephone calls to be transmitted over data networks using the standard Internet protocol (IP). VOIP is widely written about in technology media. Most telephone system manufacturers have products to offer that use VOIP technology. But what does it mean to you and your small- to medium-size business? Beyond the hype, technical jargon, and theory, what can VOIP do for you?

The answer actually breaks down into two simple and practical applications. One provides a way to make long-distance phone calls over the Internet at no per-minute cost. The other allows your to buy a phone system for your office that runs on a computer network where the phones plug into network data cable runs.

Wide-Area Network VOIP

Using VOIP technology, a business can make use of wide-area network (WAN) data interfaces (VOIP routers, switches, hubs) that will pass telephone traffic along with their data traffic. In most cases, the VOIP-enabled interface connects to phones or phone systems at each of a customer's multiple sites. The sites can then talk to each other across the WAN. No long-distance charges are incurred (on top of the cost of the WAN connection itself), no matter how far apart the two sites are.

Another application for the technology is teleworking. Install a VOIP-enabled device at a remote worker's home on a high-speed Internet connection and the remote worker could take and make calls through your business phone system from home. In theory, you could have an employee working from anywhere in the world there's a viable Internet connection.

There are also service providers in various cities and countries across the world who will terminate long-distance phone calls cheaply if they are originated on a VOIP connection. You make a VOIP call into their local phone switch in the city you want to call, they pass the call to a standard phone line and complete it locally for you. You save a lot of money on long distance.

IP PBX

Inside the building, VOIP technology has been adopted by phone-system manufacturers to create complete VOIP PBXs. The telephones and the Key

(continued on next page)

(continued from previous page)

Service Unit (KSU)(the brain that provides the phone system's functionality) talk to each other in VOIP over the local-area network (LAN).

One advantage is that, when cabling workspaces in a new office or building, you would only need one wiring infrastructure. Because the phones plug into network data drops, you only need data cabling (no additional phone cabling).

The phones and the KSU address each other differently from a traditional PBX. In a standard PBX, your extension number is determined by which port on the phone system your station cable is physically connected to. In an IP PBX, the phones address themselves virtually (using IP addressing such as computer networks to identify the location of users). The system and the phone "sense" each other when first powered up, allowing all your features, button programming, and security rights to transfer if you move your phone from one location to another.

Many manufacturers have extended this concept in their VOIP PBX. Now, a user can, in many cases, plug his standard office desktop phone into his high-speed Internet connection at home. The office system (if also connected to the Internet) will sense the phone, then allow it to operate as it normally would in the office. A remote teleworker, instead of just being able to process calls, can be a full extension off the phone system.

Another advantage of VOIP PBXs, because they are born of the information technology world, is that they are often managed the same way as computer technology is. Traditional phone systems often have telephone-based programming or complex and proprietary programming that requires special training or limits you to using vendor-certified technicians to administer them. VOIP PBX manufacturers may provide a simple, Windows-based program to manage the system, an interface very familiar to the information technology and network managers often responsible for such a system.

So Why Isn't VOIP Successful?

Based upon the wonderful benefits of the technology, you'd think that customers were lining up to buy and install VOIP. They're not. In an informal poll, there was a less than two percent installation rate of this technology. Less than two of a hundred medium-size businesses had purchased or installed VOIP technology.

The lack of success is not for lack of manufacturer effort. The good ones have pressed their development of VOIP products over the past five years. Almost all offer robust, fully functional solutions for both WAN and LAN VOIP. So what are the reasons this technology has not been adopted as quickly as the industry first anticipated?

Not because of quality. Sure, when the technology was first introduced, the quality of a telephone call was horrible; the technology had not yet been perfected. Calls were choppy, tinny, and often failed. The first IP PBXs also had limited feature sets and couldn't compete against even the most basic phone system. (Imagine buying a phone system where you couldn't transfer a call from one extension to another?). But today is a different story. Although not perfect, call quality is acceptable. IP PBXs now compete feature to feature with standard phone systems.

Maybe it's the bandwidth issue. Because the phone calls are converted into a data protocol to be transmitted over a data network (be it a LAN or a WAN), they can use up data bandwidth. An improperly conditioned or designed LAN or WAN may have trouble when thirty or forty phone calls start hogging precious bandwidth. Some network managers might be queasy allowing that much bandwidth go to nondata traffic.

Maybe the issue hurting the industry is the seeming incompatibility of VOIP technologies; the lack of adoption of a single VOIP standard. Manufacturers don't all write their devices to identical variations of VOIP. This means you would have trouble trying to build a conference call when multiple VOIP connections are concerned. Or you are precluded from making VOIP to VOIP calls (bridges) between yourself and another company using VOIP (but not your kind).

Security may also be a concern. Manufacturers of IP PBXs and VOIP WAN interfaces still need to completely settle eavesdropping and hacker access issues.

Maybe the biggest reason has been cost. Although recently pricing for such technology has fallen into line with the rest of the telecom equipment world, the trend has always been that VOIP technology is expensive. On the surface, IP PBXs have mostly cost more than their standard counterparts. VOIP routers and gateways for WANs cost more than ones that deal with data only.

Whatever the reasons for its slow acceptance, when considering all options for new phone systems or any WAN equipment purchases, the benefits of VOIP technology make it a viable and attractive option. Just know that there will be questions to settle in your mind before taking out the checkbook.

5.4 Defining the Three Types of Vendor

Selling telephone and call-center equipment has been a major part of my professional life. To me, success in sales does not mean always the absolute highest dollar in revenue sold. To me, success in sales means you did the right thing for more potential customers than anyone else and earned your living with integrity and a clear conscience.

I think most salespeople in the world of telecommunications would view success this way. They are more interested in finding a good opportunity, to serve a customer with a real need, with the authority to make a decision and with the budget to justify the expenditure, than in lining up people to pawn off the latest gadget a manufacturer is giving away prize points on. The fun part of the job is developing creative solutions to business problems or enhancing businesses through our specialized knowledge in telecommunications systems.

As a telecom manager, your role is to manage the telecommunications infrastructure. Much of the tasks that role creates are ones you handle by yourself. Sometimes though, the tasks created require turning to a service company to come in and help. For you to be able to face the telecommunications marketplace, it's important to show you how the supply side of the equation works.

As you may have already experienced in your business career, when you need a new phone system or parts and service on an old one, you don't just run the aisles at Office Depot and pull down a new phone system. There is a certain breed of company you turn to: the telephone system vendor. Your needs don't end with the simple purchase of equipment either; it must be installed, programmed, and set up to meet your needs. And what about changes down the line, when you need more phones on your Panasonic digital phone system, need to turn up a new software feature on your dialer, or require a new call flow designed and implemented in your IVR server?

There are three typical business models for the companies out there selling, installing, and servicing telecommunications equipment, each of which will be discussed in the following sections.

Manufacturer Direct

These suppliers are the local or regional direct branch office for a large, maybe global, manufacturer of telecommunications equipment. A good example was Lucent when they were a company who sold, installed, and serviced business telephone systems (in 2000, it split into Lucent, Avaya, and Expanets, fracturing the large and small systems manufacturing roles from the service side of the business).

The good of the manufacturer-direct distribution model was that you are dealing with the source. Generally, a company that large also has the resources to pump a ton of dollars into research and development of new and existing product. If you buy into the company's latest and greatest, you can be pretty well-assured that it is state of the art and the company will be around into the future (although with the ever-increasing pace of merger and acquisition, it may not be owned by the same company or named the same thing as it is today).

The manufacturer distribution model seems to serve multinational or national companies with a lot of branch offices well, those who need consistency of technology across their enterprise for management and support reasons. The downside of these companies is their size. The service organizations are merely branch offices of a national corporate structure and their pricing, both for equipment and especially for technical service, tend to be higher priced than locally owned companies—when you are the only outlet for service or additional equipment for a certain product in a market, you set the pricing based on what the market will bear, without worry of true competition.

There is also the control and flexibility issue. There are circumstances in the purchase of telecommunications equipment in which negative issues arise. To get them resolved, you may need to "go to the top." In such a large company, local managers do not always have ultimate say in issues such as billing disputes and escalated turnaround to fix technical failures at installation time.

Trunkers

On the small end of the distribution scale are *trunkers*. A lot of times the trunker is someone who used to work as a technician for the phone company and now has a small, one or two man operation selling and installing small telephone systems, running jacks and computer or telephone wiring, and servicing the older systems of his former employer.

The new product that a trunker sells is often a phone system model that he purchased over the counter at the local electrical supply house. Panasonic and Vodavi are two manufacturers that make a basic, simple phone system that anyone, with or without any knowledge or experience in telecom, can buy over the counter and re-sell to customers.

Trunkers also are the most active outlet for the resale market, locating old systems through private sale or from used-system dealers and turning them for a profit. A trunker is generally a competent and knowledgeable ex-technician. He may be the cheapest option for some simpler installations.

The flip side is, of course, that trunkers are usually companies of only one or two people. If you are not its only customer, you may have trouble with response times. If you are the only customer, watch out; if he has to make a boat payment, you may find him offering more and more work to you that you may or may not need.

The final down side is that trunkers do not necessarily have to be certified by a manufacturer to sell a product. Which means, because they have made no formal commitment to be a dealer for a specific manufacturer, they may not be trained by the manufacturer, may have no special access to technical support, and could leave you with no manufacturer recourse for issues such as warranty should they disappear.

Dealer Distributor—Interconnect

The happy medium is a locally or regionally based *interconnect*. Interconnects do not manufacture the equipment they sell and install, they become dealers for one or more telephone system manufacturer, sell, distribute, and servicing those products.

With interconnects there is the advantage of local ownership. If there is any kind of a problem with the sale, install, or support of your purchase, the ultimate authority in the company is locally available.

Manufacturers who distribute their products through interconnects tend to be smaller in scale than their manufacturer-direct competitors. This could be advantageous in that they must please their dealers to stay competitive, and dealers are pleased when they have products and support from manufacturers that help them earn business and make money from their customers.

Manufacturers who distribute through dealers will often sign multiple dealers in any given geographical market. This gives you a choice if, after a purchase, you are dissatisfied with the service being given by your vendor. Manufacturers will usually control the number of competitors they sign with, though, to allow dealers some exclusivity and to keep their product in the hands of the most qualified interconnects.

To be a manufacturer distributor, dealers will have to produce certain volumes of sales with the manufacturer; some levels just to be a dealer and higher levels to earn deeper discounting on the product.

The risks for you in doing business with an interconnect are that, because these are local companies, they may fail and you will lose any long-term warranty the dealer gave you. Some dealers are now circumventing this problem by awarding warranties underwritten by third-party insurance carriers, which can revert to another dealer should the original dealer no longer exist.

Another risk is that, because the dealer handles multiple products, the technical staff will not become absolute experts on the system you bought. Meaning that a guy who does nothing but service Toshiba telephone systems is, after so many years, going to have seen every conceivable problem that can occur with Toshiba and may cost you less, in diagnosis and repair time, for service. Too many dealers change products too often for the techs to get a complete handle on each one.

An interconnect is also more likely to hire journeymen technical staff, new to telecom, and give them on-the-job experience as compared with the national companies that have more resources to provide formal certification and training programs for new hires. In defense of the practice, hiring inexperienced technicians and training them on the job is not necessarily bad.

There is one important exception to the traditional, locally owned interconnect that should be noted. There are companies, which may or may not have begun as single, locally owned interconnects, that have grown and added locations to become a network of dealers across the country doing business under one name. In essence they are structured the same as other interconnects: manufacturer-dealer distributors.

Buying Used

Another outlet for the purchase of telephone equipment is the used and refurbished market. Refurbished is a loose term for equipment that supposedly has been remanufactured back to new standards. Refurbished may mean something more along the lines of "cleaned, painted, and tested to still work."

What happens to old phone systems when they are no longer needed? Occasionally, a business shutting down, moving, or growing will put its old phone system equipment up for sale. Companies at the end of a five-year lease may decide they want upgrade to a newer model instead of buying out the lease and keeping what they have.

Because of the rapid pace of technology, a phone system just five to eight years old may be all but obsolete. But if your needs are simple and you are able to clearly define what you want, buying a used system may not be a bad idea. Just know that there are four headaches that come along for the ride.

- **Install and service:** Remember, it still has to be hung on the wall and configured to work how you need it to work. Add the cost of installation to the cost of equipment (unless you plan to do it yourself). This means finding someone technically qualified on the system you buy and who has access to the technical documentation for the system (because it rarely comes with it; dealers usually keep the technical docs for their offices and don't leave a set at a customer site. If they do, they're long since lost).

- **Warranty:** If you buy an old phone system direct from a private individual or business, they cannot stand behind the product they've sold. And most used system dealers will extend to you ninety days on the equipment only.

- **Parts:** Because telecommunications system manufacturers are constantly looking for ways to remain competitive and always developing for the future, there is a finite number of years they will make parts for their older models. For some manufacturers, that could be fifteen years. For many, the length seems more like five to seven. Parts may be tough to come by for an older system. Therefore, the real use for a used system market becomes access to parts. A big advantage in the used and refurbished equipment market is access to parts for older systems. It allows companies stay with older technology that continues to suit them year after year by extending their access to parts. It also provides a source to keep that new-used system alive for a normal life span.

- **Future innovation:** After a system has been deemed obsolete by its manufacturer, its capability has been frozen in time. For example, I once owned a 1972 Ford Maverick. It was bright orange and had a carbureted in-line, six-cylinder engine and I loved it. But it was never going to have an air bag, ABS brakes, or computerized fuel injection. Get the picture?

5.5 Defining Your Phone System's Capability

It is time to get a handle on the telephone system in your office. This is a somewhat daunting task because of the many different phone system types out there. You could, for example, have a KSU-less phone system, which are business telephones with multiple line appearances and, along with other basic features, the ability to intercom, with no central processing unit to tie them all together. Sold via catalog and at large office-supply department stores, KSU-less systems are easy to install and give an office with as few as three or four lines all the phone system sophistication they need.

You could have a wireless telephone system, a variation of a KSU-less system where all the handsets are cordless telephones. You could easily have a complete software or PC-based telephone system.

Regardless of the type of system you have, this chapter will help you identify the resources and questions to ask to achieve your goal: identify the capacity, limitations, and capabilities of the telephone system you currently own.

This information will be critical in making decisions about possible improvements and the merits of any proposals for changes and additions that come along. It will be the framework on which to troubleshoot complaints and problems that will come up in the day-to-day operation of the telephones. Some of this information may be used to apply responsible financial management of any work done on the telephone system by vendors. The information may even allow you to make minor changes and additions to your system without the need to hire in your vendor.

To your employees, the telephone system is the telephone on their desk, the lines they use to dial, the intercom and speaker features, the voice mail box people leave messages for them in. For telecom managers, there's more to it than that.

The basic building block to the telephone system is the cabinet. This is the box that all the pieces go in to make up the phone system's "brain" that hangs on the wall in a back room somewhere. Inside, cards (modules in some smaller systems) are used to connect telephone lines, proprietary manufacturer telephones, single-line or analog telephone devices such as fax machines, modems, standard cordless telephones, and peripheral interfaces for devices such as music-on-hold sources, paging amplifiers or speakers, printers, or computers to gather call data output by the system.

Also inside is a software program that runs this platform, to make use of all the interconnected devices, which brings you the features and applications that make the phone system useful.

To learn about your system, first understand that almost everything you want to know about it is well-documented. You may even have on hand some of the documents that are most helpful. These include the following.

- **Sales brochures:** The glossy slick, single-page document that came with the original proposal for the telephone system can provide an effective summary of your telephone system's capacities and features.

- **General description:** Most manufacturers of telephone equipment produce a comprehensive guide called a general description. It is used as a marketing piece—a white paper to distribute to dealers, salespeople, and customers. It usually contains material significantly deeper than the general sales brochure. Not overly technical, a good general description will run fifty pages or more. It will also be the most valuable document to help in your understanding the telephone system and will cover every aspect.

  - **Physical layout:** Usually a graphic representation of the systems line and station capacity, a list of all peripheral equipment that can be connected to the system, and pictures of the components that make up the various possible configurations.

  - **System features:** An early section will cover the software capabilities that work on the system as a whole, programs such as least-cost routing, toll restriction, night ringing, universal call distribution, and on and on.

  - **Station features:** Another section should list all the supported telephone devices along with their specific features and capabilities.

  - **Display features:** Some phones come equipped with displays and some do not. The extra features and capabilities, like caller ID displays and soft-key menus, will be explained in a separate section.

  - **Special applications:** If the system supports station-message-detail reporting, sample data may be shown. If there is a hotel/motel program available for your system, its features may be covered separately, as would any unique or special application built into your system.

- **User guides:** These brief, pamphlet-style documents encapsulate the features of your telephones in a more concise manner than a general description, giving specific instructions on how to work each. Many vendors will also make a cheat sheet when they first install a telephone system—a single page or two that gives instructions on the top handful of features a user is likely to encounter.

- **System administrator's guide:** Similar to a user guide, this booklet may touch on features only an administrator would need or have the right to access. Items such as the date-and-time programming on your telephone-system's displays or accessing the system-wide-speed-dial program may be included.

- **Installation manual:** The technical manuals that the installer used to initially program your system are a valuable resource and usually guarded by the vendor. Sets of installation manuals (or an electronic version accessed via compact discs or a Web interface) usually never accompany the purchase of a telephone system. If you purchase or own a significantly priced system though, you may ask your vendor for copies. Many simple programming tasks can be accomplished without the help of a vendor if you have good documentation and a basic understanding of the systems programs.

  Many manufacturers offer a software program to simplify the process of maintaining and programming your phone system as well. Installed on a PC and connected to the phone system, the software allows you to simply review, change, and back up the systems programs.

- **Cut sheets:** When installing your system, the vendor creates a document that instructs the technician on how to set up your lines and extensions. It's a short-hand, written description of the phone system program and could be one of the more helpful documents in your search to understand the capacity and capability of equipment. If documented properly, it will list each of your telephone numbers and which port each one corresponds to on your telephone system, your telephone extensions and the port they relate to, as well as the jack location in your office of each connected device.

  You might not even need to remind the vendor for this. A copy of this document is usually kept on site somewhere near the main cabinet. I have found them in a nice plastic sleeve, taped to the top of the main telephone cabinet, in a three-ring binder tucked on a shelf, and rolled up and stuffed inside the cabinet itself.

■ **Schedule A:** As helpful as a cut-sheet in determining what is connected to your phone system, the *schedule A* (the legal description of all the pieces and parts that accompanied the contract you signed when purchasing your telephone system) may be the best help in determining an inventory of what you should own. A correct schedule A lists every cabinet, all software options, every circuit card or module, each telephone, and any peripheral devices bought with the package.

What can be gleaned from your documentation will be answers to questions about what your system can do. How many lines, phones, or devices are now, and can be in the future, supported. For this, start with a physical inventory.

Open the telephone system cabinet and look inside. Write down the model numbers associated with each card. Look for a system model, number, revision, or version number. How many line cards are there? What type of lines do they support? How many lines does each card support? Note also how many empty spaces there are where other cards or modules look like they could slide in. The physical inventory will give you the system's equipped capacity—how many physical lines, telephones, and peripherals can be connected to the system.

Then count your telephones, your lines, and your peripherals. Subtract the actual count of devices from the total available ports that support that type of device. What results is your excess capacity.

Do you have, as an example, four, eight-line digital telephone station cards yet only twenty-nine telephones attached? Then you could grow your system by three additional digital telephones without adding another card.

Be aware, though, that an empty slot in a cabinet does not automatically mean that the system can be expanded by the capacity of an eight-line station card or a four-line central office line card. There are sometimes rules as to which slots can be used for which cards and you must understand them before knowing how much excess capacity is available to you. For example, in a couple of systems, if one slot is occupied by a T1 interface card, the slot or two next to it must be left free.

The importance of this information relates to future

planning of telephone system–affected projects. Know the difference between your system's current and its absolute maximum capacities (the highest limit of telephones, lines, and peripherals supported by your make and model telephone).

5.6 How the Wiring in Your Office Comes Together

The world is all wired together in a way that has dissolved previously insurmountable physical barriers. From my desk in Queen Creek, Arizona, I can connect with my brother in Devonshire, England, by telephone. I can reach my mother in the morning as she travels between her home in Bothell, Washington, and her office in Everett. I can produce a single written communication and release it through the Internet into the electronic mailboxes of the thirteen members of my mountain-bike race team with one press of a "send" key on my screen.

At any given time during the day, I can transmit, at the least, my voice to all corners of the world. I have a phone in my car, several in the house, dozens on every floor in every office in the building where I work. There are even interfaces to the voice network outside many corner stores and roadside stops along my path from home to work.

This network is pervasive. It is organic. It began in a handful of cities and grew outward. It is simply a collection of interconnected switching stations—intelligent computers that take incoming signals on one side, decipher their destination, and pass them along to the next switching point in succession to their end point.

The switches are linked together to switch. The links are sometimes hard-wired: copper, coaxial, and fiber-optic. Sometimes they are wireless: microwave, laser, and satellite.

The only requirement to become part of this global network is an on-ramp, a jumping-on point, a device or utility that allows connection to the geographically most convenient switching station.

For the effective telecom manager, the telephone system is, in effect, the final link in the great, global network as far as your business is concerned. And this final termination is your domain.

And, much like the great public network, it takes infrastructure to bring all the pieces of our domain together. Let's take a tour through the office and see what I mean. While running through the elements, keep your own telecommunications systems in mind and pick out the specific example in your business for each one.

The dmarc

The first stop on our tour through the telecom infrastructure of the office is the point of demarcation *(dmarc)* between your telephone company network and you. This may be a junction box affixed to the outside of your building or, if conduit was provided to the carrier upon the original construction of it, mounted inside. In buildings with multiple tenants, the dmarc tends to be in a common place for all tenants. In multistory buildings, it may be a lower level floor utility room. Wherever it is, as far as the telephone company is concerned, its responsibility for your service ends at this dmarc.

The Backboard

Your business telephone system is usually mounted on a wall to keep it out of the way of your day-to-day operation, protected from the elements, with access to power, and access to all the wiring for the lines, stations, and the equipment it connects to. It usually ends up in a back room, a computer room, or, in buildings with multiple tenants, a common building phone room. Usually mounted on a wall, a thick plywood backing is used by your vendor to hang your phone system equipment. The backboard serves as the main distribution frame for your office wiring. If your carrier's dmarc is not located in the same place, tie-line cables must be run to bring the telephone service over.

MDF/IDF

The wiring for everything that is to be connected to your phone system must end up in one common place. This is the function of the *main distribution frame* (*MDF;* usually located at the main backboard).

Sometimes, in businesses with huge numbers of stations and installations where wire runs may extend hundreds of feet or in buildings with multiple floors, the distance is too great to conveniently terminate every station run individually to the MDF. It is sometimes easier to use *intermediary distribution frames (IDFs)* or intermediary wiring points to gather and distribute wiring.

For example, there is a prominent corporation headquartered in five floors of a twenty-three floor high-rise building in downtown Phoenix. The phone room (therefore the backboard and MDF) is located in the lowest of the five floors. There are somewhere between thirty and seventy employees per floor. Every telephone jack outlet on each floor is wired to a closet near the elevator shaft. Instead of running seventy-two pairs of individual station wires down the conduit through the floors (ending up with more than 300 individual wire runs to punch through to the lowest floor), the stations are cross-connected (spliced using punch-down blocks) onto one hundred pairs of tie cables at IDFs. The tie cables take up less space and are easier to manage.

This use of IDFs and MDFs allows an efficient distribution of wiring through a larger business so that, again, everything ends up at the common telephone system.

Some phone equipment manufacturers enhance this IDF/MDF idea by allowing their phone system to be broken up into individual cabinets or nodes distributed throughout a business to place hardware ports where the users are. Mitel PBXs are one example. The main phone system is housed at the MDF. A peripheral cabinet, merely an extension of the phone system that houses its own station and line cards, can be placed on another floor, in another building, or on the other side of a large facility, then connected back to the main cabinet with fiber-optic cable. Now there's only a hair-thin wiring run needed to provide connections to everyone served by an IDF.

Punch Down and Terminal Blocks

Wall-mounted *terminal blocks* are used to terminate all the station and line cabling so that it may easily be organized, identified, and maintained. There are different types. Sixty-six blocks are about the height of a Big Gulp cup, the width of a cigarette pack, and filled up the center with four rows of metal pins to connect wiring to. One hundred ten blocks organize wire in horizontal rows. And there are others, but all serve the same function, so that wiring is interconnected in an orderly, organized fashion.

Every jack throughout the office terminates to a *punch-down block*. Every line card, every station card, most peripheral ports on the phone system, are wired off the phone system onto punch-down blocks, grouped together and labeled. This way, all lines, ports, and peripherals can be interconnected using cross-connect wires to join the pins at one position on one block to the pins at a correlating, connecting position on another block.

Station Cabling

There is more than one type of wiring that can be used to interconnect a telephone system as listed below.

- **Unshielded twisted pair (UTP):** You've probably seen the wire that technicians use to run jacks in most homes and businesses. It's usually sheathed in a beige, plastic, or polyvinyl chloride (PVC) shroud. If you ever opened up one of the jacks, you'd find either four or eight wires per sheath sorted into pairs of color. Most telephone jacks are wired using the same stock colors and color schemes (green and red, black and yellow, blue and blue-white, orange and orange-white, green and green-white, brown and brown-white). The number of wires needed for telephone devices varies by type and manufacturer. A typical home telephone, for example, uses just two wires: one for the transmit and one for the receive side of the analog telephone signal. An older key system may use two pairs of wires to the telephone set; one pair to carry the transmit and receive of the telephone conversation, the other pair to carry instruction from the phone system controlling the buttons and lights on the phone itself. A modern, digital business system usually requires only one pair of wires, with the control information being buried in the signal with the voice transmission.

- **The category rating system:** Not all twisted-pair wiring is useful for the same purpose. Because of the advancement of telephone systems and the use of copper station cabling to interconnect computers in businesses, a category rating system is in place to measure the data carrying capacity of twisted-pair wire. Category 3 wiring, with a carrying capacity of 10 megabits of information per second, is adequate for most voice applications. Higher categories, such as category 5, 5e, 6, and 6e, are rated for the speeds at which information must travel on a local-area network.

  The ability of copper wire to carry higher speeds of data does not lie only in the grade of copper or even the thickness of the wire, it relates to how many twists per inch are wound into each inch pair of copper wire. Consistently spaced and carefully controlled patterns of twisting in copper wire enhances and secures the carrying capacity of wire.

  So then why not just use the highest grade wire everywhere and hedge your bet? Higher grade wire is more expensive to produce. For most completely new office wiring jobs, companies will install combinations of category 3 and category 6 and above wiring, matching the runs to where telephones and computers will be placed.

- **Plenum and nonplenum:** The construction of commercial office space is governed by a permitting process. These permits require certain methods and standards to be used for the construction of any building or workspace. Many cities and states have rules governing the use of low-voltage wiring as well. It may be, for example, required in your state to run all low-voltage wiring through electrical conduit.

  One common law though, is the use of special UTP coated in fire-proofing plenum material. Plenum-sheathed UTP resembles standard PVC wire but reacts differently in high temperatures. Needing to use plenum-rated cable in your wiring projects can increase the cost of materials fifty to one hundred percent.

- **Other station cabling (coax, fiber):** Computer networks operate on wiring standards beyond that of simple copper wiring. In an effort to bring even higher speed connections to a desktop, fiber-optic cable may be installed in some applications. Because the other wiring methods are necessary mostly for data applications, consult other texts that specialize in data networking to cover them thoroughly.

- **Wireless:** Infrared, microwave, radio frequency—the future of desktop-to-system or desktop-to-server communications is, of course, wireless connections. There are many exciting developments commercially available that will replace wired infrastructure networks, be they supporting voice or data applications or both. Doing away with a wired infrastructure in lieu of transmitters and receivers connected to formerly wired telephone and computer workstations would reduce clutter and complication in every telecom manager's world.

- **The end—jacks:** The end of the line of these station-cable runs is, of course, the jack. Yours may be flush mounted (the cable ending in a box recessed into a wall so the face plate of the jack sits flush with the wall), or surface mounted (a small box glued or screwed to the wall). They may be mounted into the floor, high up on a wall where a phone can hang, or broken out of a plastic strip that hides the wires in places where wire cannot be run through the wall (glass, solid concrete walls, steel shell walls). Whatever the type, be sure to crack one open and understand how the corresponding wires in the run need to be connected to the pins in the jack. The effective telecom manager can wire his own jacks if necessary. And knowing which is the primary and secondary pair on any two-pair jack will help you connect additional devices at the desktop to the phone system at the punch-down blocks in the back.

Billing Breakdown
FIGURE 5-2 **Complete the Wired Journey**

The completion of a simple phone telephone call is a miracle. Understanding how this miracle occurs, learning the path a phone call must make through the public switched telephone network, can be helpful to the effective telecom manager. Only through a basic working knowledge of a system can you hope to make informed decisions about how best to use it or how best to figure out what's wrong with it when it's broken.

To that end, I invite you to follow me on this wired journey; follow a telephone call from my desk at work to my brother's house in Devonshire, England.

I initiate the call: I lift the receiver of my handset and select line two on the button pad of my office telephone. A signal travels through the base cord of the telephone to the modular connector in the jack on the wall behind the conference table that serves as my desk.

It continues through the connecting pins on the jack to the corresponding wires on the station cable running up the wall, across our ceiling, back down the wall in our computer room and to the punch-down block on which my extension cable is terminated.

The signal is then transmitted across the jumper wire to the station position on the punch-down block where the station card on our phone system is broken out. It moves across the twenty-five–pair wire to the phone system where the software of the telephone system connects my station to a central office (CO) line.

My signal travels out the twenty-five–pair wire of our phone system's CO line card to another punch-down block. It is then jumpered to the dmarc punch-down block and connected to the second line in the six-member hunt group of lines we have in service with Qwest.

The signal then travels through Qwest's neighborhood wired infrastructure to the CO. I hear a dial tone on my telephone and I input my brother's telephone number. The switch determines that I am dialing long distance, looks up on my telephone line's program to see who is my long-distance carrier and switches my call across a tie line to the carrier's nearest point of presence (POP).

The carrier interprets the number I dialed and sees that it is an overseas call. It moves the call, switch by switch, across its nationwide switching network until it reaches tie lines it has in place with an international hauler it uses to terminate all European-bound telephone traffic. My call is switched across an undersea, fiber-optic transmission line and delivered to the carrier's European POP.

The signal is transmitted through this carrier's network, switch by switch, until it reaches an interface with the local telephone company that serves Devonshire. The call is handed off across a tie line, then moved through the local network, until it reaches the CO servicing my brother's neighborhood.

The port in the CO corresponding to my brother's telephone fires and electrical current is sent down the wire, through the streets, until it reaches the telephone terminal block mounted under an awning at the back of my brother's house. It then moves across all the extension wiring in his house, across a base cord to the three telephones there.

The telephone in my brother's house rings. All this happened in mere seconds.

It's a wonder the whole thing works, isn't it?

For the Toolbox

FIGURE 5-3a Trouble Report for Phone Problems

Trouble Report for Phone Problems

Reported by:

Date / Time: /

Best way to contact you for more informaton:

Device   Line   Modem   Voice Mail   Telephone Call   Equipment

Affected location

Description of trouble (include all known variables)

When reporting trouble, it is important to know as much specific information about the problem as we can. For example, if you are having trouble dialing a long-distance number, do you receive a recording or a busy signal? If a recording, what exactly does it say? What line were you on when calling? Does the same thing happen if you dial a different number? Use a different line? Call at a different time of day? And so on.

This section for the telecom manager only:

Resspsonded to by: _____   Date / Time: [/]

Specific Details:

Date / Time	Action	Follow up needed	When
/ /			
/ /			
/ /			
/ /			
/ /			
/ /			

For the Toolbox

FIGURE 5–3b Trouble Report for Phone Problems

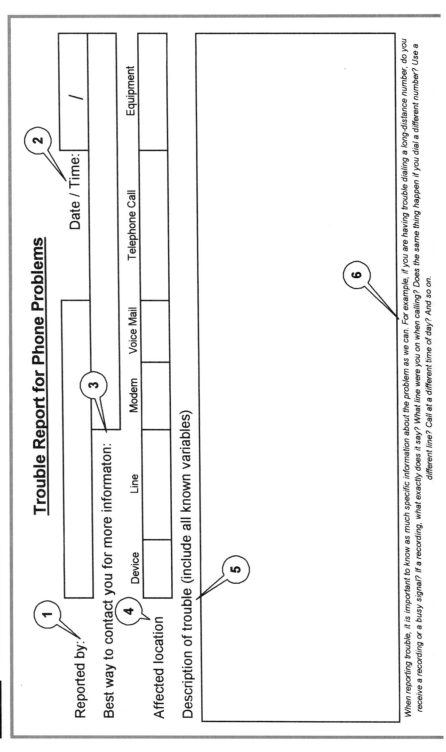

Trouble Report for Phone Problems

① Reported by:

Date / Time: /

④ Best way to contact you for more informaton: **③**

	Device	Line	Modem	Voice Mail	Telephone Call	Equipment

Affected location

Description of trouble (include all known variables) **⑤**

⑥ *When reporting trouble, it is important to know as much specific information about the problem as we can. For example, if you are having trouble dialing a long-distance number, do you receive a recording or a busy signal? What line were you on when calling? What exactly does it say? Does the same thing happen if you dial a different number? Use a different line? Call at a different time of day? And so on.*

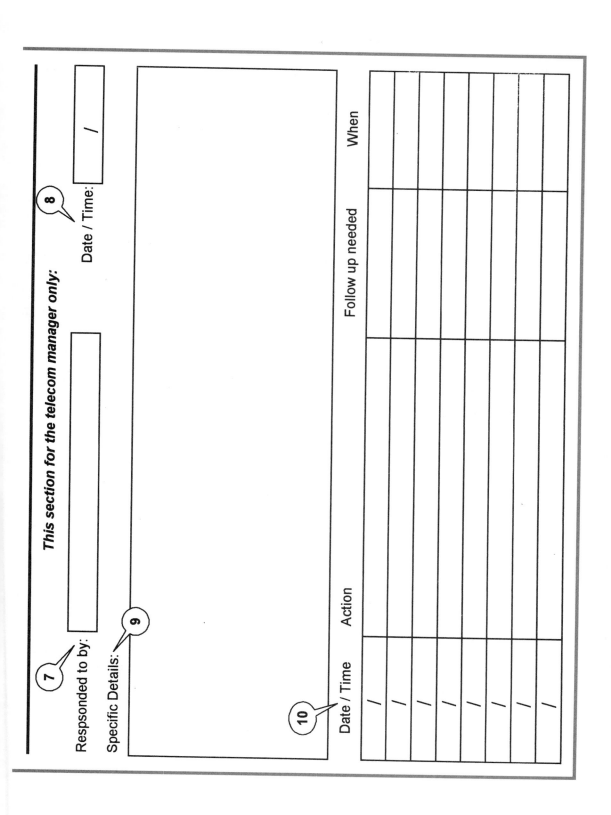

Billing Breakdown
FIGURE 5-3c   **Using the Trouble Report Form**

Use the attached form to collect information from an employee reporting any kind of telephone trouble and track your action through to the trouble's end. The form is appropriate whether you have the complainer fill it out or you use it as a tool to question someone reporting trouble to you.
   The columns are intended to be used as follows.

1. **Reported by:** Who has the problem?
2. **Date and time:** When did the problem occur?
3. **Best way to contact you for more information:** Some problems cannot be resolved immediately. You may have follow up questions for the reporter. Your vendor may need additional clarification. Ask them if phone or email, and what number or address, is the best way to get them later.
4. **Affected location:** Telecom trouble can occur in numerous ways. Ask the user to tell you what specific device or location is the problem. Are they having a problem with:
   • Their telephone device (desktop extension, cell phone, cordless phone, etc.)
   • A specific telephone line
   • A modem

 Billing Issues

The billing issues surrounding our relationship with equipment vendors are relatively simple. They perform tasks for telecom managers who buy telephone equipment and parts and pay them to install, maintain, and program. Therefore, every invoice from an equipment vendor will be a sum total of some version of these elements (with taxes and fees added on) and should be simple to understand, audit, and pay.
   There are different types of billing documents from vendors, though.

Purchase Agreements

Telecommunications equipment salespeople find a prospect, analyze their needs, present them with the information about

- A voice mailbox
- A telephone call of a specific type (local, long distance, international) or to a specific number
- Any other piece of telecom equipment (headset, cell phone battery, pager, etc.)

5. **Description of trouble:** In as much specific detail as possible, can the problem be described?

6. **Notes to the reporter:** See the examples in case a user is filling out the trouble report for you.

7. **Responded to by:** Who owns responsibility for fixing this problem?

8. **Date and time:** When did you first hear about it?

9. **Specific details:** Use this section with the user to get as much additional specific information you need to work the problem.

10. **Actions taken (date and time, action, follow-up needed, and when):** What did you do about the problem (call a vendor, tried to duplicate the problem, switched out the phone)? If the action requires a future follow up (verify solution with vendor, retest the problem in a few days), list what is needed and when.

Keeping copies of completed trouble reports in your telecom book will make you infinitely more effective in resolving similar problems in the future.

systems so they may make an informed decision then field any questions or concerns they may have about the proposal.

If the proposal is agreeable, a sale is complete. Except for one thing: the *purchase agreement*. This legal document covers the terms of the agreement, payment options, total price, address where the system is to be installed, when ownership takes place, how disputes will be handled, and force majeure (the "Acts of God" clause in a contract).

The agreement should also list all the equipment included in the proposal, labor line items, and warranties. From this document, you should be able to determine exactly what you will be charged and exactly what you will receive for the amount. Look also for the following twists.

■ **Line-item pricing:** Don't accept a simple, single price. Ask for individual parts to be assigned their individual value. This allows, should you need to make modifications to the configuration before or shortly after installation, you to know the exact financial impact of your decision.

- ▪ **Pre- and postcut pricing:** Vendors are sometimes given special package deals by the manufacturer they are a dealer for. This can have an impact on the price of equipment with an initial install (as part of a complete, packaged system) and piece by piece add-ons down the road. For example, a Samsung telephone system could be a four-line, four-phone Samsung DCS Compact system, with a built-in voice mail system, for just a couple hundred dollars more than voice mail would cost all by itself. Attractive, competitive packages to customers who fit this system can then be added on. Individual parts, added after the fact, however, cost a premium from Samsung. And because the customers usually go to their original reps for add-ons, the rep charges a premium for such parts.

Service Invoices

Any time a vendor's technician visits, regardless of the work he is to perform or the issue he was called out for, his time and any materials he uses to perform his duties must be accounted for by the vendor.

Usually, this work is captured and managed through a system of work tickets. For example, you call your vendor because a telephone in the accounting office is completely dead. You tell the person who answers the nature of your trouble. That person writes out a work ticket and assigns it to a technician. Many companies' work ticket systems are computerized for simplicity and accuracy, then tied into other systems such as their inventory program (so parts can be located and assigned to your job automatically) and accounting (so billing is simple on the back end of the job).

The technician arrives on site with a paper copy, completes the task at hand (if he has the parts and knowledge to do so), and makes a note of his time and materials used.

Vendors usually require that their technicians review and have you sign off on the work order. This is done so the tech can collect a check should you be a cash-on-delivery customer or, if you have an ongoing account, you have authorized the charges. An adjusted copy should then arrive in the mail for billing exactly what your original copy says.

When looking over that work ticket and later reviewing the actual invoice, you should find these elements that relate to the charges you should pay.

- **Standard labor rate:** The rates at which vendors charge you for the time and experience of their technicians will have a base amount. It varies widely from company to company and from city to city. A two-man interconnect in Benson, Arizona, may only need to ask for forty dollars per hour to cover his expenses and profit adequately for his work. The Arizona division of Expanets, servicing Lucent, the most popular models and brands of business telephone systems, charges $110 for an hour of work in Phoenix. The standard labor rate is the cost all labor formulas are based on. Standard labor rates are usually the applicable service cost for work performed during a vendor's normal hours of operation.

- **Overtime:** Work that falls outside of normal hours of operation may call for a premium labor rate from your vendor. Time-and-a-half is standard. The justification from the vendor is twofold: they may be paying the technician an overtime labor rate or a bonus to be on call.

    Sundays may call for an even steeper overtime rate. Holidays such as Christmas or New Years might call for a steeper rate still (double-time versus time-and-a-half, for example).

- **Minimums:** Vendors have a starting point, or minimum, for every service ticket. The minimum ensures your vendor that, at least, his raw costs for that technician, with all his tools, his vehicle, the gas, insurance, medical benefits, workspace, and overhead back at the office, is paid for. A one-hour minimum may seem reasonable in your market. An hour-and-a-half may not.

- **Billing increments:** For service calls that extend beyond the minimum, what increments of time are to be charged for the additional work? Again, increments of an hour may seem reasonable, but increments of a quarter-hour or half-hour may shave valuable dollars off the back of the invoice.

- **Trip charges:** Another approach vendors use to cover the base expense of delivering a technician to you is the trip charge. The justification for a trip charge is usually travel time to the customer's office. Know the vendor's trip-charge policy and be sure that if they expect you to pay it, you are comfortable for what you are receiving in return.

- **Shop fees:** Some vendors include an innocuous item in invoices: a general surcharge to recover the cost of the small, unbillable material all vendors use in their day-to-day work. Items such as jumper wire, screws for jacks, or electrical tape. Small items that would look silly individually listed on an invoice.

  Not many vendors charge a shop-items fee and those who do automatically add a specific, universal percentage amount to every invoice. The concept is that a small amount spread over every customer will add up to cover the money spent on all those little throwaway items.

Warranty Work

Not every visit from your vendor is cause for a charge. When you purchase telephone equipment from a reputable dealer or installer, you should expect that dealer to stand behind the sale. Most will pass on a manufacturer's warranty expressing that the equipment you purchased is free from defects.

A defective part will fail one of two ways. Either straight out of the box or some time in the first weeks or months of operation of your phone system. Therefore, most warranties cover parts out to a year or two. Beyond that, too many factors, such as the temperature and humidity of the room in which it is located, user abuse, interference from other devices, and so on, can affect the operation of equipment.

Vendors should also stand behind their ability to install and program the equipment to work as designed. Therefore, they will usually offer a warranty to cover the labor portion of any equipment that fails as well as cover any failure on their part to program the system to the stated application.

But not all vendors and manufacturers extend warranties the same way. Ask what coverage comes with the system and for how long such coverage is in effect. Know what the rules are for asking for service in a situation that may be claimed as covered by warranty. This way, when receiving service on the system later in your relationship with the vendor, you will know exactly what and what should not show up on an invoice.

In this discussion of warranty, you may hear some variation of the following.

- **Traditional warranty:** The manufacturer stands behind the equipment for a year or two. The dealer may add in labor coverage to replace warranted parts.

- **After-hours warranty:** Even if a dealer does not, in normal practice, charge labor for time spent working on warranted equipment, it still may charge the difference between their standard and overtime rates if such work happens outside its normal business (standard labor) hours.

- **What's covered, what's not:** Some systems have different coverage lengths and rules depending on the component. For example, a system processor, an internal component that rarely has problems, may be warranted for five years, yet line and station cards for only one. Station sets may have different coverage rules (user damage not covered, for example) than their system component counterparts. Ask if the warranty is universal and covers all equipment equally.

- **Don't forget the peripherals:** If you purchased single-line telephones, a call-accounting system, a channel service unit for your T1, or any of the dozens of possible adds and enhancements to a business telephone system, understand that these devices may carry entirely different warranties. Ask for a definition of warranty by equipment to be sure you aren't taken by surprise.

- **Extended warranties:** Many vendors now offer warranties extended beyond the traditional one- and two-year versions that used to be commonplace. The trend began in the mid-1990s when underwriters stepped forward and offered for sale a warranty that a customer could buy as part of the initial purchase price of a telephone system. The policy would extend the equipment's warranty out to five years. A vendor who participated in the program would add the cost of the warranty premium (a lump sum, usually five to ten percent of the retail price of the system) to the sale.

If a warranty claim was made, the customer would be required to pay a small deductible (usually fifty dollars or so). The vendor would submit the claim through the underwriting company and be reimbursed for the cost of replacement parts and labor.

These types of warranties fell out of favor within the industry when vendors complained of slow to nonpayment of claims by the underwriters. But customers generally liked the idea of no equipment replacement costs for five years; it fit well into many annual budgets. So manufacturers stepped up and began offering a five-year warranted version of their parts to dealers. Dealers pay a small premium to the manufacturer for the equipment they sell, pass the increase on to customers in the retail price, and process warranty claims straight to the manufacturer (where they encounter less back-end resistance).

If you have the option to invest in an extended warranty, know the true cost before writing a check. Understand what the claim rules are—when warranty can be applied and when it cannot. And ask if there are deductibles.

The Maintenance Program Add-On

A warranty is a nice thing to have on your expensive and complicated business telephone system. It gives you peace of mind and can help control your budgeted capital spending on telecommunications equipment. But understand it does not absolve you of the possibility of paying for service. There are still many issues that can occur with a telephone system that cannot be directly blamed on failure of the system or vendor and therefore charged away on warranty. You could experience line problems. Programming could need to be altered or corrected for a previously unknown problem. The cable to your workstation can experience failure. And so on. And remember, not all vendors throw in their labor when working on warranty-related equipment problems.

To help avoid the time-and-material bill, to give you fixed telecom expense, many vendors will offer you a maintenance agreement after your primary warranty period is over. Usually billed as a monthly or annual expense, this agreement entitles you to call your vendor for service, without being billed, for practically any equipment-related issue.

The cost of these maintenance agreements amounts to about two dollars for every line and station your system is equipped for. For example, a business with a telephone system with twelve telephones and eight lines, may pay its vendor forty dollars per month for a maintenance agreement.

You pay every month, whether you need service or not. And there *still* may be occasions that are not covered.

Know what the true cost of a maintenance agreement is, what the coverages are if they extend beyond any warranty that is still valid, and what the rules of engagement are (only good for standard-business hours for example). Many customers may be overpaying for maintenance agreements based upon the likelihood that in any one year they would have to replace the most expensive part on a telephone system. But if the maintenance agreement makes sense and is within budget, it may be nice to not have to worry about unexpected telephone equipment service expense.

What Else to Know About Moves, Adds, and Changes

No chapter on billing issues for purchasing equipment and services from vendors would be complete without touching on a couple of key points about add, move, and change pricing.

- **Mark-ups:** When you are soliciting proposals to purchase entirely new telephone systems, vendors competing against each other will lower their profit margins to try to get your business. Depending on the market, vendors may be only adding a 30 percent to 60 percent mark-up on their raw cost.

  After you are an existing customer, in most vendors' eyes, you are a captive audience. They may feel that, because they maintain and service the system you purchased through them, you have no alternative to whatever they decide to charge. Some vendors take advantage of this position and mark-up the price of individual cards, stations, and peripheral telecom equipment 100 percent or even more.

- **Prequote:** To keep them honest and let them know that you have an eye on the finances, ask your vendors to prequote any add-on work or parts to your phone system.

- **Shop around:** Nothing says you have to accept what the vendor wants to charge for that extra telephone or station card. If you have the choice of more than one vendor for service and add-ons, call and ask for a quote from each. Hold your preferred vendor to the best price.

- **Other circumstances:** Beware of using the open competition approach too liberally. When under warranty, you may be restricted to using only the original installing dealer. Don't burn a relationship with a good vendor to save a few hard dollars on a new telephone

Billing Breakdown
FIGURE 5-4   **What to Watch for on Phone Vendor Service Billing**

The relationship with your telecom equipment vendor is vital to your business. As a telecom manager, you rely on vendors for support and service. Such support comes with a price, however. Whenever a vendor's technician comes to work on your behalf, his time and the materials he uses to perform his tasks must be paid for.

You may have a warranty that covers the work. You may pay a monthly maintenance agreement that entitles you to his work. Sometimes, though, you will pay for his work on a time and material basis.

Most vendors use some kind of written or computerized ticket system to account for, track, and bill their customers for the work their technicians do.

In many cases, the technician uses a form of this ticket or invoice to track his time and materials when working on a job and can leave a copy with you when he is done. In fact, your vendor may actually require you to sign off on the ticket (acknowledging the charges) before the technician leaves your building (so there's no surprise when the bill comes). Assuming you're not a cash-on-delivery customer (have to pay the technician when he comes to your office), the actual invoice you pay from, the statement that comes in the mail, needs a quick audit before you write a check and mail it back.

Run through this checklist and apply any of these suggestions that are relevant to the style of time and material invoice you receive.

1. Is the total cost in line with my expectation?

set. Those vendors tend to pay for themselves in softer ways (like taking less billable time to resolve problems because they are more experienced at what they do).

Auditing Vendor Invoices

Be sure you have eyeballed the following items on your vendor invoices.

- **The technician's work ticket:** The easiest first audit for any vendor invoice is to make sure the pricing elements and amounts match the ticket you signed for the technician when he or she completed their work at your office. It should reflect the time and material information the vendor then used to produce your bill (Figure 5-4). From there, look at the individual elements.

2. If you received a paper copy of the work ticket, does the invoice match the tech's handwritten notes?
3. Is the charge for labor calculated correctly for
   - rate per hour,
   - any time increments and minimums correctly applied,
   - time for this specific job calculated correctly, and
   - overtime or holiday time adjusted (if it applies)?
4. Do you understand all materials and parts listed on the invoice? If you were quoted pricing before the service was performed (or have an agreement with the vendor for certain pricing), do your quotes and the invoice match?
5. Is the date and time of service listed correctly?
6. Does the invoice reference your purchase order or list the person at the company who authorized the service?
7. Are any credits you were expecting from previous billings subtracted from the total?
8. Are the references to terms of payment correct and correspond to your agreement with the vendor? Not adhering to vendor terms of payment (due dates, grace periods, net 30) can trigger financial penalties and denial of service. Make sure that the billing reflects the understanding you have with the vendor.

Billing Breakdown

FIGURE 5-5   What to Watch for on Phone Vendor Equipment Purchase Orders

When you have decided on a new telecommunications technology purchase, there will come a moment in the process called "the close." This is the time to sign the actual purchase agreement with the chosen vendor and make arrangements to pay him for what you will be receiving.

Vendors, of course, use many different variations of purchase agreements, but the elements of all should be similar. When sitting down at a close, your last diligent responsibility is to, as effectively as possible, know exactly what you're signing.

You wouldn't have come to this moment without doing everything you can to ensure you're getting the best deal for your company from the best available supplier, but run through this short checklist with your final agreement before handing over the check and scheduling the install.

1. Is the total cost in line with expectations?
2. Are the elements of the invoice in line with proposals and bids? Match the agreement to your proposals:
   - Equipment elements
   - Labor elements
   - Other elements including cabling costs and training

■ **Time:** Is the time you are being billed correct? Was a technician really on site for time spent above the minimum? Is the minimum correct? Is the time rounded to the correct billing increment based on your understanding of your vendor's billing method? Was the labor rate correct based upon the time of service (standard, overtime, double-time)?

■ **Parts (materials):** Are parts and equipment priced correctly? Do they list on the invoice as individual line items so you can make sense of them (see Figure 5-5)? Do you understand all the parts and their necessity to your job? Do the prices match your original quote (you'd be surprised, especially with vendors that have pricing leeway, because of the normal operations of most vendor accounting departments, how often the invoiced amount doesn't match the quoted amount)?

3. If this is to be a cash purchase, are the payment terms per the proposal (amount of deposit, when payments are due)?

4. If this is to be a lease purchase, are the monthly payments, deposit, and end-of-term payment options correct?

5. Has the lease been approved already? If not, do you understand what you've obligated to by signing the agreement should the lease not be approved (will you have to pay cash, will you forfeit the deposit, will the agreement just be cancelled)?

6. If there are any promised freebies, discounts, or promotions, are they listed on the agreement and the amounts calculated into the total?

7. Is the warranty spelled out correctly (years and coverage) on the agreement?

8. Is the installation date and time noted? Does it concur with the plans to install this equipment?

9. If the agreement contains legal language, paragraphs of verbiage covering issues relative to the purchase, do you understand it and its consequence to this project?

10. Are there any other written or typed notations on the agreement that affect the purchase?

■ **Taxes:** As part of labor and as part of parts, are the taxes correct based on your state tax rules for this type of business? Are there any other taxes, fees, or surcharges that need explaining to your benefit before everything is understood?

5.8 When Is It Time to Make Changes?

The perennial question. When is what you have in place right now good enough and when should it be traded for something newer, better, and faster?

Telephone system manufacturers invest considerable resources developing enhancements to their product lines. The result is that phone systems are getting more sophisticated, more interconnected with computer systems, and more mobile. Phone systems have advanced so fast that the one you purchased four or five years ago may be rendered completely obsolete by the models available today. But not all the latest technology is necessary. When is it time to tinker with the telephone system? Consider these three driving forces.

The first is physical capacity. If your business grows, at some point you may be faced with the reality that your telephone system can no longer meet the physical needs of your growth.

The second good reason is age. At some point it will make more physical and financial sense to replace a decaying telephone system that is constantly under repair.

The third good reason to make a change goes back to the beginning of this chapter: innovation. When you take a good look at your needs and what is available in the telephone system world and see than it can better accommodate your needs than what you own right now, it is time to change.

Evaluating Today's Phone Systems

The best place to receive a thorough analysis of your current system and an accounting of the desires and needs of your business is through the eyes of your employees. They use the stuff every day. They can let you know what works and what doesn't. The terms they use may not be kind but they will tell you the issues about your infrastructure affecting them. Assuming that your employees have had more than one job, chances are they also have seen and used all different types of telephone systems and can give you valuable input into the good and bad of what other companies use.

Reach out to your employees through a simple survey or questionnaire (see Figure 5-6). Be sure and cover the following topics.

- **Phones:** How would they rate the ease of use of your telephones? Is the layout of buttons and displays logical? What would they change if they could? What other system do they like better and why?

- **Outbound calling:** Is the process for making an outgoing call (pressing 9 for an outside line, selecting a line key, for example) logical and simple? Are the users familiar with another way of doing it on another system that is easier and why?

For the Toolbox

FIGURE 5-6   **Questionnaire for Employees About Telephone Systems**

When it is time to begin the process of buying a new phone system, you will learn the most about what your business needs by asking the people who use the phone system in their everyday lives: the employees of your company.

An efficient way to gather such information is through a short questionnaire. The one following is not meant to be exhaustive or precise for every situation; it is meant to guide an employee through the thought process of evaluating your current system and determining what needs to be improved and how it might be improved. It is meant to facilitate creativity, draw from your employee's experience with the telephoning world, and provide you with the best possible blueprint to work from when defining to vendors exactly what you want to buy.

Many of the responses will seem repetitive, obvious, and, some of them, a complete waste of time. Mostly though, you will find a thoughtful, creative, detailed definition of your new telephone system.

Name of respondent: _____

We have decided to investigate the possibility of improving our telephone systems. The purpose of this questionnaire is to give you an opportunity to voice your opinion on what works and doesn't work today. Share your knowledge of what other technologies exist in the world that we should consider during this evaluation process. Answer only what you can or want. Please be as thorough and complete as possible.

Thanks for your input.

Phone Operation

1. Overall, do you like the phones we have today?
2. What would you change if you could and why?
3. Score the importance of these features on a scale of 1 to 5 (5 being most important, a feature you could not live without or a feature you desperately want us to add to the system). Please add any comments you feel would help us better understand your rankings.

(continued on next page)

(continued from previous page)

- Account codes (1 2 3 4 5)
- Call announce over intercom (1 2 3 4 5)
- Call forwarding options (1 2 3 4 5)
- Caller ID (1 2 3 4 5)
- Conference (1 2 3 4 5)
- Direct inward dial (1 2 3 4 5)
- Do not disturb (1 2 3 4 5)
- Executive override/Barge-in (1 2 3 4 5)
- Hold/call park (1 2 3 4 5)
- Intercom (1 2 3 4 5)
- One touch record (record-a-call) (1 2 3 4 5)
- Paging (overhead) (1 2 3 4 5)
- Paging (over the phones) (1 2 3 4 5)
- Redial (1 2 3 4 5)
- Repeat redial (1 2 3 4 5)
- Speed dial (personal or system) (1 2 3 4 5)
- Transfer (1 2 3 4 5)
- _____ (1 2 3 4 5)
- _____ (1 2 3 4 5)
- _____ (1 2 3 4 5)

4. Are there features or functions you would like to see added to our phone system and why?
   - _____
   - _____
   - _____

5. Do you use a headset? Frequently / Infrequently / Never
6. Is there anything you would change about the way your headset operates?
7. Are there any improvements you would make to our music on hold (and why)?

Handling Telephone Calls

1. Is it simple to make a call from your desk phone? (If not, why?)
2. Is it simple to make a conference call from your desk phone? (If not, why?)
3. As a company, do you feel we efficiently handle incoming telephone calls?
4. If not, what are the challenges or problems our callers encounter?
5. Is it easy for you to handle incoming calls? (If not, why?)
6. Do we efficiently handle calls at night?
7. If not, what would you change?
8. Do you know of another company that does things the way we should (a model we can copy)?

Interoffice Call Flow

1. Do you use the intercom function of the phone system to talk interoffice with people at other phones?
2. Is this easy to do? (If not, why?)
3. Do you know of another company that does things the way we should (a model we can copy)?

Voice Mail

1. Overall, do you like our voice mail system? (If not, why?)
2. Score the importance of these features on a scale of 1 to 5 (5 being most important, a feature you could not live without or a feature you desperately want us to add to the system). Please add any comments you feel would help us better understand your rankings.
   - Delete   (1 2 3 4 5)
   - Distribution lists   (1 2 3 4 5)
   - Fax mailbox   (1 2 3 4 5)
   - Forward to another mailbox   (1 2 3 4 5)
   - Pager notification   (1 2 3 4 5)
   - Password protection   (1 2 3 4 5)
   - Retrieve and listen to messages   (1 2 3 4 5)
   - Save   (1 2 3 4 5)

(continued on next page)

(continued from previous page)

- Skip, rewind, or forward while listening to messages   (1 2 3 4 5)
- Time stamps on messages   (1 2 3 4 5)
- _____   (1 2 3 4 5)
- _____   (1 2 3 4 5)
- _____   (1 2 3 4 5)

3. Are the menus simple and logical?
4. Is it simple enough to change your greeting?
5. Is it simple enough to change your personal settings (password, pager notification number, recorded name, etc.)? (If not, why?)
6. Do you know how to forward a message to someone else in the company from voice mail?
7. Is the way the system notifies you of new messages (message waiting light on your phone, pager notification, other notifications) convenient and reliable?
8. Do you know of another voice mail system, a model we can copy, a company you know of that has a system in place that does things the way you think we should do it?

Unified Messaging (for those who have it)

1. Do you use the integrated unified messaging software (the program that puts your voice mail messages into your e-mail inbox)?
2. Is the program simple to use? (If not, why?)
3. Is the handling of messages (retrieving, listening, forwarding, saving, deleting, etc.) convenient and reliable?

- **Inbound calling:** Does this employee answer incoming or transferred calls? Does the phone indicate the difference between a ringing call, a recalling call, a transferred call, a hold-ring-back call in a way that is easy to understand?
- **Moving calls around:** Do they know how to transfer calls to other stations or to voice mail when fielding a call for someone else?

4. Are there any features or capabilities of unified messaging you could not live without?

- _____
- _____
- _____

5. Is there another unified messaging system you know of that does things the way we should do them?

Integration When Outside the Office

1. When you are working away from the office, is your experience simple, convenient, and conducive to productivity when:
   - Checking voice mail or retrieving messages?
   - Calling into the office to speak with a coworker?
2. Is there anything about the experience of calling into our office that needs to be brought to our attention?

Specific Complaints and Extra Suggestions

1. Please list any specific problems with our current phone system that have not been covered by this questionnaire.
2. Please list any other feature or function of our current phone system that you could not live without that has not been covered by this questionnaire.

- **Intercom, paging, and transfer:** Can your employees call across the intercom to another station with ease? Do they know how to access the paging function? Can they transfer calls without fear of dropping callers?
- **Extras:** Do they ever use other, more sophisticated features on their telephone set (such as the conference calling, call forwarding, or do-not-disturb features)?

- **Display options (caller ID):** Would caller ID be helpful and why? If they do not have a display on their telephone, how do your company's employees feel it would be of benefit to them or their callers?

- **Wish list of features:** If they could have or do anything new with the telephone system what would it be? (This will elicit a variety of suggestions from things they think phone systems can do, have heard from

Billing Breakdown

FIGURE 5-7a   **Telephone System Inventory: System and Vendor Profile**

Accumulating a proper inventory of your telephone system and peripheral equipment arms you to make better decisions about what equipment to evaluate and buy when looking for improvements to make in your telecommunications infrastructure. Use this form to break down an inventory of your telephone systems.

The columns are intended to be used as follows:

1. **Phone system vendor:** What is the name of the company who installed or currently provides service on your telephone system?

2. **Address:** Their address.

3. **Service telephone number:** The main telephone number you call to get service on your telephone system.

4. **Customer service rep:** If there is a specific person who handles customer service issues or dispatches technicians to work on phone systems, list them here. If they have a direct telephone number, other than the vendor's main number (such as a cell phone), make a note of it.

5. **Salesperson:** Who sold you the phone system?

6. **Direct telephone number:** What is their direct, pager, or cell phone number?

7. **Installing technician:** What was the name of the technician who either installed your system or is the normal tech to perform service on your system?

8. **Direct telephone number:** Do they have a direct telephone number?

their friends and colleagues that *their* systems do and yours doesn't, or practical experience with others. This question will bring you some of the real gems for your request for proposal. Unfortunately, however, many of the suggestions will not be useful.)

Figure 5-7a shows a sample telephone system inventory.

9. **Manufacturer:** What company manufactures your telephone system?

10. **Model number:** What model is yours?

11. **Equipped lines:** How many telephone lines can you hook up to your phone system in its current configuration — before it would need to be expanded? Use this to compare to the actual lines listed on this system inventory to know your current capability for expansion.

12. **Equipped digital stations:** How many digital (proprietary, desktop telephones) can be installed on your phone system without expansion?

13. **Equipped analog stations:** How many single-line (analog) station devices such as modems and fax machines can be connected to your system before it would need to be expanded?

14. **Additional peripherals:** What other telecommunications system peripherals are added to your phone system — property management interfaces, administration terminals? If any of the peripherals are of the following four categories, list them below.

15. **Voice mail system:** Manufacturer, model, and number of ports or mailboxes.

16. **Call accounting system:** manufacturer, model, software release number, any specific limitations for stations supported or records stored. If you receive support directly from the manufacturer, list any pertinent contact or account information.

17. **Paging amplifier:** Manufacturer, model, number and type of speakers.

(continued on next page)

(continued from previous page)

18. **Music on hold source:** Radio, CD player, digital music on hold system — manufacturer, model, and any details that seem relevant.

19. **Cabinet map:** Diagram the location within your system cabinets of all peripheral cards. Describe their individual function at the bottom of the page if necessary (i.e., DTIB24 = 24 digital stations, LCOB = 8 CO Lines, etc.).

Telephone System Inventory: Lines

1. **Telephone number:** List each telephone number (or channel on a T1) connected to the telephone system.

2. **Hunt group:** How are the lines grouped by your carrier into hunt (rollover) groups? Or, for outbound trunks, how are they grouped in your phone system.

3. **Trunk number:** The number assigned to the line in your phone system's programming.

4. **Port number:** The physical port, on which card, in which cabinet of your phone system, where the line connects.

5. **Line designation (or location):** What do you call the line internally (line 1, line 3, main line, Harry's private line, etc.)?

Telephone System Inventory: Stations (all station ports)

1. **Ext.:** The extension number assigned to the device in your telephone system's programming.

2. **Phone (name and type):** What type device is assigned to the extension (twenty-button digital speaker phone, single-line phone). If the extension relates to something other than a phone (voice mail port, SMDR port, etc.), list the port usage instead of the device type. What is the name that needs to appear on the display when other extensions call this station (if relevant).

3. **Ringing (R-D-N):** During your day, night, and other ringing modes (if your phone system is capable of this feature) does the

station ring always (R), ring only after a delay (D), or not ring at all (N)?

4. **Port number:** The physical port, on which card, in which cabinet of your phone system, where the station connects.

5. **VM:** Is there a voice mailbox assigned to the extension?

6. **LD:** Is long-distance calling allowed at the extension or is it blocked?

7. **Physical location:** Where in your building, in terms relative to you, is the extension (receptionist desk, John's office, laundry room, etc.).

8. **Features:** Are there any specific features required at this extension that are worth noting? For example: Is it the number of a hunt group? Does it need call forwarding to an off-site location? Does it need direct station select buttons? Does it have a CTI link? Is it a main answering position?

Telephone System Inventory: Voice Mail

1. **Mailbox number:** List each mailbox programmed into the voice mail system.

2. **Owner's name:** What person is the mailbox assigned to. List the designation for mailboxes that have no specific owner (auto attendants, audiotext mailboxes).

3. **Ext.:** If relevant, what telephone extension does the mailbox answer for.

4. **Pager notification to:** If it is a personal mailbox, list any call-out notification numbers the user has programmed for when he receives messages.

5. **Name directory:** Does the user wish to be listed in the dial-by-name directory?

6. **Features (or dial-option destinations):** Is there any specific features or programming applied to the mailbox that are noteworthy? For mailboxes with single-digit dial-through options (press 1 for sales, press 2 to be transferred to my cell phone, etc.), list each and the corresponding destination (be it another mailbox, a telephone extension, or a telephone number).

FIGURE 5-7b   Telephone System Inventory: System and Vendor Profile

Cabinet Map

Phone System Vendor

Address

Address

Service Telephone Number

Customer Service Rep

Salesperson

Direct Telephone Number

Installing Technician

Direct Telephone Number

Manufacturer

Model Number

Equipped Lines

Equipped Digital Stations

Equipped Analog Stations

Additional Peripherals

Voice Mail System

Call Accounting Software

Paging Amplifier

Music On Hold Source

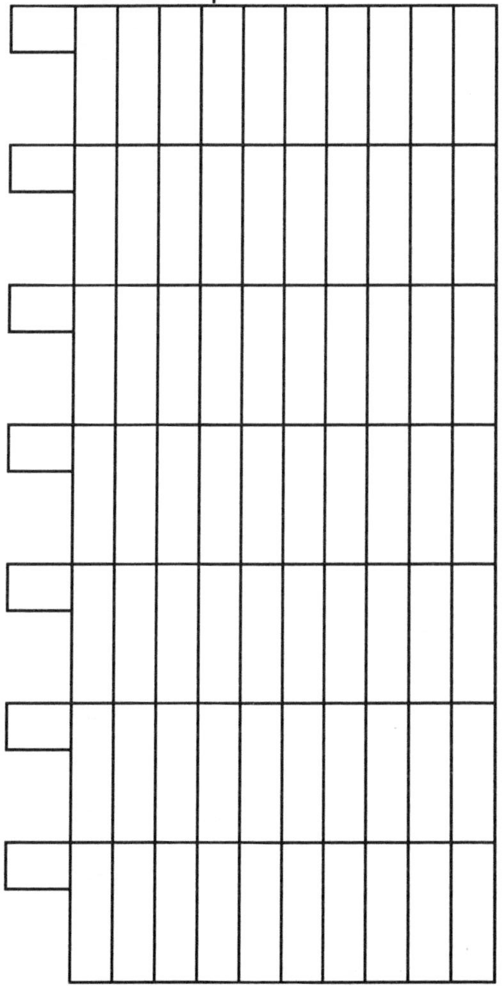

Telephone System Inventory: Lines

Telephone Number	Hunt Group	Trunk Number	Port Number Cab	Slot	Port	Line Designation (or location)

Telephone System Inventory: Stations (all station ports)

Ext.	Phone Name	Type	Ringing (R-D-N) Day	Night	Other	Port Number Cab	Slot	Port	VM	LD	Physical Location	Features

Telephone System Inventory: Voice Mail

Mailbox Number	Owner's Name	Ext.	Pager notification to:	Name Directory	Features (or dial option destinations)

FIGURE 5-7c **Telephone System Inventory: System and Vendor Profile**

Cabinet Map ⑲

①									
CPU (MPB1)	LCOB	LCOB	DTIB24	DTIB24	DTIB24	SLIBE	T1		

Phone System Vendor ① Vodavi Direct

② Address 1800 West Broadway, Suite 1

Address Tempe, AZ 85281

③ Service Telephone Number 480-443-8191

④ Customer Service Rep Steve

⑤ Salesperson Stephen W. Medcroft

⑥ Direct Telephone Number 602-570-6467

⑦ Installing Technician Bradford Pete

⑧ Direct Telephone Number none

⑨ Manufacturer Vodavi

⑩ Model Number XTS

⑪ Equipped Lines 1 T1 x 16 CO lines

⑫ Equipped Digital Stations 72

⑬ Equipped Analog Stations 12

⑭ Additional Peripherals none

⑮ Voice Mail System Vodavi Pathfinder version 9

⑯ Call Accounting Software Trisium Call Analyst – CS# 877-439-9338

⑰ Paging Amplifier Valcom 24v single zone

⑱ Music On Hold Source CD Walkman

Telephone System Inventory: Lines

Telephone Number	Hunt Group	Trunk Number	Port Number Cab	Slot	Port	Line Designation (or location)
T1 Channels 1-24	A1 - A24	100-123	1	8	0-23	DID's 602-555-1000 to 1099
602-555-1100	B1	124	1	2	1	Toll-free line pool
602-555-1101	B2	125	1	2	2	
602-555-1102	B3	126	1	2	3	
602-555-1103	B4	127	1	2	4	
602-555-1104	B5	128	1	2	5	
602-555-1105	none					Fax machine - MAIN
602-555-1106	none					Fax machine - Accounting
602-555-1107	none					Fax machine - Mr. Stephenson
602-555-1108	none					Alarm system

Telephone System Inventory: Stations (all station ports)

Ext.	Phone Name	Type	Ringing (R-D-N) Day	Night	Other	Port Number Cab	Slot	Port	VM	LD	Physical Location	Features
2000	Reception	30 butt / D	R	N	N	4	4	1	Y	Y	V10	
2001	John K.	30 butt exe	N	N	N	4	4	2	Y	Y	V30	
2002	Joe A.	8 butt exec	N	N	N	1	4	3	Y	Y	V31	
2003	Gary A.	30 butt exe	N	N	N	1	4	4	Y	Y	V32	Sales Pool
2004	Brian K.	30 butt exe	N	N	N	1	4	5	Y	Y	V44	Sales Pool
2005	Patrick M.	30 butt exe	N	N	N	1	4	6	Y	Y	V63	
2006	Debra F.	30 butt exe	N	N	N	1	4	7	Y	Y	V65	Call Coverage for Greg R.
2007	Scott B.	30 butt exe	N	N	N	1	4	8	Y	Y	V10	Sales Pool
2008	David L.	30 butt exe	N	N	N	1	4	9	Y	Y	V11	Sales Pool
2009	Shane S.	8 butt exec	N	N	N	1	4	10	Y	Y	V12	
2010	Omar A.	8 butt exec	N	N	N	1	4	11	Y	Y	V33	
2011	Chuck F.	30 butt exe	N	N	N	1	4	12	Y	Y	V24	Sales Pool
2012	Lobby	8 butt exec	N	N	N	1	4	13	Y	N	V71	
2013	Lunchroom	8 butt exec	N	N	N	1	4	14	Y	N	V14	
2060	Voice Mail Port 1		D	R	R	1	6	17	N	N	phone room	
2061	Voice Mail Port 2		D	R	R	1	6	18	N	N		
2062	Voice Mail Port 3		D	R	R	1	6	19	N	N		
2063	Voice Mail Port 4		D	R	R	1	6	20	N	N		
2064	Voice Mail Port 5		D	R	R	1	6	21	N	N		
2065	Voice Mail Port 6		D	R	R	1	6	22	N	N		
2066	Voice Mail Port 7		D	R	R	1	6	23	N	N		
2067	Voice Mail Port 8		D	R	R	1	6	24	N	N		

Telephone System Inventory: Voice Mail

Mailbox Number	Owner's Name	Ext.	Pager notification to:	Name Directory	Features (or dial option destinations)
2000	Reception	2000		N	Covers '0' Mailbox as well
2001	John K.	2001		Y	
2002	Joe A.	2002		Y	
2003	Gary A.	2003		Y	
2004	Brian K.	2004	480-555-9786	Y	
2005	Patrick M.	2005		Y	
2006	Debra F.	2006	602-555-1794	Y	
2007	Scott B.	2007	602-555-8749	Y	
2008	David L.	2008	480-555-1893	Y	
2009	Shane S.	2009		N	
2010	Omar A.	2010		N	
2011	Chuck F.	2011		Y	

Callouts: 1, 2, 2, 3, 4, 5, 6

Including Questions about Your Voice Mail System in Your Survey As voice mail systems have become more popular and accepted in business, you may find your users have equally sophisticated requirements you should consider (see Figures 5-7b and 5-7c on pp. 216–223).

- **Menus:** Voice mail is an answering machine to the people calling you. They hear ringing, they hear a greeting, they hear a beep, they leave a message, they hang up. There's not much to it. The power in voice mail lies in the user interface. How do your users like their message menus? Do they know how to save, skip, and forward messages? What features, such as the ability to slow down a message to carefully listen to a fast-talking caller's phone number, do the users think would be a valuable addition to voice mail?

- **Automated attendant:** Does your voice mail system act as an automated attendant for any part of the day? Have you called your own office lately and listened to the attendant? Do the single-number dial options you're given make sense to your callers? Is the most popular menu choice the first option presented? Does dialing zero lead to a person, a mailbox, or does it loop around and lock callers into "voice mail jail?" You may also survey a few customers about this one, ask what their experience is with your company versus others and solicit opinions on how to make the automated attendant as helpful and friendly as a live one.

- **Reliability:** Some manufacturer's voice mail systems are notorious for lost or delayed messages. How about yours? Can users count on voice mail, on messages to be delivered and received in the way the system should work?

- **Accessibility:** Can users access voice mail any time they need, night or day? Are users receiving busy signals at certain times of the day? Are callers complaining of problems when trying to leave messages for your employees?

- **Ease of use:** How easy is it to change your personal greeting? (Can it be recorded daily, for example?)

- **Models:** Again, is there a company anyone knows of that has a voice mail system with better reliability, accessibility, and options than yours? Ask for suggestions on who, what, when, where, and why.

Understanding What's Available

After you have a firm grip on what the issues are with the current telephone system, and before you put pencil to paper or fingers to keyboard on defining what you want in a new system, it may be prudent to get a feel for any new telephone system technologies in the market. Look for information about new technology in the following ways.

- **Listen:** Your surveys contain important information.
- **Find models:** Yes, this again!
- **Media:** Telecom technology is well covered in the media. Telecom manufacturers invest huge resources ensuring exposure. Are you connected to the Internet right now? Pull up a search engine and type in "business telephone systems" or "telecom magazine" or any number of critical keyword combinations and page through the thousands of responses. You can page through manufacturer and dealer Web sites. You can read online reviews of products.

    There are also numerous books and magazines on the shelf at the nearest quality bookstore ready to break down the possibilities.

    Also, look to the index of this book covering periodicals related to the telecom industry. Many offer online content or free subscriptions and provide sometimes exhaustive studies of the latest available technology.
- **Preliminary visits from vendors:** Invite two or three vendor salespeople to visit your office. Keep the conversation to concepts, ideas, and technologies.

    Ask for references and call on the potential vendor's clients. Use the references as models. Ask how they made their decision to buy the system they did and what issues and applications were accomplished with the purchase.

Defining the New Telephone System

As discussed in the chapter on the purchase process, the best approach to effectively communicating your needs for a new system is to write, in as plain English as possible, a description of your needs.

Be sure and approach the Request for Proposal with these thoughts in mind.

- **Tell them what you have today:** A brief summary of your current environment (phone system, peripherals, and how you apply them) will give a vendor a reference point. Unless you're buying a system for a brand-new facility, the successful implementation of an equipment installation, with minimum risk of downtime, depends on a smooth transition from an old system to a new. So list your phone system's basics. Let them know what telephone line services you have in place today.

- **Clearly and separately, cover your physical needs:** How many telephone handsets are you looking for? What, at a minimum, do those phones need to do (speakerphone capability, hold button, caller ID)? What types of telephone network services do you expect the telephone system to support? What peripheral devices do you need connectivity for (such as hold music or call accounting)? And, probably the most important physical requirement of all, estimate your needs for growth and expansion in the system for the next five years. This nuts-and-bolts configuration will be used first by the vendor as a basis for pricing.

- **Communicate what you're trying to accomplish with the purchase:** Speak only to your needs, the application to be served. A good way to visualize the applications approach is to explain to your vendors in your own words what you want your customers, vendors, and colleagues to experience when calling your company. This picture can be drawn with words or with a flow-chart diagram.

  Anticipate various calling circumstances. Describe then the experience you wish your company to have with this system, what you wish users to be able to do with callers (transfer, intercom to another desk, build conference calls). Do you want a live person to answer or do you prefer an automated attendant? Do you want employees to have private telephone numbers for customers to reach them directly, bypassing a front desk all together?

You may have seen several preliminary telephone system proposals. Pick any items, concepts, or ideas that strike you about certain systems and define them in your request for proposal. But, again, keep the language plain.

Should you see a system with attractive cordless handsets and you see the application for it, state in your document the application.

A creative vendor may come up with a cheaper, better, faster way to give you the same result (so don't tie his hands).

- **Time frame expectations:** Tell your vendor when you want your system installed and working.

5.9 **Quick Hits for Telephone Equipment Purchases**

The checklist that follows, if considered in the purchase of telecommunications systems, will assure a well-informed, appropriate, and productive basis for telephone equipment purchases. These ideas and concepts may help you avoid many of the miscommunications and hidden expenses that can accompany the sale and installation of new telephone-system technology.

Live Demo

Before signing final purchase documents for telephone equipment, insist on either visiting a customer who has a similar system installed or having the vendor give you a live demonstration on a working version of the system at the manufacturer's or your office.

Guaranteed Installation Timeline

Ask your vendor to give you a step-by-step timeline for the installation. It should include all the necessary steps the vendor needs to complete the fulfillment of the purchase including all training classes, technical meeting and on-site technician time. It should clearly state all customer responsibilities. This timeline will be used to manage the cutover, so it's important that it be realistic and complete. Getting a timeline from the vendor avoids unnecessary confusion on who was supposed to do what and when.

Meet the Installer

Having a working relationship with the installer or project manager of your install can help to ensure that the cutover goes smoothly. If you meet in an informal setting, you get to see whether you're comfortable with the vendor's resources, get valuable direct contact information, and, hopefully, give the installer a human dimension to his or her work. So much of the common miscommunication that occurs on technical systems installs can be avoided by the principal players, you and the installer, working together directly.

Meet the Service Dispatcher

Introduce yourself. Take donuts into the vendor's office one Monday morning. The service dispatchers in vendor's offices are the people who have to deal with a hundred customers all day long who get nothing but phone calls about problems. It helps to make yourself a person to them more than just a customer. Say hello and be nice; when the time comes in the future when you need them, you'll ring a little bit softer in their hearts when you call.

Itemized Price Breakdown

Most telecommunications systems are built by assembling components within a contained system (line cards, station cards, voice mail systems). Understand what is being proposed down to its elemental parts. Know the price of each. You can then make educated changes to the final proposal.

Pre- and Postcut Pricing

The cost for components rises when they are purchased individually after the installation. Ask your vendor to tell you what the cost of individual components are if you add them to the total package before the installation is complete compared with adding them after. For postcut pricing, ask for a time guarantee. If a telephone for your PBX with ACD costs $225 before cutover and $292 after cutover, can the postcut price be guaranteed for one year from the install date?

Turn-Key Price

When you and your vendor agree on the total bottom-line price, be sure that it is a turn-key price. This is the total amount you will be asked to pay for the system, to be completely installed and working as the documentation says it will. If you're purchasing a sixteen-station phone system with a four-port voice mail, the price should include everything that is needed to make it run the way defined in the literature. All installation, programming, setup, training, and miscellaneous costs (wires and jacks and so on needed for the installation) should be included.

Hold Out Percentage/Position

There is usually one or two nagging details left to wrap up at the end—a training class still needed, one phone that doesn't yet work, one auto-attendant menu tree not completed.

On cash purchases, insist on a percentage you can hold out (say, 10 percent) to use as leverage to see these final issues resolved without being considered delinquent on payment of the system.

If you lease or finance the system, do not sign the final delivery and acceptance (the legal document that tells the lease company to release payment of the system to the vendor and begin billing you for your monthly payments) until all issues are resolved.

Extended Warranty

Most manufacturers of telecommunications equipment provide a minimum one-year warranty coverage through their dealers. Many dealers, to have a competitive advantage in their markets, will extend the warranty to two years. Some vendors have also formed underwriting cooperatives and are purchasing a form of insurance on new systems (approximately five percent of the total cost of a new system is placed into a collective escrow and used to reimburse warranty claims to any member of the group), which means warranties in the five-year range are now being given.

Expect, as part of your purchase, the longest warranty being given by competitors in your market. Then ask if the vendor will consider extending it by another year. This is a low-cost option for the vendor and a great value add for you.

Free Coordination with Carriers

Changes in your telephone systems often require coordination with and sometimes changes in your local or long-distance telephone service. Insist that your vendor be the one to work out any details with your carriers. These issues can be frustrating time wasters for you. Vendors deal with carriers all day long. They know how to make the proper requests and changes to service. They speak the same language. They can make things go much smoother for the cut. Besides, this way if something happens to go wrong, it would be on the vendor to correct it.

6

Data Lines and the Internet

Connecting Computers

Most of what telecom managers deal with is telecommunications technologies. Some of them may also, or alternatively, deal with the computer world for our businesses.

There are thousands of resources already available to you. Books such as: Newtons Telecom Dictionary, *Data Networking Made Easy—The Small Business Guide to Getting Wired for Success* (Aegis Publishing, May 2000) by Karen Patten or the titles of Microsoft Press, to name a few. Many community colleges offer courses on computing, the applications of business, and information technology (IT) management. There are people who have dedicated themselves to years of theory, study, and practice to become day-to-day professionals.

But there is an interplay between information technology and telecom, one that must be addressed in a book meant to be specifically a resource for telecom managers. Computers are sophisticated tools for business. Telecom managers keep data about customers, products, and employees on computers. They use software applications to track business relationships, communicate, manage all aspects of accounting, and handle hundreds of other business needs.

Years ago, businesses began connecting their computers to each other (in local-area networks [LANs]) so employees could share the information and resources held there. Companies with multiple locations soon widened their networks and interconnected the LANs creating wide-area networks (WANs). Companies could then share information and resources enterprise-wide. Then they added in the Internet's implications in business communications, marketing, product development, manufacturing, and delivery.

This interconnectivity of computers has aroused the imagination of developers, engineers, and designers so that numerous applications have made it into the everyday lives of businesspeople. These applications, in turn, drive the need for carrier base services to allow the interconnection of computers and systems.

Following are examples of the relevance of these applications.

- **Databases and systems:** When you are first introduced to a new client or customer, you should create a record in a database. Record the basic information you might need about them: address, name, phone number, e-mail, types of products and services they have that you might be able to help them with in the future. Make a record in the database about the interactions you have with them; meetings, phone calls, and projects that you perform on their behalf. When you process orders for services for this customer, all the relevant documents and paperwork are stored in your network server. Submit these orders to your vendors through a variety of methods including accessing an order-entry database through the Internet or by dialing in with a modem.

Most businesses of any decent size use databases and computer-storage systems in their day-to-day lives. This dependence upon stored electronic data has created huge demand for connectivity.

Credit-card companies are a good example of this demand. When you make a purchase at a retail outlet using a credit or check/debit card, the store swipes your card through a reader that calls up the database of the credit-card authorization service and makes sure you are entitled to make the purchase. For the system to work, each retail outlet must have instant access to the credit-card authorization database to determine a buyer's eligibility. This is made possible through carrier technology, or computer-to-computer interconnectivity.

- **File sharing:** When cold calling, you may find that many of the offices you visit are branches of a larger company. These could be small, one-of-a-hundred branches for a multinational corporation, or large, regional hubs, or one of a handful of offices within the city for a local company.

It is no longer surprising to find so many businesses that are part of a larger entity. As proud of we are of our diversity and individuality, Americans are, at heart, a generic nation. If a business offers a product or service that is relevant to a specific community, and must be represented in the community itself to be successful, there is no reason to believe that it cannot also succeed equally in any other community.

If a sign-making shop can make enough profit to survive in Flagstaff, Arizona, why can't the same company provide the same service in Tucson, Arizona? Look at Starbucks. It would seem that you can place one for every square mile of metropolitan America and have it be successful!

This duplicative nature of most businesses creates companies with distributed offices, workforces, and presence, which creates demand for the sharing of information. Beyond the databases, businesses share marketing and support material, process manuals, forms, letters, and so on. Because much of the tools of communication in business are created electronically today, sharing the tools between remote offices creates a demand for interconnectivity of computer systems. Many companies constantly access shared documents. All of that paperwork (customer order forms, internal paperwork) can be placed on servers as templates, as can training programs and all marketing material.

- **Interface to partners and colleagues:** Imagine you are a brokerage or agency for a number of insurance carriers. Or an installation and service dealer for an elevator manufacturer. Or a franchise branch of a mailing-services company. The parent, partner, or colleague company you work with may want to extend access to information to you. It may want to allow you access to its stored files. To make use of centrally stored information, you'll need connectivity into that company's system to gain access on your own to the necessary files.

- **Internet access:** We all know the impact the Internet has had on business. Specifically, it has become a great tool for businesses to market their products; communicate electronically with customers, colleagues, and vendors; streamline the purchase process of their customers; and use as a research tool. But use of the Internet by business creates a demand for access to it. You can't get anything out of it if you can't get to it.

- **Intranet:** Businesses often create a private version of the Internet called an intranet to allow partners, subsidiaries, and remote workers access to proprietary services and information. An intranet looks and feels like the Internet, it uses browsers and Web pages to display information and interface with the users. Yet it is closed to public access, only available to those on the WAN or those granted secured, protected access from outside the network. Many customer support, marketing, and internal systems can be accessed through the intranet.

- **E-Mail:** As an extension to Internet and intranet functionality, any business computer with carrier access to the rest of world should be able to send and receive e-mails on a public platform.

     E-Mail is like the fax machine of yesterday. When

fax machines first came out, they were clumsy, expensive, and slow. But they were cool. And the business application, being able to send an image of a document immediately to another location through a telephone line, drove them to become cheaper, faster, and better.

The same goes for e-mail. Companies first adopted it on their LANs as an effective way to manage written communication. When the Internet opened the world to us, e-mail soon widened to become a company-to-customer, colleague, and vendor communications tool. It is a business standard, a must for any businessperson, to have access to e-mail.

For many companies, almost all internal communications are accomplished through e-mail. It is simply more convenient than the coordination of scheduling meetings with people spread throughout the country. More convenient also than the game of phone tag (no matter how fun a game of tag sounds). (And, as a bonus, e-mail comes with a paper trail.)

Do you have these applications in your business? Would you like to? If so, how do you plan to implement the tools and infrastructure needed? Which carrier products and services will you implement?

One infrastructure you may make use of is a WAN. To create one, you may purchase private line circuits between your offices from slower than 56k to faster than 155 megabytes in capacity. In lieu of building a private network, you may use a carrier's frame relay offerings, or make simple modem dial-up connections between locations to interconnect computers and networks.

A second infrastructure needed for some of these applications is the Internet. You may purchase Internet access from carriers.

Third, you may combine the first two concepts to build a private network using the public Internet as the transport medium. In a virtual private network scenario, each location accesses the Internet (whether through high-speed connections or as dial-up clients) and special software is invoked at each point to provide a secure connection, through the public Internet.

Computers are traditionally the domain of the IT manager, yet the effective telecom manager should be educated on, and maybe responsible for, managing a variety of data lines and Internet access services provided by carriers.

In each section of this chapter, the application of that particular technology as it relates to either Internet access, WAN, or both will be discussed.

6.2 Internet Access Technologies

The Internet is nothing more than great, worldwide, public interconnection of computer systems and networks. It's a network of servers, e-mail systems, databases, Web pages, and the users who are accessing those things. When you are connected to the Internet, you become part of the Internet.

To become connected, whether you dialed up using a modem on your home computer or are connected at the office through a high-speed line shared with everyone on the LAN, you must access the network through a carrier service of some kind.

Access is a two-layered product.

First, you must have a link, or physical connection, to the Internet. There are many different telecommunications technologies that your computer or network can use to physically connect to the Internet. From simple dial-up to high-speed wireless microwave links, it will be covered in this chapter.

The speed in which information can flow between your computer or network and the Internet itself will be determined mostly by the physical link (although, as you will read in this chapter, speed is determined by other factors as well).

The second piece of the puzzle in using the Internet is the right to connect to the Internet through your physical link; that is, access to the greater network. This access is provided, as a service, by companies that control the core network that makes up the backbone of the Internet. Well, that's not entirely true. The carrier or Internet service provider (ISP) that can grant you access to the Internet may be buying its access in turn through one of the companies that controls the core network that makes up the backbone of the Internet. Or, your ISP may actually be reselling or wholesaling access through one of the companies buying access through one of the companies that controls the network. You get the point. Access comes through a provider. The physical link comes through a carrier. Most of the time, the two sides are provided by the same company. Not always, though.

Dial-Up

Many of you have had experience with dial-up networking. Local telephone and cable companies may have not yet equipped rural neighborhoods for faster options.

The modem in your computer is a telephone device. Its distinction from the telephone on your desk is that the computer communicates across the telephone lines using a language only other modems can understand (the squeals and squeaks we hear when our modems connect to others).

This technology allows basic connections to the Internet. ISPs purchase equipment capable of receiving modem calls, attach them to local telephone service, and allow customers to establish a connection to their network. Their network, in turn, is then connected to, and subscribers are granted access to, the Internet.

This dial-up Internet service can range in price from free to twenty-five dollars per month per account and higher. In business, and as it relates to a telecom manager, dial-up Internet is meant for small or remote offices that have little use for Internet access or minor e-mail requirements. Dial-up accounts vary by carrier so ask for the details. You may see differences in the following.

- **Access time:** Some carriers limit the number of hours in a billing period you can be connected.

- **E-Mail accounts:** Most dial-up packages come with e-mail accounts that can range from one free e-mail address to seven or ten or more. Other restrictions may be placed on how many messages you can store (or how much data in terms of volume your stored e-mails can amount to) on your providers e-mail server.

- **Web storage space:** Ever had a business idea that you thought would make a good Web site? Many dial-up Internet accounts provide you with a few megabytes of space on a Web server to post your site.

- **Content:** America Online and Juno are examples of ISPs that provide content—a proprietary software program you use to access their service. Compared to just using off-the-shelf browsers and e-mail programs to access the Internet, a content-based service can be good or bad. Good because the software often has additional features (filters, security, mail, instant messaging, links to specific sites) that make the Internet easier to navigate and simpler to manage for the end user. Bad because the interface can become a barrier with the potential to slow your experience getting through to sites.

All else that is required to use dial-up-Internet access is a computer with a modem that is connected to dial tone. For a business, that dial tone could be in the form of standard analog telephone lines or analog station extensions off your telephone system.

Modems today can provide data connection speeds of up to 56k (56,000 bytes of data per second) or more. Because of the less-than-ideal quality of analog telephone service, though, you will rarely experience the full carrying potential of your modem. Your actual speed will depend on the quality of your telephone line, something you may not be able to control.

Installing a separate telephone line for every modem user in your business can be expensive. For a single-computer business, the extra line may be warranted. For an office with multiple modems, there are less costly alternatives.

Most users in a business environment are casual. They need intermittent access to the Internet. They send e-mails individually throughout the day or maybe in a burst, checking and returning e-mail first thing in the morning before heading out for the day. Because of this typical intermittent use, it is not always necessary for a modem to have its own dedicated telephone line. Share a line between several users and have them split the time they use their modems to save money.

Better yet, install analog station ports in your phone system and make your modems simple extensions. This way, when a dial tone is needed for Internet access, it will be granted to the modem by the phone system from the pool of lines everyone shares. This saves the need for dedicated lines all together.

ISDN

The *basic rate interface* version of an Integrated Switched Digital Networking (ISDN) is a copper-based telephone service that provides three channels of communications between you and your phone company.

The digital (d) channel is used to pass signaling and control information. The bearer (b) channels carry information. Because ISDN is a digital service, it cannot be connected to a standard telephone device; it must terminate into an ISDN modem or telephone. Because it is a digital service, it then provides controlled, conditioned speeds at which information can pass. This means ISDN-based Internet access can allow you a connection of up to 128k (two 64k bearer channels) or 144k (2b plus one 16k d channel).

ISDN is a dial-by-call telephone service, so ISDN Internet access is similar to dial-up. But to make use of ISDN as an Internet-transport service, it must be offered by your ISP. It must be equipped to allow ISDN modems to connect to its network. Your local phone company must also be able to provide ISDN telephone lines (not all do because of the network capabilities of the serving central offices [COs] under their purveyance).

Because ISDN is a premium telephone line service, expect to pay more for the line and access than you would for simple dial-up.

Digital Subscriber Line

A *digital subscriber line (DSL)* is a term for a technology that uses the same installed copper telephone wire used for stand-alone telephone lines and ISDN service, but increases the bandwidth. A special interface unit *(digital subscriber line access multiplexer [DSLAM])* is installed in a local exchange carrier's (LEC) central office. A DSL modem is installed on the line at your business. The two devices communicate with each other across standard telephone wiring, at speeds of up to 7 megabytes per second or more.

There are several different versions of DSL with different data transmission characteristics. *Asynchronous DSL (ADSL),* for example, has a higher bandwidth capability for information coming downstream (from the network to you) than for data passing upstream (from you to the network). Think of the application for Internet access here. When connected to the Internet, the information you pass upstream is relatively small; key strokes, mouse clicks, a few typed words into a search engine. What comes back is pages of pictures, graphics, animation, sound. Therefore ADSL would be a great technology for Internet access.

If yours is a business and either hosts a Web site or sends volumes of e-mail, you may want *synchronous DSL (SDSL),* in which the upstream and downstream data transfer rates are evenly matched.

These two basic DSL technologies make use of existing copper infrastructure. SDSL ties up the line, dedicating the copper to its purpose. ADSL allows you to also use the line for voice service and therefore has an advantage.

There are almost a dozen other iterations of the technology. If it works better for your need, *high bit-rate DSL* or *very high bit-rate DSL,* versions with the highest data transfer rates to date, might be more your speed. Or even *rate-adaptive DSL.* Which one you choose will be more a question of what is offered by carriers in your area. There are three questions affecting the answer: First, has your carrier equipped the CO that serves your business to provide DSL? Second, what technology did it base its offering on? Third, are you within range for DSL at all? By the nature of the technology, there are physical limitations to deal with. It only works, at the speeds it is designed for, when the length of cable the signal must pass through—between you and the CO—is below the signal strength limits of the technology.

For example, SDSL has a reach of approximately 18,000 cable feet. Beyond that distance, the signal is generally too weak to carry data. This means cable feet, which in turn means that you may be physically close to the CO but if the route of the cable in the street between you and the CO makes many curves, it may stretch beyond the limit and take you out of DSL range.

DSL can also be adversely affected by other devices installed onto telephone wires. *Bridge taps* connect different paths of wire together that may have been necessary to make a bad telephone line work again, but interfere with DSL signals. Load coils, pair gains, and amplifiers are all used to clean up or boost voice signals. Each one, if installed on your line, can make DSL unusable. So expect limitations when looking into DSL as an Internet access option for your business.

If you can get, or already have, DSL, you'll be enjoying high-speed Internet access which can be connected to a single computer or to a network of computers using a DSL modem or router.

Most often, DSL is offered by your LEC, by competitive local exchange carriers (CLECs), or by an ISP who has colocated its own DSLAMs in a LEC CO and is buying access to the copper-wired infrastructure to make the service work. Some ISPs resell LEC-based DSL and offer it under their own pricing and branding.

Pricing varies based on market and speed, but DSL can range from twenty-nine dollars per month to $150 per month and up.

DSL packages also usually come with options for e-mail service and Web space options similar to dial-up or ISDN accounts. Each provider's offerings will differ. Be sure you understand the details before signing up.

Dedicated

Some ISPs and carriers may offer *T1-based Internet access.* A T1 is an on-all-the-time digital telephone circuit that carries twenty-four multiplexed channels, each with a carrying capacity of 64k. For Internet access, that makes a pretty fast connection: 1.536 (1.544) megabytes per second.

Carriers and ISPs usually call this service *dedicated access or dedicated Internet,* because you are connecting to their network on a dedicated T1 circuit. With dedicated Internet, you'll usually be charged a separate fee for the circuit itself and a separate charge for the ISP service. Some carriers may even charge a port or network-connection charge on top of the rest. This doesn't take into account fees for additional services such as e-mail support or static Internet protocol (IP) addresses. The pricing tends to be about $1,000 per T1.

A carrier may offer to save you some money on the ISP charge by only turning up a fraction of the T1's total capacity (say twelve of the twenty-four channels for a bandwidth of 768k).

T1 is more appropriate for companies with networks of computers that all need a shared, high-speed Internet access connection. Companies that host their own Web site or e-mail server sometimes use T1 so their servers are available to users on the Internet with relatively high reliability and speed.

All else that is needed to make the service happen is a T1 between you and your ISP or carrier, Internet access on the far end of the T1, and equipment on your end to terminate the service. A T1-compatible router, usually offered for purchase or lease by the carrier, provides a termination point for the circuit, deals with the channelization of the T1, and interface to your LAN. Routers also often come with firewall and security software so you can protect your business network from intrusion through your Internet connection.

Cable Modems

Another industry that has wired the world to provide service to the American doorstep are cable television companies.

A telephone network is wired like the branches of a tree. A main line down a major street would feed branch cables into side streets, which may feed smaller branches into a wire center that serves a small neighborhood. From this wiring pedestal, cable runs down your street and terminates at your business.

A cable network is built on loops. A loop would be run throughout your neighborhood, with each business or residence it passes on the way connecting in at the nearest point.

A digital signal is fed along the cable that carriers use to send the hundred or so channels of programming to your home. The box on top of your set is encoded to pick out the channels within that signal that you have paid for the right to access.

Many cable companies have retrofitted their networks and the set-top boxes have grown in capability to extend this digital signal and allow bidirectional communication between your box and the cable company. The box now has extra connections in the back—one that can be connected to a computer or to a computer network. The cable company will, in turn, provide you with access to the Internet.

The advantage to this option is speed. A cable modem can deliver access speeds similar to, or greater than, DSL without the same distance limitations.

The downside of cable modem Internet access is that cable company networks were primarily built to serve residential com-munities. Availability is spotty in business-dense neighborhoods. Although, because of the potential profitability of this new technology, cable companies are looking to extend their networks to hit commercial markets.

Another disadvantage may be some of the security concerns. You may want to involve an information-technology specialist on this, but because of the loop network nature of the service, you must take steps to ensure adequate protection of your computer and the information you pass to the Internet. You're sharing a neighborhood loop with hundreds, maybe thousands of other users. Be careful about the security implications of that access before choosing cable modems as an Internet access choice.

As for pricing, high-speed Internet access costs about forty dollars per month. After a quick survey of other providers nationwide, it seems cable-modem Internet access prices more competitively than DSL in most places.

You also need a cable modem to terminate the service. These special routers can usually be rented or purchased from the carrier at nominal cost.

Wireless

The concept of transmitting information by radio waves between two transmitters or receivers bears so much promise for development, this is where much of the future innovation in telecom will come.

The technology, as it has been adapted by carriers and ISPs for Internet access works simply. A modem, connected to your computer, is wired to a transceiver mounted high on your business. The transceiver is aimed so there is a line-of-sight path to the receiving site for the carrier. The receiving site gathers and sends encoded signals to all the customers the carrier serves. Transmission speeds similar to DSL are possible with fixed wireless.

As with DSL, wireless is an "always-on" technology; after the connection is established, it stays connected unless specifically interrupted. Therefore, wireless is a good technology for business for which sharing high-speed Internet access with all users on a LAN is desirable.

Because the standard wireless technology used is microwave, line of sight between the customer and the carrier is critical. A tree, lamppost, or building impeding this line of sight can limit you from making use of this Internet access option. This means there are specific geographic limitations to wireless that may preclude it from being an option in your market. Because, with wireless, information passes through the air, there are environmental risks to the stability of the technology as well; deflection of the signal off bodies of water and severe weather storms can affect transmissions.

As a counterpoint to the negatives: because (and here's the sexy part with all the implications for the future) it uses radio transmissions through the air to connect both ends of the service, wireless bypasses carrier wired lines. Which means you won't be paying both an LEC and an ISP for the two halves of the service. And because a competitor to an LEC can bypass the existing wired infrastructure, this technology could be adapted to bring voice to businesses. In the near future, you may be able to buy a local or long-distance T1 while never paying for a wire-based T1 to transport the service.

When used to provide Internet access, wireless prices out somewhere higher than DSL yet below fractional or full T1-based dedicated products. There is also the usual assortment of add-ons and features associated with Internet access: e-mail service, Web space for hosting, static IP addresses that allow you to host your own Web site or e-mail.

The equipment required (transceiver dish, mounting hardware, interface cable or card for the computer or network) usually comes bundled with the service. You will probably be offered the option to buy, rent, or lease it, or earn credits to pay for the equipment by signing longer term agreements for service. The only outstanding LAN or equipment issue for your company then is to provide for the same protection and security concerns of other "always-on" LAN-shared interaccess options.

Other Internet Services

There are other products or services you might buy along with Internet access. Following is a handful of products you might expect to encounter on a carrier bill.

- **Web hosting:** Does your business have its own Web site? If so, where are the actual files stored that people view when they select your Web site on the Internet? Many carriers that offer Internet access also offer Web-hosting services.

  What you're buying, in its basic conception, is storage space on a hard drive in your carrier's data center. It comes in three versions. With shared Web hosting, you buy a portion of a hard drive. The remaining space on the server is sold to other customers. Many times, you pay a varying rate depending on the amount of space, amount of data that can be transferred from your site, and various peripheral services. A carrier may offer a variety of packages, each with a fixed monthly cost. You pick the one that suits you the best.

  In dedicated Web hosting, the server that houses your site is dedicated to you. You pay based on the size and complexity of the server and also pay for bandwidth, either for a specific amount of bandwidth allocated to your server, or a package price that allows so much data to be transferred from your server.

  With colocation, you place your own servers inside the carrier's data center. The carrier then sells you access to the Internet out of its data center.

- **Domain name service:** The Internet is built upon a numbered addressing scheme. Every computer, router, hub, and switch directly connected to the Internet has an IP address. Through your browser, you can type in the numbered address of any of these devices and be connected directly with it.

  To read it, the numbering system is based upon four sets of numbers separated by decimal points (a 32-bit number expressed in four octets with decimal notation, to be precise). The numbering is controlled by a central organization (the *Internet Assigned Numbering Authority* globally and the *American Registry for Internet Numbers* [ARIN] in the United States) and no numeric addresses will work on the Internet without coming from the assigned and governed ranges. Because using the numbers to navigate the Internet would be incomprehensible to most users, a scheme was created to allow people to use names for the location of the computer (or a specific folder destination within a computer).

A domain name is made up of a unique name for a Web location followed by one of the domain suffixes that help determine what type of destination the domain name is (dot-com, for example, denotes a commercial enterprise; dot-org, a nonprofit organization; dot-gov, a government Web site; dot-uk, a British Web site, and so on). Domain names have to be registered with one of the cooperating organizations that make sure that no duplicates exist.

Computers still need to address each other numerically. But within the Internet, there are numerous servers (*domain name service* [DNS] servers) that act as interpreters, translating the names we type in to the numbers computers need.

Carriers that provide Web hosting will usually update and maintain your site's information in their DNS database.

- **Static IP:** Should you decide to host your own Web site, you must provide a fixed, permanent address for your Web site files to reside to make it work. To allow you to have an Internet-addressable computer at your own office, your carrier must issue you a fixed, permanent (static) IP address (or a block of addresses) from ARIN-assigned blocks.

- **Branded e-mail:** Carriers sell support for your e-mail accounts to allow people to address you by your private domain name. For example, if you register the domain name XO.com (as CLEC XO did), and your Web-hosting company provides branded e-mail transport, routing, and storage, you would be able to publish <u>yourname@xo.com</u> e-mails for people to communicate with you.

- **E-Commerce:** Some carriers, along with their Web-hosting packages, will provide tools and software to allow you to run transactions for products and services you wish to sell online. This service may include a merchant account allowing your customers to pay you through your Web site using credit cards.

6.3 WANs

The world is full of networks. Think of them all: the public telephone system is a network that allows your speech to be transmitted to another phone somewhere else. When you purchase items at a retail location with a credit card, the credit card machine is networked back to a server that authorizes your purchase. Banking machines are networked in the same way. Cellular telephone networks. Cable television. The Internet.

For business, networks pervade in three types. When you interconnect the computers within a private space — an office, a school campus, a home — you have created a local-area network (LAN). If the reach of your connection spans all manner of borders (cities, states, even countries), you have created a wide-area network (WAN).

There are many different technologies that allow WAN. Many of the connectivity technologies adopted by the Internet access industry began their lives as members of the WAN family. Here's a rundown of the most common.

Dial-Up

There are dozens of software applications and tools that allow dial-up telephone connections to be used to connect private computers and networks. Microsoft's Remote Access Services, part of the Windows desktop and server operating systems, allows companies with remote workers who need secure, direct access to a corporate network to use dial-up connections back to the corporate network.

Dial-up networking is the same technology used to create dial-up Internet connections. The only difference is that the remote user is calling into a private network, not a carrier or ISP access point to the Internet. After the connection is established, the remote user logs into the LAN as he would were he in the office. From this connection, he can use most, if not all, the resources of the LAN.

If you are familiar with a software called PCAnywhere (from Symantec Corp.), you are familiar with another form of dial-up WAN. With it, a remote user creates a connection to another single computer and "takes over" the screen, mouse, and keyboard remotely. The remote user can work and manipulate the connected computer as if he were sitting right in front of it. This is an ideal technology for employees who travel, who can now connect to their base computer back at the office and work, albeit slower, as if they had never left.

There are, of course, many more software applications that allow computers to network using dial-up connections but with a more secure basic concept—a remote user dials into another computer or a network access point and becomes a remote node on the network.

Private Line

A telecommunications circuit, leased from a carrier and wired between two points (remote offices of your company for example), are called private line circuits. They are used for both voice and data communications between the points and are dedicated by the carrier to the leasing customer. Other terms for private line circuits include leased line, point-to-point circuit, and tie line.

Tie lines come in several forms.

- **Analog:** Applicable mostly for voice traffic, there is an analog version of the technology. Based upon standard copper telephone wiring, analog tie lines are single-channel lines leased alone or in bundles. They create voice pathways and can be connected to telephone or data modems with extremely low data bandwidth requirement (old-fashioned, IBM terminal access to a mainframe server, for example).

- **DS0:** When the need is data, the analog, copper-based circuit becomes conditioned by the carrier for data, certified to carry 56k or 64k of data. The circuit is terminated to a channel-service unit (much like the channel service unit [CSUs] used to terminate T1s).

DS0 circuits can be configured in a couple of different ways to accommodate a variety of uses. In a loop configuration, each location to be interconnected has a DS0 installed to the next location in a loop from first to last. This allows all connected locations to share information on the open circuit all the way along the pipe. A loop configuration is equipment-efficient (each location only needs, at most, two CSUs—one for the line from the last point on the loop, one to the next point on the loop) but has vulnerabilities. If one location loses its piece of the loop, no information can pass through them between other sites on the network, which kills the network beyond the failure. Also, information is restricted to move across the network only as congestion will allow it. If multiple locations are requesting files from a server somewhere down the line at the same time, chances are the network will bog down because all the packets of data attempt to make it along the loop.

In a star configuration, a hub location is designated. Each remote site has a DS0 installed back to the hub. This creates an equipment-intense application because the hub location will need a CSU to terminate every remote DS0, but increases the effective bandwidth between the hub and each remote. Faults in one segment, one DS0, are isolated to the affected location only and don't bring down the entire network.

Analog tie lines and DS0 circuits are provided by both LECs and interexchange carriers (IXCs). Their cost depend upon the mileage between the two points you wish to connect. They are usually one of the least expensive, "on-all-the-time" connections you can base your WAN on.

- **T1:** Using T1 (DS1) circuits for point-to-point networking provides several major benefits. First, you will be receiving the full 1.544 megabyte capacity of T1 for your network. Second, because it is a standard telecommunications circuit, it is available practically everywhere there is a serving CO.

Because of the ready channelization of T1 into twenty-four 64k circuit segments, point-to-point T1s are useful as more than just data connections. Circuits on each end of the tie line could be segmented from the twenty-four and allocated (using a special CSU called a *drop-and-insert CSU or a channel bank*) to the phone systems at each point, allowing station-to-station voice calling between two phone systems.

Putting together a T1 tie line is relatively simple. A T1 circuit is installed at one end, terminating at the customer location and at the serving central office. The same thing happens at the far end. For a point-to-point circuit between two offices within a local telephone company's local serving area, a circuit is provisioned through the local network between the two COs and interconnected through the local network to complete the link.

For a point-to-point connection between offices states apart, an IXC must be involved to complete the link. One LEC delivers a T1 to the IXC's local point of presence (POP). The IXC provides a T1 through its interstate network and delivers it to the LEC for the remote office; who, in turn, completes the circuit on a T1 local loop.

T1 tie lines are charged by carriers in two ways. There are three elements to the service; local T1, local T1, and T1 transport between the two points. For an intra–local access transport area (LATA) service (T1s between two points within the same LATA), you would probably be charged one lump sum. The amount depends on your mileage between points.

Traditionally, you buy inter-LATA or interstate T1 tie lines from an IXC. On billing, expect to see three line items. Two recover (pass-through) the local T1 costs from the LECs. The third charges for the transport of your service between the two LECs. Expect again to pay an amount proportionate to the mileage.

- **Bigger pipes:** The exact concept that brings point-to-point DS0s and DS1s can be applied to larger carrier circuits as well. The next transport circuit in the telecom world, for example, is a DS3; a digital circuit capable of carrying 45 megabytes of data between two points. When multiplexed, it breaks down into twenty-eight T1s, each of which, of course, can be broken down into twenty-four individual 64k circuits. That's a tremendous amount of either data for a network, or telecommunications connection between two points.

DS3 is not the ultimate. If you had the need, and the locations you wish to connect are within the physical reach of a carrier network, you may be able to buy access to a *fiber-optic network*. On which you could buy optical carrier network segments in varying capacities that give tremendous carrying capacity. The optical carrier standard OC3, for example, provides a carrying capacity of 155 mb.

It may be hard to conceive of a need for such a huge WAN, but there are applications that warrant it. For example, in Phoenix, the local newspaper, the *Arizona Republic,* has its headquarters. The *Republic* prints several different local editions, at different printing plants across the valley. A local, fiber-based network is used to move the massive amounts of data that make up the layout of that day's paper out to the printing facilities.

The pricing elements of large-pipe private line is usually similar to that of other private line (albeit on a much larger scale). One difference is that where a carrier has a large construction investment to build new facilities to accommodate your request for high-capacity private line, you may be asked to pay the construction costs to the carrier or sign a long enough term commitment that the costs are recovered from you over time.

■ **Multiplexing and inverse multiplexing:** Some carriers offer advanced hybrids of private line service. What if one T1, or one DS0, is not enough bandwidth for your WAN? If 1.544 megabytes of bandwidth between two points was not enough for your application, you could order two or more T1s to make the connection. If you do, however, you will need to employ an inverse multiplexer (a device that, instead of splitting the channels of a single digital circuit, binds multiple circuits together) to create one larger pathway for your data to travel through.

Frame Relay

The cost of private line service can be overwhelming, especially when the remote offices lie at great distances from the host.

Frame relay is similar to private line data service in that it provides a link between two points. The difference is that the network itself is a shared resource. Your information moves across network connections between frame relay switches along with every other customer of the carrier. The pathway between your locations is no longer dedicated only to your traffic.

As a customer, you buy access to the network and pay for the right to move your information through the network to another location.

To separate your traffic from another customer's traffic, it is divided into frames—chunks of data—and marked with a set of control information that allows the network to distinguish it from others. These headers and footers tell the network where the data came from and where they are destined.

The launching point for your data is a *frame relay access link,* a circuit installed between each of your office locations and the carrier's nearest frame relay network POP. Because you pay only for access, and not mileage between locations, links tend to be inexpensive in terms relative to private line.

Your access link should be configured based on what is the maximum bandwidth you may want to push in and out of that location. It may be a DS0, on which you pay for 32, 56, or even 64k of network access. Your link may be a T1, which you pay for however many channels you need as a pipe for data (128k [two channels] or 768k [twelve channels]).

The price of the frame relay service is then determined by how much bandwidth you want guaranteed through the network. Because the network is shared among many customers, the carriers oversubscribe it to spread the costs around (which means that if you added up the bandwidth size of all the access links of all the customers on the network, you would exceed the total capacity of the network several times over). This oversubscription works in practical application because not every customer needs all of its bandwidth all the time; bandwidth is only used when actual data are passed between two points.

With frame relay service, you buy a guaranteed bandwidth (called *committed information rate,* or CIR) for your access links. You can operate at the CIR all day long.

Network allocates CIR through the use of permanent virtual circuits (PVCs). A PVC is a logical address or pointer within the network that establishes a pathway for data to travel. Your point A is assigned a PVC to your point B. Data are now permitted to pass (at the CIR of the PVC) between the two points.

To build a simple, star-design, multilocation frame network, you assign PVCs from the host to each remote and a PVC from each remote back to the host. In this design, information can travel between remotes by moving through the host *(hub)* location. Some customers may wish to "mesh" their network. That is, to create PVCs between remotes as well as from hub to remote so data can travel in multiple directions, enhancing the performance of the network and reducing the risk of service-affecting failures.

Policing the CIR is handled by the carrier's network in the addressing of your frames through a small element of the packet of information contained in your header called a *discard-eligible bit*. Frames coming across an access link above the CIR (up to the full bandwidth capacity of the access link) are marked as eligible for discard by the network. Should the network be congested along pathways your data would travel, the discard-eligible frames can be rejected by the carrier's routers and the remaining data (up to your CIR) be allowed to pass.

To help you manage the possibility that some of your valuable data may be thrown out by the network, the control packets contain information telling the receiving router (sometimes known as a frame relay assembler/disassembler or frame relay access device) how many frames of data make up the current transmission. Should any frames not arrive (discarded by the network), a retransmission request can be sent back to the original source.

The other major advantage of frame relay is equipment investment. Because the interconnection of multiple sites is handled logically, each point on the network has only one physical link. Therefore only one set of hardware is needed at the host to interface the service.

You may be able to purchase your frame relay network from the LEC or an IXC. Or some hybrid of both; most carriers have network to network links tying their frame relay networks together. This interconnection allows them all to offer broader coverage than their own networks, or Federal

Communication Commission regulation control local area versus long-distance coverage, allows.

In billing for the service, you are usually charged for an access link, port charge, and CIRs (in the form of PVCs).

Asynchronous Transfer Mode (ATM)

Should your WAN need to carry real-time critical information (such as video and real-time audio) as data, you may need to turn to ATM as the WAN technology of choice.

ATM is a protocol somewhat similar to frame relay; a language into which data are encoded on one end, switched through a carrier network, and interpreted on the other. ATM breaks down the data stream into small, predictable chunks (53-byte cells). Because the chunks are small and predictably sized, switches, hubs, and routers can be manufactured to move data in the ATM protocol faster than other protocols allow (less thought is involved at the device to interpret the data and send it on to the next point on the network). Information that must be sent in a real-time stream (voice and video) can be relayed using ATM without breaks in the stream.

To make use of ATM for your WAN, you need special ATM multiplexers, routers, bridges, or switches at each of your connected locations. Because of the real-time capabilities of the technology, some of that equipment may interconnect directly with your videoconference equipment or even telephone systems at each site (as well as the local data networks).

As a service from a carrier, you will usually pay for the ability to transmit through an ATM network on a variety of carrier circuits including fractional or full T1, DS3, or even one of the fiber-optic, optical carrier standards (with speeds of 45 mb, 100 mb, 155 mb, 622 mb, 2,488 mb, or even 9,935 mb).

A premium service, because of its rarity and specific application, you will find ATM to be one of the most expensive WAN technologies.

Wireless WAN

In specific situations, you may turn to wireless communications links to create your WAN.

There are two key applications of wireless. First, wireless communications (in the form of adapted cellular, digital personal communication service telephone service, and digital two-way radio service) can be adapted to allow wireless dial-up connections for remote users back to a corporate network. All the concepts and rules of dial-up apply, the difference being the user is not tied to a wired telephone line.

Second, wireless can be used as a WAN technology for line-of-sight links between locations within the mileage range of high-speed wireless and microwave radio transceivers. This could mean across a public street, where you want to link two LANs and don't want the hassle of digging up a public road to string fiber-optic cable. This could also mean across a state, where you might install a series of radios and repeaters to bounce your link from mountaintop to mountaintop for hundreds of miles.

Although some carriers may use wireless links to deliver data or provide telephone service to your building, wireless as a WAN technology would more likely result in a private purchase by your company. Because, with a privately owned solution, you would contract a company to install the equipment, wireless can be a relatively expensive WAN option. But if the up-front cost and lower annual maintenance is weighed against the ongoing monthly cost of a carrier-based service of other WAN technology, it may make financial sense in your case.

Wireless also may make sense from a bandwidth perspective. Links can be broken out into several channels, providing telecom-standard T1s to interconnect telephone systems, and data-standard connections to link LANs. With today's wireless technology, links are also available from simple T1 to 10 megabit ethernet and higher is yours for the right price.

6.4 Virtual Private Networking

Virtual private networking (VPN), a hot topic among information technology professionals, has implications to telecom management. Some customers insist upon VPN when it may not be the most elegant, least expensive solution for them, but they become swept up by the excitement in the development itself. And for some, it is so perfect for their need, that no alternative makes sense. It is an exciting development because its availability is universal and it leverages the most widely distributed network for the personal use of your business: the Internet.

VPN's basic concept is that you create a WAN using the Internet as the backbone. Each of your locations establishes a connection to the Internet and communicates to the other locations using an encrypted version of the universal, global network protocol: IP.

This ability to leverage Internet access connections for your WAN has implications for two types of traditional WAN connection. For site-to-site networks, locations with two fixed sites that need to communicate (normally solved with private line or frame relay networks), high-speed Internet connections allow large, open pathways for data to travel back and forth to the Internet.

For single, remote clients (usually served with dial-up networking), Internet access is available from almost any telephone. Plus, for remote users who communicate with a corporate network from home, high-speed Internet access through DSL, cable modem, or wireless broadband Internet access may give them a huge WAN node compared with simple dial-up.

The Pieces

Assembling a VPN involves the following three things.

- **Internet access:** Each computer or LAN has to connect to the Internet, be that by dial-up, DSL, cable modem, wireless Internet, or dedicated Internet. The faster, the better.

- **VPN software:** The security of the connection is handled by software that encodes and decodes the information travelling between locations. This keeps the communication private even though it travels across a public network. There are different variations of the software required. In a simple form, and packaged with the latest versions of its Windows operating-system software, Microsoft issues Point-to-Point Tunneling Protocol. There is also a secured version of IP called *IPSEC* (Internet protocol security). Manufacturers of VPN solutions may also provide accompanying software of their own. All the solutions do the same two things: first, they encrypt (scramble) the information to protect it. Second, they establish logical, or virtual connections between computers connected to the Internet (called *tunnels*) to handle movement of information back and forth.

- **VPN equipment or appliances:** For customers using VPN in its site-to-site version who want to share their VPN connection with all the users on a LAN, a special hub, router, or VPN appliance is typically installed between the network and the Internet connection to handle the routing of traffic. Each client on the LAN still runs encoding and decoding software, but the VPN device deals with the tunnel between the two points.

Buying VPN

What you need from a carrier depends upon how you decide to implement VPN. If you have the ability and access to the software and hardware solutions to properly equip your network, you may decide to set up and manage your own VPN, in which case all you need from a carrier is the best, fastest, cheapest Internet access at each location (be it dial-up or high-speed). Refer to the chapter on Internet access technologies for a guide on the relative costs of different solutions.

For a larger, more complicated VPN, many carriers offer solutions that allow you buy everything you need as a package. Either way, there are considerations to take when putting together a VPN. Some are the domain of the effective telecom manager. Others are just good to know.

What you pay for VPN can depend upon which of the options you choose.

- **Same-network advantage:** The Internet is a great public network. It is not specifically controlled by any one enterprise. When information is passed from switching point to switching point on the Internet, you have no control over how that information is routed. Therefore, data passing from one site to another, through the Internet, may be subject to hopping from router to router before reaching their destination. At each switching point, delays, or latency, can affect the transmission time and bandwidth of your connection.

I once sat with a VPN user in Tucson, Arizona. We looked to see how many hops his data passed through before reaching their Hawaii location. The result was an average of 15. These delays not only caused a perceptible lag for the two locations accessing information from each others servers, but caused some network-based software programs to time out (thinking the transmission had failed when it only had been delayed and shut down).

Some carriers contend that if you buy Internet-access from them for each location on a VPN, they can control the throughput between locations.

Facility-based ISPs (those with their own networks) sell access to the Internet through their own networks. Your information is not immediately passed to the Internet itself. It is routed through the ISP's network to one of three places. First, it may be routed to the nearest Internet bridge and out to the public network.

Second, if the location you are sending information to (Web site, e-mail server) is hosted on another carrier's network, your data may be routed across a peering (direct, carrier-to-carrier) connection.

Third, if the location you are accessing is hosted by the ISP itself, the information may pass only across the ISP's private network to the hosting location, bypassing the Internet altogether.

The contention for VPN is that if all your locations connect to the ISP's network, your data can pass across their network only. The number of hops is controlled and limited. The end result is faster, more stable VPN connections.

- **Management of the realm:** Who will be allowed to become part of your VPN? For a large, complicated VPN with hundreds of constantly changing remote users, it may make more sense to buy VPN as a service and let the carrier manage the details.

- **Client software and end-user support:** Again, if the application is large and complex, carriers offer packages that include distribution of the client software and technical assistance to users in the set up and configuration of the software. They would also provide help in determining which access numbers dial-up clients use (which can be a bothersome chore for a travelling user every time they're in a new city).

■ **VPN devices:** For site-to-site VPN, the set up and management of necessary routers, hubs, and VPN appliances, can be purchased as a package from a carrier. This eliminates the need to worry about how all the pieces fit together and the complication of managing the time it takes to roll out a VPN solution to all of your locations.

■ **Billing issues:** All the options with VPN have implications in the cost of VPN as a service for your business.
   Specifically, look for these elements to any proposal or billing (Figure 6-1).

1. **Dial-up client:** A fixed cost for the individual dial-up user accounts. As with Internet access dial-up, you may pay a flat monthly rate for unlimited access or a price related to the time spent connected to the network.

2. **Fixed-site access link costs:** Price for the access for fixed locations may be relative to access type, bandwidth or total data transferred, or number of users.

3. **Equipment:** In many cases, any equipment that comes as part of a VPN package will be purchased by you up front. Some carriers offer lease programs, though, which means you may incur an ongoing monthly cost to cover the equipment.

4. **Installation:** Expect to pay up-front fees for the set up of your account, each location, access circuits, and the installation of any equipment and software.

5. **Managed services:** Should your carrier manage your service, expect to pay a monthly account maintenance. A high-end package may entitle you to call for support twenty-four hours a day for any reason related to the service. Another package may give you site-to-site equipment support, entitling you to a visit from a technician should you have any issues, but only allow telephone support during standard business hours.

Billing Breakdown
FIGURE 6-1   What to Look for on Your Data Services Billing

Performing a regular monthly scan of your data services billing (private line, frame relay, broadband Internet) is as short and simple a process as the scan of your local and long-distance phone bills. It can happen easily after you have completed a thorough review of your long-distance accounts (reviewed your bills and identified all services, eliminated unnecessary items, renegotiated your pricing plans).

Follow this simple checklist, looking for the things you feel *should* be checked every time this type of bill comes across your desk. And just as with other audits, if no obvious anomalies are present, the bill can be paid with good conscience.

1. Is the total amount due in line with expectations? Based upon an understanding of what this carrier provides to you in services, charges for all data services, any fixed monthly charges, features, and taxes, are there any surprises?

2. Were you credited correctly for your last payment made?

3. If any installation, one-time, or nonrecurring fees appear on the bill, did you expect them? Are they correct?

4. Review the taxes to be sure the quantities, categories, and amounts are correct.

5. Look to the detailed summary, the section of the bill (assuming this carrier provides such detail) that breaks down the total new charges into its elements. Depending on the type of service and the elements it reduces to, you may see both variable and fixed costs listed.

   For variable costs (connection times, usage charges, and data transfers, for example), you want to determine that the per-unit rates are correct. Divide the cost (after discounts but before taxes), by the total units for that category. For example, if your per-hour connection charge shows eleven hours at sixty-six dollars, your cost-per-hour is six dollars. Should you have been charged for those hours? Is this the correct rate?

Nonvariable charges are easier to audit. If the carrier agreed to provide a T1 connection for your Internet for $210 or 512k of bandwidth for $375, you want to see those specific amounts on the bill so you can quickly move on.

When reviewing the summary details, be sure to look for the following categories.

- Circuit costs (T1 or other)
- Port connections
- Billing summary charges
- Feature fees (e-mail accounts, static IP addresses, Web hosting)
- Bandwidth charges
- CIR charges
- Usage charges (volume of data passed by MB)
- Connection charges (metered connection time for dial-up)

6. Does the total of all the detail line items add up to the total new usage charges on the front of the bill?

7. For WAN products, are the number of circuits and locations correct?

8. Are there any pay-per-use features or rental line items listed on the bill? If so, are they expected and correct?

9. If you were expecting credits from previous bills, be sure they're included?

10. Is there anything left on the bill, any line item, charge, or notice, that you do not yet understand from your complete audit of telecom services? If so, call the carrier and ask for an explanation before paying the bill. (It's easier to have amounts taken off what you owe than fight for and track credits promised to be given you at some later date.)

In just a few short minutes you should be able to run through whichever of these ten questions is relevant to the specific data billing you're auditing. Staying on top of billing and maintaining your complete understanding of all products and services under your domain should then be a snap.

7

Personal Wireless Communications Devices

7.1 Today's Wireless Marketplace

The personal wireless communications industry is a moving target; difficult to freeze in one moment for examination because it's constantly changing and evolving. The industry's own short but powerful history bears this out.

In the mid-1980s, many people got their first cellular telephone—it easily weighed a couple of pounds and was as large as a desk telephone. At the time this was innovation. The previous generation of phones were carried as a backpack or shoulder pack with a handset on a cord that you talked into. But most didn't care about the weight of the phone or that the quality of sound was horrible by wired telephone standards, that it was difficult to hold a conversation through the static, or that moving too much while talking on the phone was a sure recipe for ending the call.

And that the battery lasted maybe an hour. The phone's usefulness created demand. And demand and competition drove development.

Today, most cell phones slip in a pocket. The battery will keep the phone alive for two days. Many phones receive text messages and e-mail. Many have call waiting and can build three-way conferences, display caller identification (ID) and have an associated voice mailbox. The carrier's network is based upon digital switching technology, so static is not an issue.

The technology has also been adapted in hundreds of ways. One business took wireless telephone technology and married it to global positioning technology. It can install the new device in a vehicle and, on demand, call into it and tell you where on the planet the vehicle is, what direction it is facing, and how fast it is traveling. It could lay this information over a detailed map of the area and show you a real-time picture of the vehicle in motion. It could even kill the ignition of the vehicle and render it useless to whoever, at the time, is in possession of it.

One radio-dispatched vehicle recovery outfit's field workers have hand-held laptop computers in their trucks. The laptops are equipped with a wireless modem that connects back to a corporate computer network. In real time, without having to return to a home base of some kind, they receive orders of which vehicle to pursue next along with all the supporting research and information they need. They then post, into the computer, reports of their attempts to recover vehicles throughout the day. This information is then available to the company and its clients, giving a near-immediate picture of how the efforts to recover their property is going.

There is a wireless telephone technology that is installed in specialized industrial machinery rooms and remote-transmission towers that allows alarms to be sent to service technicians should anything bad happen at the site (fire, loss of air conditioning, loss of power, unauthorized entry).

Wireless technology has limitless adaptation. Which exacerbates any attempt to capture it effectively for you in a book. What is possible, though, and what has evolved over the years of development of wireless communications, is several practical, time-proven, and generally accepted business uses for personal wireless communications. These technologies (paging devices, wireless telephones, two-way radio, and some simple cousins of these three), should the research on dollars spent in American corporations be correct, may represent a huge ledger item on your balance sheet.

For the effective telecom manager, personal wireless communications represent numerous challenges. The issues start with the complexity of the billing of these services.

There are usually two ways these services are purchased by your company. First, employees purchase their own wireless devices and services to be reimbursed by you for the expense. So then, exactly how do you audit a telecom bill if you only see the charges as a line item on an expense report? And if employees do include billing information as part of their expense-reporting procedure, how do you manage a telecom expense item while not being able to consolidate services to make the physical management, billing, and auditing of similar services easier?

Other complications for billing come when you provide the wireless communications device to the employee but your company bears sole financial responsibility for it (see Figure 7-1 for a sample policy). How difficult is it to manage a number of devices, keep track of whose hand they're in, how they're being used, and whether the billing information reflects the actual use of the device?

One effective way companies handle the issue of financing wireless is to give employees a set stipend to cover the expense, say fifty dollars per month. They receive the stipend on their paycheck and understand it is the total reimbursement they will receive for any spending on wireless. This approach allows the business a fixed expense and single-payment simplicity. It allows employees a budget to use as they wish.

This concept is not without work, however. An accountant should advise you, but the employee and employer, to avoid the dollars given being treated by the Internal Revenue Service as income, must still make an accounting of how the money was spent. So the employee must keep expense reports. Still, it seems the simplest of the alternatives in financing personal wireless communications.

Billing Breakdown
FIGURE 7-1 A Sample Wireless Services Policy

What follows is a sample wireless services telecom policy for a business that provides wireless devices to employees for use in their every day duties. Such a policy may not be necessary (or may need to be modified) for companies that do not provide wireless devices to employees but rather reimburse employees for the expenses they might incur. This policy sets down a few basic rules of use to help manage wireless usage and keep expenses reasonable.

Wireless Services Policy

- **Introduction:** This policy governs the financial and physical responsibility for wireless devices for this company.

- **Eligibility:** Employees of the company may use wireless telephones and other wireless devices for the benefit of the business in the performance of their duties. Such use is limited to employees approved or required to use the services by the employee's direct supervisor. Supervisors must determine that a wireless telephone or device would be necessary to the employee's function within the company or that such a device would significantly enhance an employee's productivity. Such business need could be, but is not limited to, frequent business travel, employees who work in the field, employees who must be on call after hours.

- **Selection of plan:** There are many service plans available from your selected wireless provider(s). A plan will be selected by you and your supervisor that best matches the usage required by your position. It is the employee's responsibility to understand the usage rules of the plan and manage the use of the company-provided wireless device to optimize the

But why not take the easiest route: let employees find their own way through the wireless landscape and write off the expense at the end of every month?

It may not be so easy to let it go. You need to balance the decision against the compelling reasons why you would want to exercise some control over wireless communications yourself, such as the following.

- **Track innovation:** The wireless industry is a buyer's market. It is an ultracompetitive industry. Competition is fierce. What cost a dollar per minute a decade ago financial benefit of the plan. Plan selection should never be overbought or inflated to make sure it contains sufficient usage allowances.

- **Selection of equipment:** In many cases, a carrier will provide equipment free of charge to the company with the initiation of a new service plan. This option will be selected when available. If a carrier does not provide free equipment, the least-cost option will be selected. An employee who wishes to upgrade his equipment to higher priced options offered by the carrier may do so at his own expense.

- **Personal use:** Personal use of company-provided wireless devices is permitted but is to be infrequent and should be deemed necessary to the users' productivity in their role as employees of the company. Personal use of wireless devices means any use that does not directly relate to the employee's primary job function. During the regular monthly audit of an employee's wireless device billing, the employer may, at its own discretion, calculate the total personal usage for the device, and charge back the cost to the employee. Charge back for personal use on a device that has a fixed monthly service plan may be calculated as a percentage (division of the personal use minutes by the total minutes used to determine a percentage) of the total service plan price.

  An employee may, at his own expense, have a second line of service added to the company-provided wireless device by the carrier for unrestricted personal use.

- **Management:** It is the employer's responsibility to perform regular audits of all wireless devices billing to ensure that this policy is being followed by each employee using company-provided wireless devices.

costs pennies today. Features that once cost a premium now are freely included with service. Devices that once cost hundreds of dollars up front now are given away as incentives to sign up service with a particular provider.

Managing telecom based on the merit of a particular technology's benefit versus its cost is confused by the constant changing of offerings by carriers. Companies providing wireless simply don't sell the same services in the same way, so it is nearly impossible to reduce their proposals and plans to common elements for comparison. It is difficult for a sole employee to make choices of technologies and applications that are coherent with the company's mission.

Why leave the decision to every employee when the same research and understanding of both the issues of the business and the offerings of the marketplace are needed? Who better to consolidate that effort than you?

- **Leverage pricing and promotional plans:** Although under the care of the FCC and your state's utility or communications regulators (as are all telecommunications industries), the wireless community is relatively free to price and package its services as it sees fit.

  Does it make more sense that a carrier will offer favorable plans and pricing to an individual shopping as a retail customer or to a business customer needing one hundred telephones or pagers? Bulk purchasing power is used to leverage better pricing out of the competitive marketplace in all other aspects of telecommunications, so why not wireless?

- **Control the communication between the business and its customers:** When you hire an employee, especially one who deals with customers, the relationships he forms with clients are for the benefit of your business. By allowing employees to purchase and control their own method of communicating with these clients, you give up total control of the relationship. If you assign a phone to an employee, and that phone's number is the one printed on your employee's business cards, the one customers come to associate as a way to reach your company, the communication stays under your control should the employee separate from your company.

This chapter attempts to capture the spirit of personal wireless communications, covers the application to business of the products available, and addresses the management issues brought up by these products.

There are many specialized applications or devices that may not be covered in this chapter. There may be products offered by carriers in your market not covered here. You will need to take an active role in this chapter. Spin the message of this chapter into something specifically relevant to you. Look for examples in your personal and professional life to hold in your mind.

7.2 Paging Services

A pager is a simple device; it is technology that has been part of our modern world and has remained relatively unchanged for more than two decades. Pagers give a simple communicating experience to their users. Conversely though, the ability to ring a device on the belt or purse of a person is a powerful and useful tool.

How Pagers Work

To understand how this technology works, first understand that a pager is nothing more than a small, low-power, radio receiver. It picks up transmissions sent within a certain band of frequencies through the air from paging transmitters (see Figure 7-2). In dense metropolitan markets, there can be so many pages bursting in a day that there is a transmission on the airwaves almost all the time.

The way a pager knows when a signal is intended for a specific person is that the individual transmissions are encoded to specific devices. A pager listens to all transmissions long enough to read the encoding to know which it can ignore. Those intended for a specific pager are interpreted into (in most cases) the numbers to display on its screen.

Paging company transmission networks (interconnected radio towers and central processing terminal switches) are distributed into zones. A provider may transit messages to you across a local, statewide, or even a national zone; this is usually determined by the package of coverage you purchased with the service.

Most pagers are designed to receive messages only, although some have both a receiver and a transmitter to allow two-way communication.

Billing Breakdown
FIGURE 7-2   Wireless Frequencies Chart

The entire U.S. radio spectrum is divided into segments (bands), the use of which is governed by the Federal Communications Commission (FCC). Some frequencies are set aside for government use (military, maritime, public safety). Some frequencies have been placed in the public domain and are free to use by anyone (CB radio, family mobile radio).

There are also unlicensed frequencies available for commercial use, although the FCC licenses many commercial frequencies and strictly controls their use.

The list of bands relative to telecom managers is short. The capability of each frequency range (strength versus distance characteristics) determines the application of technology that uses it.

There are three terms that may be new to you. The first is MHz, an acronym for MegaHertz. The second is GHz, an acronym for GigaHertz. Both are measurements of radio frequencies and refer to how many times per second the radio signal cycles as it is passes through the air. The transmitter and receiver of a signal must be tuned to the same frequency for information to be effectively passed between two points. A Hertz is one cycle. MegaHertz measures in millions of cycles per second. GigaHertz measures in billions of cycles per second.

The third new term is narrowband. The term relates to technology that takes advantage of very narrow frequency bands to transmit and receive between two points (in counterpoint to broadband, which refers to technology using a wide spectrum band).

Following is a summary of telecom managers–relevant frequencies.

Cell phones:

- Cellular—824–849 MHz for mobile units to communicate to their base stations and 869–894 MHz base to mobile
- PCS—901–941 MHz narrowband, 1850–1910 MHz mobile to base, and 1930–1990 MHz base to mobile
- GSM—935–960 MHz and 890–915 MHz

Citizens band radio:
- 26.865 – 27.405 MHz

Cordless telephones:
- 27 MHz — original frequency range
- 46 to 49 MHz — second-generation cordless
- 900 MHz — modern cordless
- 2.4 GHz — today's cordless telephones

General mobile radio service (GMRS) radios:
- 462 – 467 MHz

Pagers:
- 30 MHz, 150 MHz, 450 MHz, and 930 MHz

Two-way radios (commercial two-way radio systems):
- Frequencies within the 800 and 800 MHz ranges

Wireless local-area networks:
- Bands within the 2.4 GHz (2.400 – 2.483) and 5 GHz ranges
- Bluetooth technology also uses bands within the 2.4 GHz frequency range

Wireless wide-area networks:
- The unlicensed 902 – 928 MHz, 2400 – 2483.5 MHz, and 5725 – 5850 MHz bands are most commonly used, although there are higher frequencies (bands between 2 and 38 GHz) available for longer range applications (that require licensing)

There are many tools on the Internet that show the entire radio frequency spectrum and how it is divided for use by the FCC. One good place to start is the FCC's own radio spectrum chart. You can download or view it at *http://www.ntia.doc.gov/osmhome/allochrt.html.*

Types of Services Available

Paging companies provide a variety of devices and corresponding services. When in the market to apply paging technology to your business needs, expect to encounter the following options.

- **Numeric:** A simple pager that allows only numbers to be displayed from callers. It may be all that is needed. People often use a numeric pager if most of their business contact is through the office. People call and leave voice mail messages at work. The voice mail system in an office then pages the user to let him know that he has a message waiting for retrieval. For clients and colleagues that may have an urgent need to reach the user and who use a pager as a way to reach him, entering a simple callback number is sufficient.

- **Alphanumeric/text:** For businesses that need to communicate information to field employees without wanting the expense or time consumption of calling them via cell phones or radios, a text-message pager may be more appropriate. With it, a user enters a typed, text message into a software program or Web site interface that, in turn, dials into the paging system terminal and relays the message out to the pager. For users who have no access to the software interface, carriers may provide operator assistance; agents take messages by phone and relay them, in text form, to alphanumeric pagers.

  One example of a company using text messaging is a commercial real estate broker in Phoenix. The representatives are often in the field for hours at a time. The business owner insists on a human interface for callers. Receptionists, therefore, transmit phone messages out to the alpha pagers to the reps.

  Another company's dispatcher uses alphanumeric paging to communicate with field technicians; she sends them their next assignment, the address, a description of the problem, onsite contact, and keeps them away from the office (the only place they don't make money for the company).

- **Associated voice and e-mail services:** Many paging services come with optional or additional voice mailboxes. Callers can, instead of entering the digits of a callback number, leave a voice mail message. The paging system then pages to alert the recipient of the message. Some enterprising carriers provide an e-mail address for users to send messages that will then be relayed on to the pager.

- **Voice:** The original pagers were more like one-way radios; they had a small speaker through which played a short, recorded voice message from the caller. Voice paging is still available and may be useful to convey detail, context, and texture to messages that might not be available with numeric or alphanumeric-only pagers.

- **One way versus two way:** With the Internet so easy to use and e-mail–style written communication prevalent in the back-office operations of the business world, two-way alphanumeric/text pagers have been developed. All developers needed to design was a small, low-power transmitter to wire into a paging unit and retrofit paging terminals to receive communications from the devices they traditionally only transmitted to. Two-way pagers make a great mobile–e-mail interface. However, the cumbersome nature of the tiny keyboard interface most of these devices come with and the inability to manage attached documents limit their use.

- **Coverage areas:** Providers organize their paging networks into zones or grids. Before signing up with a certain carrier, understand over what geographical area your message will be transmitted. Throughout your city? Statewide? Regional? Nationwide? For traveling employees, the difference between coverage areas can be critical.

7.3 Wireless Telephones

Just by their sheer pervasiveness and an almost overwhelming flood of availability and options, cell phones have proved themselves as a business tool.

Where are you right now? At home? At work? On a bus or plane? In the passenger seat of an automobile? On a bench at a park? If you happen to be in a public place, chances are you can spy a handful of people with cell phones either in their hands, clipped to their belts, or pressed to their ears. What are they using them for? Are they talking to clients? Are they being reached by their offices? Are they following through on promises to return calls? Checking the status of an order a customer is worried about? Walking someone back at corporate through the login process on a computer they're having trouble with? Are they staying in touch with their loved ones while at work?

This ability to continue working (communicating as your role for your company) beyond the boundary of your office has been revolutionary to business.

How Wireless Telephones Work

The term cell *phone* is a holdover from cellular telephone (which is a hint at how the technology works). The devices now communicate via either analog cellular radio systems or its digital scion *personal communications systems (PCS)* spectrum wireless-based networks.

Wireless telephone networks are similar to paging networks in that a carrier sets up radio transmission stations throughout a service area and can provide service to subscribers with compatible handsets within reach of their network.

One major difference is that wireless telephones require two-way communication to be effective, so cell sites (transmitter tower locations) are equipped to be receivers as well. Another difference is that wireless telephones operate at a lower radio frequency range than pagers; a bandwidth with much shorter effective range. The coverage network therefore needs to be populated with many more transceiver locations than a paging network.

Yet another difference is that the device makes itself known to the network when it first powers up by transmitting a registration signature out on the frequency picked up by the nearest cell site, establishing a continuous, low-power link to the carrier. Pagers perform no such registration.

This connection replaces the need for a cell phone to "listen" to every call to determine which are meant for you. When a call comes in, a control signal goes to your phone. The network tells it which of the hundred or more channels within its bandwidth range it will pass the call to. Your phone adjusts to that frequency and the call is then yours.

The issue for the technology then is, because it is a mobile device, how to keep the transmission going when you move out of range of the current transmission site. This is accomplished by the network "handing off" your call to the next transmission site you come in range of. As you move into the range of a new cell site and out of the range of the old, the network moves your call to an open channel on the new cell site. Your phone is instructed of the change and adjusts. The switch happens in a millisecond and is rarely detectable by the user.

Cell sites are hardwired back to central switching stations where calls are processed for that carrier's coverage area. This switching office is where the processing of all calls happens. Similar to the wired telephone switches that provide dial tone to our homes and businesses, this switch is a programmable computer. It accounts for all your calls and reports them to the carrier's billing system. It provides all the necessary logic to set up, complete, and tear down your various types of calls. It can also be programmed to provide a variety of features useful to you should you have a compatible telephone.

Wireless telephone technology has advanced rapidly in the past few years. When faced with managing wireless telephones and service for your company, expect to make decision on, deal with, and understand the following issues.

Analog Versus Digital

The original wireless telephone technology—analog-based cellular radio systems—was widely deployed. The digital PCS technology was developed and deployed later; therefore, in some rural areas, the network has not yet caught up with technology. If, in your covered area, you have a choice, digital wireless will bring you better quality telephone service, more features with your phone and service, and generally cheaper rates.

The following is a list of features for wireless services.

- **Phone features:** Wireless phone providers now offer, usually packaged with the basic service price, a wide variety of features to make your phone more usable. Options include voice mail service, caller ID, three-way calling, call transferring, and so on.

- **Text messaging and paging:** Wireless phone manufacturers have incorporated paging applications into many cell phones. You can now receive, on the display of your phone, numeric and alpha pages. Some carriers offer e-mail messaging as well.

- **Web interface:** Wireless applications protocol (WAP), a protocol suite used by mobile phones that includes a wireless markup language (WML) for displaying Web sites, has been developed to allow a properly equipped wireless phone to be used as a Web browser. Your service provider establishes a data connection between your phone and the Internet through its network. Special Web sites are formatted to be displayed on the tiny screens of wireless applications protocol (WAP)-compatible devices. From your phone, you can access search engines, e-mail services, corporate product pages, or any Web site formatted to display correctly. A company might consider creating an intranet Web site in WAP-compatible formats to allow mobile employees access to tools relevant or important to your business.

Pricing Plans

When you subscribe your wireless telephone device to receive service from a specific carrier, you're buying, in essence, access time to its network. Access is measured in minutes. Most carrier service plans are therefore built around the mathematics of minutes.

Basic service gives you the right to use the network for a certain amount of allowable minutes—usually called airtime—and managed with rules.

The next cost elements of service are the many available additional features.

The third element is the charges related to use above and beyond the first two. This could include long-distance service, calls made above and beyond your allowable packaged minutes, and calls made either outside your coverage area or through another carrier's network. Here are the issues related to service plans.

- **Anytime versus night and weekend:** The minutes that come along with your plan are usually divided by time of day or day of week. Most plans split the block into minutes you may use during peak hours (Monday–Friday, 7 a.m.–7 p.m., for example), and minutes assigned as viable for night and weekend calls.

- **Long distance:** Much the same as for wired local telephone service, you are usually billed by the minute for long distance for qualifying calls (in addition to airtime). Unlike wired local telephone service, wireless providers do not always allow you to choose an alternative carrier for long distance. In the wired world, you leverage your choice and make carriers compete for your business to drive rates down. In the more restrictive wireless world, without the same complete freedom of long-distance carrier, rates are open for abuse.

  Don't worry though; carriers generally don't take advantage. Most, in fact, offer long distance either completely free of charge or give you a separate bucket of minutes. Carriers are leveraging the fact that their wireless networks are connected coast to coast, and they don't really incur additional costs to move your call across the country. Expect free long distance as part of your service plan's package or ask for the ability to designate the carrier. That way, you can negotiate the rate for long distance separately and combine cell phone long distance with your general business long distance spending for higher volume discounts.

- **Mobile to mobile:** As an incentive to lure customers, many carriers give you a separate minute allowance for calls placed between their subscribers. Again, this is the carrier leveraging the network. As an incentive to a business, having all their employees use the same provider may greatly reduce wireless phone expenditures.

- **Mobile to home:** Many carriers also allow calls back to a specific designated telephone number (usually the subscribers main listed home or business telephone number) at no charge (that is, it is not accounted against the bucket of available minutes). Again, for a company whose employees are talking back to the office all day, getting mobile-to-home minutes included and credited for calls to the main business number can greatly impact the cost of cell phone spending.

- **Membership groups:** Another incentive to tie all your employees together offered by carriers are various forms of pooled service plans. The basic concept is that, instead of individual buckets of allowable minutes assigned to each phone, a larger bucket of minutes is assigned to the corporate account as a whole. All calls made by any plan phone are deducted from the bucket. If plan amounts are selected carefully, at the end of a month, the under-plan users balance out the over-plan users and the company spends no more for wireless services than it has to.

- **Prepay:** A relatively new trend is prepaid wireless telephone service. The basic concept is to pay for a bucket of minutes in advance and use your phone until the plan is exhausted. For business, this seems impractical to manage but may be useful if, because of the nature of your business and your wireless phone use, you need to apply absolute spending limits to individual phones.

Coverage

For marketing purposes mainly, providers may propose different calling plans based upon different coverage options.

- **Local calling area:** Most carrier's local calling coverage areas are actually multicity or multistate mini-regions. Service plans restricted to local calling areas (calls originated from within the local calling area) are generally cheaper than those plans that allow you access to a wider-reaching network.

- **Nationwide carriers:** These carriers may offer a coverage area spanning the entire nation. Many carriers have either deployed nationwide networks or have formed relationships with other regional carriers so they can offer coast-to-coast wireless service. This is an especially useful option for frequent travelers. In a nationwide calling coverage option, all calls are generally treated as if they are made from the home network—meaning charged against your allowable usage counts or billed under one flat rate.

- **Roaming:** When you are making a call from outside your service package's allowable coverage area, if your phone is set up to allow you to do it, you are *roaming*. Roaming could mean that your carrier is allowing you to make calls on another geographic segment of their network. They will usually charge you a per-minute rate, over and above your plan's basic minutes, for the privilege.

For example, my local calling area covers Arizona from top to bottom, some areas of New Mexico and Nevada as well. When I travel to Southern California, Verizon's So-Call network picks up my phone and allows me to make and take calls as if I'm home. I just pay a premium on my next bill for any usage.

Roaming could also mean that another carrier is allowing the call to go across its network and will, in turn, bill the call to your carrier at a wholesale rate. Your carrier will, in turn, add a charge-per-minute retail rate onto your regular monthly statement. For phones that are not set up to allow roaming, you may still use your wireless phone outside your calling area, with a caveat.

To stay with the example of my own service, I made the day-and-a-half drive to Washington state a couple of years back. For long stretches of the Northern Nevada/California highway system, I was out of reach of the Verizon network. I could still make calls, roaming on some regional carrier that had good signal strength through the area. My next bill included a whopping cost for the calls, three times what I pay for roaming on my own carrier's network.

Equipment and Accessories

For all these service plan options and features to mean anything, of course, you need a telephone. Most carriers offer discounted or even free telephones with the initiation of service accounts. Expect any offer to earn your business to come with the equipment you need. To earn a multiphone business account, many carriers should make concessions on equipment. They can also be convinced to add a few minor, yet important accessories. So ask for car chargers, carrying cases, and headsets; you may be surprised what can be yours just for the asking.

Management Issues

The employees and principles of our companies thirst for wireless telephones. To put the service and equipment options into perspective, look at wireless telephone service for your business from an effective telecom manager perspective. Be sure to address the following issues in the day-to-day management of the technology.

- **Retain physical control of the devices:** If you own the device, you subscribe to a wireless provider as a corporate account, and secure and issue telephones for your employees to use. Be sure to create a master inventory of devices. And don't just list the make and model of the phone and who it is assigned to. Register the serial numbers, which are usually found under the battery. (A carrier can use this information to disconnect service from a lost or stolen device without you having physical possession of it.) List the accessories you assign with the device so they can be accounted for should the user leave the company (or billed to the employee if lost). Have employees sign an asset responsibility form whenever they receive equipment as mobile, damageable, and losable as a cell phone.

- **Understand the elements of your bills:** Insist on seeing complete copies of all wireless telephone bills before your company pays them. For company-provided phones, this should be easy. For employee-provided phones for which you reimburse one hundred percent of business expenses, expect a complete copy of the bill. The only way to catch mistakes and fraud in telecommunications spending is by careful, even if quick, monthly review of all billing; looking for anomalies in the bill (discrepancies with what you know should be billed) is the fastest way to stay on top of problems.

- **Educate users on the things that always cost extra:** Roaming, directory assistance, and long distance are often charged on a pay-per-use basis for wireless phones and could cause additional charges on bills. Know, above and beyond the calling plan basics, what you could be charged for and educate your users. Include this education on your asset responsibility or wireless phone assignment forms. State whether there are rules or limits to this spending and where the employees responsibility starts and ends. (The stipend idea is looking particularly good again, isn't it?)

- **Occasionally review your calling plans:** To remain competitive, carriers are constantly tweaking their service packages by increasing allowable minutes, reducing costs, and adding new, free features. Many carriers will allow you also to switch plans (up or down in value) if you find a new one better suited to your actual calling patterns. Make a habit of researching new plans every couple of months. If you make a switch, trigger your next audit to be sure the plan was applied correctly to the account.

- **Fight roaming charges where applicable:** If you find roaming charges for calls made, check the carrier's coverage map. If you were within the coverage area, fight the charges. There are two ways this billing error could happen: another carrier's network-transmission towers are so strong they overwhelm your carrier's network and fool the phone into roaming. Or, the carrier had coverage holes within its territory, which allows roaming to happen. Either way, unless you catch it on the bill and dispute it with your carrier (charges they are more than happy to pull off the bill), you might overpay for service and never know.

7.4   Two-Way Radio

My stepfather was an air-conditioning repair technician. He carried a weighty brick of a radio with him at work. He even brought it home at night. When it was turned on, we could hear the back-and-forth banter of half a dozen workers out on jobs. Occasionally, he would catch a phrase or question that meant something to him and would wait a beat, press a talk button, and converse with the speaker. This was two-way communications twenty years ago.

So many technologies have come along to displace this method of communicating, but because something is old-fashioned and appears outdated does not mean it isn't useful. As two-way radio goes, the opposite may be true. There may be more two-way radios in use today than two decades ago; the application of this technology from a more simple time is more prevalent, more relevant, and more useful than ever.

So the effective telecom manager must look at two-way radio, even if briefly, to understand its application and think through the challenges of its management.

Simple Two-Way Radio

The first application of the technology is simple. Organizations that employ service personnel (construction, systems installation and service, computer technicians) may use short-range two-way walkie-talkies to allow employees working on the same job to communicate with each other. These simple devices allow, for example, a wire puller at one end of a conduit let a coworker at another end know when to stop feeding wire. A dish installer on the roof of a building may radio to a colleague in a conference room asking for signal-strength status relative to his positioning of the device.

The radios themselves are useful, inexpensive, and readily available today. Radio manufacturers leverage two frequency bands released by the FCC in 1996 for such devices.

- **Family radio service (FRS):** FRS-band radios are limited to one-half watt of transmission power (restricting their range to less than two miles even under ideal conditions). This frequency carries no licensing fees and the radios cost as little as ten to twenty dollars.

  FRS was established to give the general public access to radio technology they can use for short-range, mobile communications. At home, you might use FRS radios to keep tabs on your kids in the neighborhood, at a park, or on camping or hiking trips. For business, they make a cheap two-way communication tool for any team of employees contained in a geographically limited space.

- **General mobile radio service (GMRS):** GMRS allows radios that transmit at two watts of power, extending the range to five miles under ideal conditions. This makes GMRS ideal for golf course management, school or corporate campus, or for any team of people that needs coverage beyond the reach of FRS.

  GMRS is also a frequency open to general use but the FCC asks for a licensing fee from users. Legally, you should abide by FCC rules and register to use the frequency if you purchase GMRS radios for your business.

The good news about both GMRS and FRS is that neither require you to subscribe to a carrier for airtime access; therefore, you will not incur monthly or per-minute usage charges. The bad news is that, because these are open, public frequencies, what you say across them is not private and can be heard by anyone who is both within range and properly equipped to listen.

Two-Way Radio Service

Simple, short-range walkie-talkie radio is just not going to cut it as a communications tool for every situation. Think of the organizations and businesses that use two-way radio on a larger, farther-reaching scale, such as

- Emergency services
- Schools and colleges
- Taxi companies
- Local trucking companies
- Towing companies
- Couriers

To achieve the greater transmission distances, radios for these types of applications must use a higher set of frequencies and make use of a transmission network.

The individual radio itself transmits on a channel within the licensed and approved frequency within its geographical territory. The network comprises relays or repeater sites that boost the signal, thereby expanding the radio's reach. Anyone monitoring the correct channel can transmit a reply along the same frequency and two-way communication is achieved.

To implement two-way radio in this fashion for your own organization, you have the following two choices.

- **Build your own radio network:** First, you could buy your own two-way radio system and implement it. This approach requires securing the necessary equipment. Your shopping list would include radios, be they hand-held models, base stations (fixed, higher power radios), or mobile (vehicle-based) radios. Next on the list would be any necessary transmission towers and repeaters needed to extend the reach of your network to make it relative to the travels of your employees. Should multiple repeaters be needed, you would invest in trunking (telephone lines) to interconnect repeaters and provide dial tone access to properly equipped radios. Usually coordinated by the vendor you would buy equipment through, you would also need to deal with the licensing issues to make use of the airwaves (securing the right to use and paying for).

- **Buying two-way as a service:** The other (and maybe the easier) approach would be to lease equipment and buy access to the frequency and the associated transmission network from a service provider. Generally, you'll pay a monthly fee for the access, regardless of minutes or airtime used. The rate you pay may be affected by the number of radios you have issued to your company.

The management of both approaches has their issues. Buying and maintaining your own two-way radio system requires dealing with equipment and asset management, along with service issues. On the other hand, leasing equipment and paying for service means another set of options and services to understand, another billing statement to audit, and another set of responsibilities to bear.

Two-Way Push to Talk

There is also hybrid two-way device and service.

Nextel (and other carriers) is a hybrid handset that provides facets of both wireless and two-way radios. The handset works and acts just as a mobile phone and comes with all the features a normal cell phone would. In addition, though, there's a walkie-talkie–style button on the side. With it, you can communicate, two-way, in much the same fashion as any two-way radio system.

The way it works is that, to initiate a two-way call, you bring up on your display a list of other phones in your call group. When you've found the phone belonging to the person you want to talk to, you press your two-way button. A signal is then sent to the other device. Their phone doesn't ring. You don't get voice mail if they don't answer. They simply push their two-way button to talk back and forth (one person at a time) with you.

This hybrid is extremely useful for companies in which both two-way radio and mobile phone usage would be appropriate but carrying two devices would not. Say you have field service technicians. With the two-way feature, they could communicate among themselves and back to their dispatcher in real-time. Should a field technician need to make a phone call, the device allows them to do that as well.

Nextel, because they were the first (and for such a long time, the only) commercial provider of such a hybrid, has been extremely successful with their product. Competitors are on Nextel's heels, though. As the competition upgrades their networks to operate with a two-way feature and be able to release handsets to catch up with Nextel's years of development, costs should drop significantly.

Be careful not to get swept up in the application if it's not completely appropriate for your business. Push-to-talk providers, because their service is so useful, are in a position to charge per minute for two-way calls as well as charge for cell phone usage on the phones they provide. This increases the overall cost to business for wireless service.

7.5 Other Wireless Devices

Wireless technology is in use everywhere—the cordless telephone, the wireless computer mouse and keyboard, and garage-door openers are just some everyday applications in use now. Can you imagine a television, VCR, DVD player, cable box, or satellite receiver without a remote control today?

On the telecom side, there are wireless PBX (meaning private branch exchange) telephone systems, complete with cordless handsets from which you could hold, transfer, intercom, conference, and do all the things you've come to expect from high-end business phone systems.

The computer industry has been hard at work extending the concept of clipping the wires from, and therefore our chains to, the working desktop.

By attaching and building transmitters and receivers into computer devices, industrious enterprises have brought new applications to the table. And new challenges to the effective telecom manager.

Following are three major applications for wireless-enabled computing.

Wireless PDA

The first such logical fit for wireless technology is the personal digital assistant (PDA) hand-held computer. If you're familiar with the Palm Pilot, the most popular of such devices, you are aware that it is a hand-size computer running simple applications.

The devices themselves are no more than hardware platforms (just as a PC or a Mac computer is). This platform runs an operating system: Palm OS or Windows CE or some other proprietary operating system (OS), depending on who manufactured the device. Software is then written to run on the OS. Applications taking advantage of the unique characteristics of the device (portability, low power requirements) began simply offering electronic calendars and contact databases. The applications have grown to be quite sophisticated, giving users so many options the PDAs now act as limited versions of their desktop applications.

Some systems have a digital telephone module attached, making the PDA a phone, a two-way pager, and able to access the Internet for Web browsing and e-mail. Users can synchronize the data in their desktop calendar and contacts into the hand-held daily. Essentially, you are carrying a convenient copy of your computer in a portable, lightweight, unobtrusive computer. This is the true power of handhelds—to be extensions of their big brother, the PC.

There are many applications for wireless-enabled PDAs. Imagine being able to log information into your contact database while out prospecting or meeting with clients and have the information be instantly synchronized back to your office computer system. Or being able to access real-time inventory and sales paperwork while standing in front of a customer.

Wireless Modem

Take the concept of mobilizing computing power one step further than hand-helds. Wouldn't it be great to work on your laptop computer, away from the office, using the same applications in the same way, without having to find a telephone line to dial into your corporate network with?

This is possible with wireless modems. Coming usually in PC-card form and sliding into your computer, a wireless modem is a specially designed wireless telephone. You subscribe to service through a wireless provider and it gives you modem-style dial-up connectivity. You can use your modem in any way you would use a wired-line modem—to connect back to a corporate local-area network or to an Internet service provider for Internet access.

Fleet Management Systems

There are devices that can be installed in fleets of vehicles (trucks, rental vehicles, overnight and ground shipping vehicles) to allow their owners to keep track of their whereabouts. These devices are another adaptation of specially designed computers now enhanced by wireless technology. They relay information about the vehicle they're attached to back to a main computer system. Usually equipped with global positioning service (GPS) components, these devices may also be wired into the vehicle's ignition and even the main computer.

The system is then able to transmit the location, direction, speed, and any other information it is wired to read from the vehicle. It may even provide two-way communication to give the vehicle operator a way to type or talk to the dispatcher about the status of travels or shipments.

The marriage of wireless and computing technology opens the way for many more applications. Children may soon be wearing a ring or watch-type device that allows you to keep tabs on and communicate with them when they are away from home.

What a world. The effective telecom manager, though, needs only worry about today. If your business decides to use these, or any other, wireless-enabled computing systems, you are bound to face the same management challenges as with other wireless technologies. When investigating possible products, solutions, applications, or service, run through the following issues.

- **Service:** Wireless devices will need to make use of a wireless network to be effective. Expect to buy access. The model plans resemble most wireless service programs complete with service fees and usage charges and additional features or rights to pay for.

- **Cost containment:** The same issues of you pay/they pay will exist (see Figure 7-3). Will it be better for you to

Billing Breakdown
FIGURE 7-3   What to Watch for on Your Wireless Services Billing

Because of the different financial arrangements under which wireless devices are paid for by businesses, you may or may not, as part of your responsibilities as telecom manager, audit wireless bills. You may not even see these bills except as attachments to reimbursement request forms.

If your company, at its expense, provides wireless devices to employees, you will undoubtedly have the unenviable task of monitoring and auditing wireless bills. But don't worry. Run through this short checklist to make sure the bill is in order before you pay.

1. Is the total amount due in line with expectations based upon an understanding of what this carrier provides to you in services, charges for all call types, fixed monthly charges, features, and taxes?

2. Were you credited correctly for your last payment made?

3. If any installation, one-time, or nonrecurring fees appear on the bill, did you expect them? Are they correct?

4. Review the taxes to be sure the quantities, categories, and amounts are correct.

5. Look at the detailed summary, the section of the bill (assuming this carrier provides such detail) that breaks down the total new charges into its elements. Just like with other telecommunications billings, you should find both variable and fixed costs on the detail summary.

    For variable costs (such as roaming and long distance on cell phones or connection times on wireless modem services), determine first that they are legitimate charges. Did you have an agreement with the carrier, a plan that should have included these types of calls? Did you exceed your plan and therefore were charged per minute (or hour) over and above the allotment in your plan?

    If any of the variable costs on the bill are legitimate, figure the cost per unit. Divide the total price (after discounts but before taxes) by the total units (minutes, hours) for that category. (For example, if your roaming line item shows sixty-eight calls for one hundred minutes at thirty-five dollars before taxes, your cost per minute is thirty-five cents.)

    Be aware: You may see both fixed and variable costs covering the same category of usage. Usage charges for calls should only be billed their variable rate after any plan allotment is used up.

    Check the nonvariable charges (per-month program and feature charges) as well. Are they legit and should they be part of your bill? If you signed up for unlimited long distance with your carrier for $4.99 per month, make sure you see $4.99 on the bill and no per-minute charges for long distance.

When reviewing the summary details, be sure to look for the following categories.

- Peak or daytime minutes
- Night and weekend minutes
- Mobile-to-mobile minutes
- Mobile-to-home minutes
- Roaming charges
- Long distance
- Directory assistance calls
- Data-related elements
  —E-Mail accounts
  —Static Internet provider addresses
  —Web hosting
  —Usage charges for data by volume
- Monthly recurring (fixed)
  —Service fee (covering the plan's basic minutes or connection allotment)
  —Promotional package pricing for long distance, night and weekend, mobile-to-mobile
  —Billing summary charges
  —Feature fees (account codes)

6. Does the total of all the detailed line items add up to the total new usage charges on the front of the bill?

7. Spot check a few detailed phone calls for
   - per-minute price,
   - minimum call length,
   - roaming charges, and
   - long-distance charges.

8. Look quickly for any extremely long or extremely expensive calls and decide whether they're worth extra investigation.

9. Are there any pay-per-use features or rental line items listed on the bill? If so, are they expected and correct?

10. If you were expecting credits from previous bills, are they included?

(continued on next page)

(continued from previous page)

11. Is there anything left on the bill, any line item, charge, or notice, that you do not yet understand from your complete audit of telecom services? If so, call the carrier and ask for an explanation before paying the bill. (It's easier to have amounts taken off what you owe than fight for and track credits promised to be given you at some later date.)

As with other bill audits, you should be able to pass through these questions in just a few minutes. Doing so will prevent any abuse, mistakes, or fraud escaping through your wireless billings.

consolidate the service plans of all the devices under your domain? Will you provide the device? If you will not provide the device, is service linked to the device (provided by the manufacturer) and therefore out of your hands? What will your reimbursement or expense policy (if any) be?

- **Control of the communication:** If users procure their own devices, and they're used to access the network, resources, tools, and applications of your business, how do you retain control?

- **Control and security of the asset:** If you provide the device to your employees, how will you assure the protection of your investment? See Figure 7-4a and 7-4b for a sample of a wireless devices inventory.

- **Coverage issues:** In addition to service issues, what are the coverage challenges with the technology you adopt?

- **Custom applications:** If your application cannot be achieved with an off-the-shelf device and software, how will you go about bringing your application to life?

Billing Breakdown
FIGURE 7-4a **Using the Wireless Devices Inventory**

The use of wireless devices in business has grown exponentially since their early adoption in the 1980s. It's important to maintain a proper inventory of such devices in use at your business, to track where all these things are and manage how they're used day-to-day. Use this form to list them all, their cost, their usage, and who they're assigned to.

The columns are intended to be used as follows.

1. **Carrier:** What company provides the service

2. **Device details:** Make, model, and type

3. **Phone number:** Useful information when troubleshooting problems or referring to billing issues.

4. **Owner:** What is your company's financing arrangement for wireless devices? Do you set up the account and provide equipment for your employees? Do you expect employees to set up their own accounts and reimburse their expenses? Which are you?

5. **Employee:** Who is the device assigned to?

6. **Monthly dollars:** On average, what is the monthly cost of service for this device? When auditing, you'll be able to give a bill a quick pass and know if it's in line with the expected charges or not. Saves your fiduciary detective work for accounts outside of statistical norms.

7. **Paid by:** You may provide equipment to your employees, but that doesn't mean you pay the bill directly. Use this column to list who has financial responsibility for the account (use an R to show that you reimburse).

8. **Contract terms:** List the expiration (renewal) date of any contract on the device and a summary of the usage amounts (minutes, features, connection hours). Use the information to compare against bills when auditing. What is the termination penalty should you be attracted by an offer to replace a service on your inventory?

9. **Account:** Make notes of the device's account or the carrier's contact phone number.

10. **Notes:** A little room for writing in information that, although helpful, doesn't fit into a neat little box.

Billing Breakdown
FIGURE 7-4b Wireless Devices Inventory

Carrier	Device Details	Phone Number	Owner CO	Owner EMP	Employee	Mo. $$	Paid by CO	Paid by EMP	Expires	Contract terms Usage	Termination
Accont:	Notes:										
Accont:	Notes:										
Accont:	Notes:										
Accont:	Notes:										
Accont:	Notes:										
Accont:	Notes:										
Accont:	Notes:										
Accont:	Notes:										
Accont:	Notes:										
Accont:	Notes:										
Accont:	Notes:										
Accont:	Notes:										

Billing Breakdown

FIGURE 7-4c   Wireless Devices Inventory

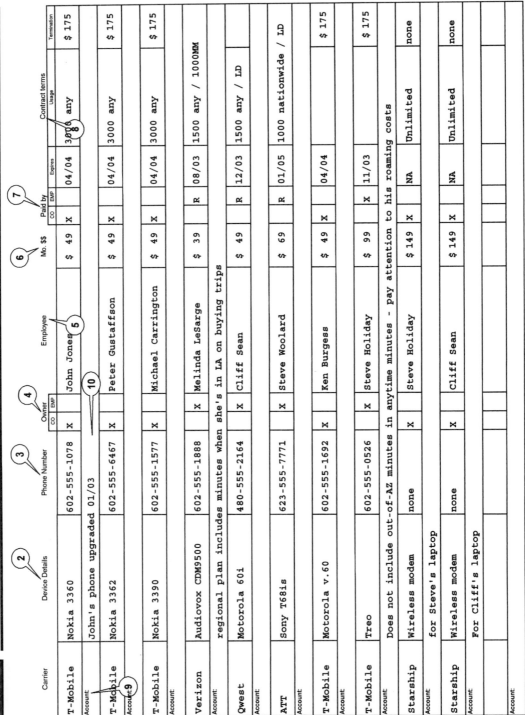

Carrier	Device Details	Phone Number	Owner CO	Owner EMP	Employee	Mo. $$	Paid by CO	Paid by EMP	Expires	Contract terms Usage	Termination
T-Mobile	Nokia 3360	602-555-1078	X		John Jones	$ 49	X		04/04	3000 any	$ 175
Account:	John's phone upgraded 01/03										
T-Mobile	Nokia 3362	602-555-6467	X		Peter Gustaffson	$ 49	X		04/04	3000 any	$ 175
Account:											
T-Mobile	Nokia 3390	602-555-1577	X		Michael Carrington	$ 49	X		04/04	3000 any	$ 175
Account:											
Verizon	Audiovox CDM9500	602-555-1888		X	Melinda LeSarge	$ 39		R	08/03	1500 any / 1000MM	
Account:	regional plan includes minutes when she's in LA on buying trips										
Qwest	Motorola 60i	480-555-2164		X	Cliff Sean	$ 49		R	12/03	1500 any / LD	
Account:											
ATT	Sony T68is	623-555-7771		X	Steve Woolard	$ 69		R	01/05	1000 nationwide / LD	
Account:											
T-Mobile	Motorola v.60	602-555-1692	X		Ken Burgess	$ 49	X		04/04		$ 175
Account:											
T-Mobile	Treo	602-555-0526		X	Steve Holiday	$ 99		X	11/03		$ 175
Account:	Does not include out-of-AZ minutes in anytime minutes - pay attention to his roaming costs										
Starship	Wireless modem	none		X	Steve Holiday	$ 149		X	NA	Unlimited	none
Account:	for Steve's laptop										
Starship	Wireless modem	none		X	Cliff Sean	$ 149		X	NA	Unlimited	none
Account:	For Cliff's laptop										
Account:											

Working with Consultants

8.1 When Is It Time to Turn to an Expert?

Consultants offer valuable services to the effective telecom manager. Consultants may be single individuals or firms; they also may be management consultants with a telecommunications subspecialty. There are also marketing firms that are agents for multiple carriers and can perform consulting tasks for you as part of or in adjunct to their core business of selling you telecommunications products and services.

A consultant is a short-term, highly expert, temporary, contract employee. You might use such an expert for one of two common reasons. First, you may need specific expertise to accomplish some project or task. This could mean hiring a consultant to write a Request for Proposal for your new telephone system or using one to research the market for the most effective WAN technology for your business application. Using a consultant, theoretically, puts the project in more efficient hands.

The second reason occurs when time budgeting will not allow you to focus on other duties. For example, the complete audit of your company's local, long-distance, and wireless services can be an overwhelming and time-consuming task, especially if your business has multiple locations. You may have the knowledge and expertise to perform such an audit, but demands on your time means that it makes more sense to keep you free to focus on your other day-to-day responsibilities.

8.2 How to Hire a Consultant

A typical client-to-consultant relationship begins when a client realizes, because of time restraints or lack of expertise, he needs to hire an expert. The job the client wishes the consultant to perform then needs to be defined. Defining, or putting formal context to your project, allows the consultant to price the work he will do for you.

You might approach this as you would when defining your applications in the Request for Proposals for buying telecom services and equipment. Your consultant should take this definition, probe you to flush it out, and present you with some form of a proposal, usually in the form of a project overview.

Recently, I had the opportunity to assist a client in setting up a new telephone call center. He had his product lines up. He had the business plan approved and his funding in place. He had the core management team hired and ready to work. He had purchased his building. He had even placed his preliminary order for the scores of lines of telephone service his operation would run on. But he needed help in purchasing the right call-center technology to allow his staff to handle the customer calls that would result from his television, radio, and print media advertising.

We talked for a while about the business, how it would operate, what his goals were, when he wanted to be up and running, the size and scope of his call center. I then wrote a project overview and attached an estimated fee. Figure 8-1 provides the consultant project overview used with this client.

* * *

For the Toolbox

FIGURE 8-1   Sample Consultant Project Overview

Consulting Project for Ballistic Ventures, Inc.
Scope of Work

Submitted 04-08-XX by Stephen W. Medcroft

Stephen W. Medcroft (herein known as "Consultant") will assist Ballistic Ventures, Inc., in securing the appropriate and most effective telecommunications systems for his new call center venture in Denver, Colorado.

Consultant will provide hands-on guidance in defining the telecommunications system(s) needs of the call center, assist in selecting qualified vendors to bid for the project, write a Request for Proposal that communicates the application needs of the business to vendors, and assist in negotiating favorable terms for the purchase of the successful bidder's system(s).

The project will involve the following steps.

Defining Your Need
- Basic service levels
- Desired call flow
- Desired employee experience
- Desired monitoring capability
- Desired management reporting capability
- Desired installation time frames and parameters
- Finding models

Writing the Request for Proposal
- Communicate the applications
- Set cost expectations
- Establish formatting guidelines for responses
- Set contact rules
- Set time frames
- Reserve the right not to accept any of the proposals

(continued on next page)

(continued from previous page)

Selecting a Provider

- Seek vendors through referral and open solicitation
- Qualify vendors by checking references and interviewing about capabilities
- Distribute Request for Proposal
- Field and respond to questions and requests for clarification
- Preview and score responses
- Invite field of vendor finalists to demonstrate (through live demonstrations or field visit to live, current customer) proposed system(s)
- Negotiate final terms of purchase
    - Itemized price breakdown
    - Pre- and postcut pricing
    - Turn-key price
    - Hold out percentage/position
    - Extended warranty
    - Guaranteed installation timeline
    - Meeting with the installer
    - Meeting with the service dispatcher
    - Work out coordination with carriers

Project Implementation

- Assist in establishing responsibilities between vendor and customer and work as a liaison and customer advocate during installation when necessary

Project assistance will be rendered by working with your company in a team approach using electronic communication. The consultant will, however, require two visits to the project site. The first will be to accompany you during vendor presentations and on-site demonstrations. The second visit may be required during system cutover to work through any last-minute, on-site issues between the vendor, carrier, and your company.

We estimate that our involvement in this project will require approximately fifty-five hours of service. At a billing rate of seventy-five ($75) per hour, plus anticipated expenses, we estimate this project to run approximately $5,000.

Our intention with the project is to bring exponentially more value to the relationship with your company than we take in compensation. Therefore, justification for our role is achieved the following three ways:

1. There are many call-center systems and technologies in the marketplace. In uncontrolled, open solicitation, you would see systems ranging in price from $1,000 per seat to $15,000 per seat. Our goal is to determine, first, which call-center system(s) will achieve the goals of the business, based on our experience and understanding of the available technology, and, second, to solicit proposals to meet your true need. By doing this, we will protect the company from overbuying call-center technology up front and save a potentially huge capital outlay.

2. By fully considering the anticipated growth of the organization, both real and projected, we will work to protect the company from making a purchase that will become obsolete by its own future plans.

3. At the point of purchase of the call-center system(s), we will work to negotiate discounts that equal more than any consulting fees the company may have incurred with us.

Thank you for your consideration of this proposal.

At your service,

Stephen W. Medcroft
Consultant
555-555-5555
stevemedcroft@mcleodusa.net

Of course, not all consulting projects need to be this complicated. You may have a one-line definition and single-line proposal in response if you need a consultant simply to audit your local telephone line accounts. Hopefully, though, this example demonstrates how your definition of the project should affect the consultant's written scope of work.

Besides defining the project, it is important to find the right consultant to work with. There are a few simple, practical concepts that can ensure that hiring a consultant is a valuable and productive experience for you. The following is what to look for in your consultant.

- **Expertise:** Of course, you want a consultant with practical experience in the area you are hiring him or her for. Be sure you know when you are talking to prospects what the required expertise should be. If you are buying a telephone system for a fifty-employee office, do you need someone who engineered central office switches for twenty-eight years? He may know the ins and outs of all things technical in telecom, but his specific knowledge should suit the project.

- **Experience:** Ask for a resume. Get a list of current or recent projects. What other companies has this consultant or consulting firm done similar work for recently? Will the same person or people who worked these projects be attending to yours?

- **References:** Talk to the companies the consultant has recently served. How did the project go? Would they use the consultant again? Did they get their money's worth?

- **Pay structure:** Consultant fees vary. Because these are private individuals or firms hiring out their expertise and experience, the value they place on their expertise is extremely subjective. The following are common practices, however.

  - **Hourly rate:** Expect to pay an hourly rate to a consultant that would be a premium over the average hourly salary for an employee with the same experience and core competency.

  - **Expenses:** The consultant will have rules to follow to be reimbursed for business expenses incurred while working on your project (such as long-distance telephone charges, copies, travel expenses, material supplies). Understand how you will be charged these fees and what ability to audit their validity you will be given.

- **Retainer:** When charging you for work done, your consultant's billing report may come as an invoice statement or a reconciliation report (called reconciliation because most consultants' proposals will ask you to retain their services and post a deposit toward rates and fees from which actual charges will be taken). What is a reasonable retainer amount? Fifty percent? The full estimated hourly amount? Whatever is asked, you must be comfortable before handing over a check. If you're not sure if the project or the consultant will work out, consider negotiating a smaller retainer to accompany a trial period for the project. Set a milestone to meet at some point into the project. You may then evaluate progress and cut a new retainer check for the asked-for amount knowing the work will be worth the money spent.

- **By-project pricing:** Even better than hourly rates, will your consultant bid the entire project at a single price? It makes life much easier if you're able to spell out a specific task or outcome for a project, then have a consultant attach a single price to it. Some consultants may not like this approach because they worry about a project running long for reasons out of their direct control and their effective hourly rate being lowered. Flat-rate billing is the simplest and most elegant way to hire a consultant because it is easier to budget and cost-justify and easier to budget and sell up the food chain in your company. The consultant should look at it as an opportunity to increase his hourly rate by overperforming and working the project so efficiently that he finishes ahead of the scheduled time.

- **Cost justification:** Expect that your consultant justify to you the expense of hiring him in hard or soft dollars. Hiring a consultant is a business decision and should be treated as such based upon return on investment. He may show you that he can accomplish a task in much less time than an employee. He may show you that he will negotiate such a favorable rate for the equipment or services you are buying that his fees will be saved multiple times. Any consultant should be able to justify his cost to you and not think it's asking too much of him.

- **Full disclosure:** Ask if the consultant has any affiliations, associations, or agencies with any of the outside companies that he will be working with on your project. Is a long-distance carrier paying him a commission to bring your business to the company? Is a telephone system vendor kicking back a small percentage of all sales the consultant steers its way? You should know your consultant's motivations when he is hired by, and working for, you.

    A consultant who has a financial incentive to steer clients to certain telecom companies shouldn't call himself a true consultant. He is an agent. Agents perform a valuable service for clients, even consulting work. But, because of their financial arrangements with vendors and carriers, they should charge customers little or nothing for any work they benefit from financially in other ways.

Signing the Consultant Agreement

The final step in securing a consultant for a project is to sign a form of work agreement. Again, this is a subjective business, so expect widely varied documents. There are a few common elements, however.

- **How, what, and when to pay:** You will have negotiated this by now, but the specific terms should be spelled out in writing.

- **Who owns the work:** When hiring a consultant for a project that results in any form of document (Request for Proposal, audit of services, training material, employee manuals), you should retain ownership of the final product. In a legal document (get professional legal assistance should this be a concern of yours), ownership is retained when your consultant "works for hire." Effectively, this means you're buying his time, not any license or right to make use of the work he produces for you. Look for clauses on copyright and ownership and be sure that the work you pay for won't go to benefit your consultant's other clients.

- **Confidentiality during and after the project:** You might also want to assert confidentiality. Successful consultants work for many companies during their careers—maybe even your closest competitor. Although it may seem to "go without saying," it should be said, in writing, that your business, concepts, ideas, proprietary information, and so on, be kept in confidence ad infinitum by your consultant.

Figure 8-2 is a boilerplate consultant agreement that should be helpful when hiring a consultant.

For the Toolbox
FIGURE 8-2   Sample Consultant Agreement

Consultant Agreement

This agreement is entered this ___ day of ___ 20XX between Stephen W. Medcroft ("Consultant") and Ballistic Ventures, Inc. ("Client"). Subject to the terms and conditions as set forth herein Consultant agrees to perform the services outlined below for Client in exchange for the compensation provided and outlined below.

Consultant Obligations:

Consultant agrees to provide each of the services outlined below. In return for the compensation noted under "Consultant Compensation," Consultant voluntarily agrees to perform the services described in the "Project Overview" attached hereto as Exhibit "A." By this reverence, all of the services described on Exhibit A are incorporated into this agreement as if set forth fully herein.

(continued on next page)

(continued from previous page)

- Consultant agrees to diligently perform the services described on Exhibit A starting on May 2, 20XX, until a purchase and sale agreement for the call-center system is executed by the customer. Consultant acknowledges that time is of the essence in completing its obligations under this agreement, but expressly disclaims any warranty regarding when the call-center system will be in place, when the services outlined by Exhibit A will be completed or when an acceptable customer for the call-center system can reasonably be anticipated.

- Procedure for adding additional work or extending the contract: Consultant agrees to provide client biweekly billing information with a statement of work performed that is sufficiently detailed to allow Client to verify the work performed to date. Consultant will make every effort to inform Client if and when the project fee amount exceeds the amount of the retainer set forth and described below but does not guaranty its ability to do so. If Consultant is able to provide Client with said notification, Consultant will attempt to provide Client with enough time prior to excess work being performed to allow Client the ability to review and approve the additions. Despite these best efforts by Consultant, Client's responsibility for paying amounts properly billed by Consultant in excess of the retainer set forth and described below is not contingent upon Consultant's notification of the project fee amount exceeding said retainer. Additional projects (such as project management of call-center system installation) can be proposed at the client's request any time prior to the conclusion of this project. Unless such additional projects are listed upon Exhibit A, such projects are not subject to this agreement and will be billed by Consultant separately at the hourly rate set forth below.

Consultant Compensation:

Hourly rate: Client agrees to pay Consultant a fee of $75.00 per hour in consideration of Consultant's performance of the services and obligations set forth on Exhibit A. All hourly billings shall be submitted by Consultant as set forth above and will be rounded to the nearest 1/10 of an hour.

Taxes: Consultant shall be exclusively responsible for the payment of all taxes incidental to the compensation paid for services performed, including but not limited to federal and state income, sales, or use taxation.

Retainer: Prior to Consultant commencing work on any of the services forming the basis of this agreement, Client shall provide Consultant with a retainer payable to Consultant of $5,000.00 to cover Consultant expected billable hours and expected expenses.

All amounts billed by Consultant on the project that is the subject of this agreement will be applied to the retainer amount until the project is completed or until the retainer is exhausted. Should the retainer be exhausted prior to completion of the project, Consultant will provide Client with its best estimate of the amount of fees and expenses that will be incurred in completing the project. Upon receipt of said estimate, Client agrees to replenish the retainer in the full amount of the estimate. Said procedure will then apply in each instance where the retainer has been exhausted. Should Client fail to replenish the retainer, Consultant may, at its sole discretion, either waive the requirement that Client replenish the retainer or cease work on the project. In such an instance, Consultant will provide written notice to Client of its election and shall have no obligation, express or implied, to complete the work outlined on Exhibit A hereto.

Should any retainer remain after the completion of Consultant's work or the performance of services on Exhibit A, Consultant will refund any remaining retainer balance to Client upon presentation and acceptance of final reconciliation statement. Consultant estimates, but does not guarantee that any refund under this section will take place within 10 business days after completion of the project.

Independent Contractor:

Consultant's relationship, and that of its employee(s) to Client is one of independent contractor. Nothing in the agreement shall create an employment or agency relationship, nor shall Consultant act as an agent or employee of Client unless such representation is outlined in the scope of services.

Consultant's services are to be performed solely by Consultant or its employees, or approved subcontractors, for Client pursuant to the terms of this contract.

Standards of Performance:

Compliance with law: Consultant's performance of services under this agreement shall be in compliance with all applicable laws or regulations of the federal, state, and local government.

Reputation and goodwill: Consultant shall not perform any contracted services in a manner that would be injurious to the reputation and goodwill of Client.

(continued on next page)

(continued from previous page)

Trade secrets: Consultant shall not in any manner disclose to any person, partnership, firm, or corporation any information concerning any matters affecting or relating to the business of Client including, but not limited to, any trade secrets, production processes, customers, pricing, or marketing plans. This covenant shall remain in effect after termination of this contract.

Waiver of liability: Neither party to this agreement shall be liable to the other on account of any personal injuries or property damage sustained as a result of any actions or omissions relating in any way to this agreement. Client shall indemnify and hold Consultant harmless from all liability for personal injuries or property damage directly related to the performance of contracted services under this agreement.

Modification of contract: No waiver or modification of this contract or of any covenant, condition or limitation herein shall be valid unless presented in writing and signed by both parties.

Severability: All covenants contained herein are severable, and in the event of any being held invalid by any competent court, this contract shall remain intact except for the omission of the invalid covenant.

Choice of law: It is the intention of both parties that all suits that may be brought arising out of, or in connection with, this agreement will be construed in accordance with and under and pursuant to the laws of the state of Arizona. The parties agree that the exclusive venue for any action brought by either Client or Consultant related in any way to this agreement shall be in Phoenix, Arizona.

Attorneys fees: In the event Client breaches any provision of this agreement or if it becomes necessary for Consultant to enforce any provision of this agreement, whether suit is initiated or not, Client agrees to reimburse Consultant its reasonable attorneys fees and costs incurred in either remedying the breach or enforcing this agreement in whole or in part.

Entire agreement: This contract contains the complete agreement concerning the services to be performed by Consultant for Client and supersedes all prior agreements or understandings, written or unwritten. By signing this contract, both parties acknowledge that they have read this contract, understood its terms, including the release, have had an opportunity to have legal counsel review this agreement, and have voluntarily accepted its provisions.

Signed

Name	Date

Stephen W. Medcroft
555-555-5555
stevemedcroft@mcleodusa.net

Name	Date

Print Name	Company Name

8.3 Managing the Consultant

When a consultant is involved in a procurement or project, it may be tougher to make the deal. Sometimes, the entire selling process is more complicated than opportunities in which you deal directly with a customer. The consultant might require answers to a more thorough set of questions. A consultant might expect conformance to a standard proposal he could use to measure all proposals equally. This means that, most of the time, you are in fair, equal, and impartial competition against other vendors. It may also mean needing to slash the profit margin to stay in consideration to the final round.

It also means throwing away most of the person-to-person interaction you normally have with customers and losing the opportunity to sell. The proposal will have to be based on the merits communicated through the proposal, marketing, and technical material only. The company will be judged on objective standards instead on how the customer feels about your competence.

Some competitors refuse to bid when a consultant is involved, considering a lower-margin sale not worth the extra work needed. Following is an example of why this may be a short-sighted reaction.

A 120-room hotel in Seattle wants to provide best-in-class technology to its upscale guests. The owner hires a telecommunications consultant to oversee the purchase.

As with most better consultants, this consultant is present in every interaction with the customer without being obstructive or overcontrolling. Her relationship to the client is to lead the client through his project, educate him about his choices, help him understand what is happening, and show him how to protect himself with the clauses she provided in her request for proposal and not just performing work for the client without his involvement.

If answers are needed before being able to respond to the request, they come directly from the customer or from the customer through the consultant. In this situation, the client is managing his consultant well. What he receives for his effort is competent proposals that he understands and can assign value to. He is then able to make an informed decision of which system to purchase and install.

The guests and employees of his hotel will continue to benefit from that relationship. As a result, his consultant has justified her expense.

What made their relationship successful and how does understanding this help you?

With a project of your own defined, a consultant selected, and a contract signed, how do you manage your relationship with your consultant to foster a similar, productive relationship? How do you get the value you need while retaining the control of the project without getting tied down in the day-to-day work that the consultant is to take on?

Here are three simple suggestions based on this hotel project scenario.

Work from the Project Overview

There are two inherent risks to the success of any consulting project: not meeting the timeline (going over budget even) and losing focus on the objective of the project.

In the hotel project, the time was taken to break the project into individual, measurable steps or stages. Time frames were assigned to every aspect of the project: bidder's responses due, questions fielded by the customer, live demonstrations scheduled, a purchase awarded, installation, and cutover date.

Be sure to do the same. Assign timelines to individual steps and track your consultant's progress. This way, if focus or timeline is lost, you'll know at the earliest possible stage.

Communication

At every stage of the hotel project, questions were to be answered by either the customer or the consultant. They should work together to make the information reliable, with no confusing responses or mixed signals. It is essential that the consultant and customer keep in close touch about the project and work effectively together. Whatever the nature of your project, there are a number of ways for professionals to stay connected. Telephones, cell phones, e-mail, and fax machines are all tools you can use to stay connected. Schedule and stick to regular communication with your consultant. Ask for updates. Review drafts of documents they may be preparing. Ask to be informed of any meetings affecting your project so you may attend if needed. Clear and common communication is the best way to stay involved in any project.

Periodic Payment Statements

Receiving biweekly or even weekly billing reconciliations or statements is an effective way to stay on top of any long-term project. It will let you know the actual work being done on your behalf and whether your consultant is meeting the projections for cost and timeline with enough forewarning to make changes (such as canceling the project) if there are serious issues raised in the statement.

Glossary of Relevant Terms

There are many terms and acronyms in the telecommunications industry. This glossary summarizes words and terms from the book. Use it as a reference and refresher for conversations with vendors, colleagues, and employees.

1FB (one flat-rate business) line: An industry term used to designate single telephone lines that provide local telephone service to businesses. Other terms include CO (central office) line and POTS (plain old telephone service) line. The "flat" means the phone company charges a flat monthly rate for the service, with all local calling throughout the local calling area at no per-minute charge.

1MB (one metered business) line: The same as a 1FB except the local telephone company charges a metered, per-minute rate for local calls made.

56k leased line: Used mainly to provide inexpensive, low-cost, up-all-the-time links between computer systems in geographically separated locations. Such 56k leased lines are the DS0 version of point-to-point (private line) service.

Account codes: Many phone systems have the capability for employees to enter, through the telephone keypad, a numeric code before, during, or after a telephone call. Typically used in conjunction with call accounting reporting, which is software that allows a company to print reports detailing call activity off the phone system.

Local or long-distance carriers may also offer account codes as a service, gathering the codes at the time a user dials a toll call, and presenting the information on their billing. Account codes as a service are traditionally offered as verified (the caller is forced to enter a code that must match a carrier-maintained list) or unverified (caller has to enter a code of a specific digit length, any combination of which would be allowed by a carrier).

ACD (automatic call distribution):   A stand-alone system or a function of a PBX, ACD answers incoming calls automatically, and when agents are not free to take the call, can play greetings, recorded messages, and hold music, entertaining and informing callers while they wait. ACD also distributes calls evenly, using algorithms to balance work flow to groups of answering agents.

ACD reporting: Manufacturers of ACD systems usually offer a reporting package to allow production of detailed reports on the call center's activity.

Agent: A call-center worker who handles the interactions (calls, e-mails) of a business. Also, an individual or business that independently represents carriers for the sale and implementation of the products and services.

Analog (telephone signaling):   The original technology of telephone signaling. Using modulation in electrical current, Alexander Graham Bell patented this technology for transmitting and recreating a telephone call across copper-wired lines.

ADSL (asynchronous digital subscriber line):   A version of a digital subscriber line service in which the upstream and downstream data rates have different bandwidth characteristics. The nature of ADSL makes it a good carrier technology for Internet access because, when browsing the Internet, relatively few bytes of information are sent (key strokes, mouse clicks), yet large volumes of data (files, graphics, animation, sound files) are being received. Another distinct quality of ADSL service is that it provides data service on a standard telephone line without interrupting the ability to use the telephone line for voice calls.

ANI (automatic number identification): Using in-band signaling (a method of transmission that embeds additional information about a call in the call signal itself), a telephone carrier can pass, to your phone system, the phone number of the caller.

ARIN (American Registry for Internet Numbers): The governing organization for the United States that manages the distribution and public and private use of Internet protocol addresses by Internet service providers and users.

ATM (asynchronous transfer mode): A packet-based data transmission signal that allows carriers to bond together voice and data signals on one carrier circuit.

Automated attendant: A stand-alone system or function of a voice mail or PBX telephone system that acts as a mechanical receptionist. Upon answering incoming telephone calls, the automated attendant plays a greeting that asks callers to dial, usually, a 0 through 9 routing choice (for example, 1 for sales, 2 for administration . . .). Some automated attendants allow dialing of an entire telephone extension as well. Advanced automated attendant, usually provided as part of a voice mail system, may allow callers to select employees from a directory of departments or names.

Automatic dialer: See *predictive dialer.*

Backboard: A wall-mounted board, usually plywood sheeting, used by telecommunications vendors and carriers to mount the equipment necessary to provide their services at a customer site.

BRI (basic rate interface): One of the two ISDN protocols. With BRI, a copper telephone line is digitally partitioned into one carrier channel for signaling information and two bearer channels to carry traffic. The traffic could be voice or data (such as a connection to a corporate LAN or Internet service provider). Because it is a conditioned, data-ready telephone line, the two bearer channels can be bonded together to establish one, 128 kbps (64 kbps per channel) data call.

Broadband: Officially, the term relates to a carrier service operating across a wide bandwidth range or a carrier network in which a frequency range is divided, through technology, into channels. In common use though, the term means any carrier service (wired or wireless), usually relating to data services and Internet access, capable of carrying data at high speeds.

Cable modem: A device used to interface a personal computer or network router to the high-speed Internet access service provided by cable carriers.

Call accounting system: A software or hardware system that captures SMDR information from a business telephone system and stores it for later retrieval as reports. Hotels use call accounting systems to track telephone calls guests make from their rooms and charge back the cost. Businesses may use call accounting to help allocate telephone costs across departments or employees.

Call center: Any business or business unit whose main function is to communicate with customers, vendors, or suppliers primarily by telephone.

Call sequencer: A device, when installed between incoming telephone lines and a telephone system, that can place ringing lines on hold until someone is available to answer them.

Caller ID (identification):   Using in-band signaling, a local telephone company can pass a caller's telephone number and name along with an incoming telephone call. The telephone or telephone system must be appropriately equipped to read, display, or otherwise make use of the information.

Carrier: A generic term for any company providing local or long-distance telephone or data services to customers.

Carrier-issued calling card: Issued by a carrier, this card allows a user to access the carrier's network from any public telephone, place telephone calls, and be charged the cost of the call on their carrier bill.

Channel bank: A device installed at the customer's premises that breaks a digital T1 line back into individual channels, so these channels may be connected to telephones or a telephone system for use as lines.

Circular hunting: See *hunting*. With hunting, calls roll from one line to the next across a preprogrammed group of lines. Circular hunting means that the call, if all lines in the group are busy, will circle from the last member of the group back to the first and continue until one becomes free and the call is answered.

CO (central office) line: See *1FB*.

CO line card: The circuit board in a business telephone system whose function it is to connect the system to carrier-provided CO lines.

CIR (committed information rate): A term given by carriers providing frame relay service for the guaranteed minimum amount of bandwidth data that can pass through their network between your network points. CIR usually amounts to a specific fraction of your port speed (bandwidth capacity of the circuit connecting each point on your network).

Data above the bandwidth of the CIR can travel through the carrier's network, but it is marked as eligible for discard by the network and can be thrown out should the network be congested, forcing retransmission of lost data.

CLEC (competitive local exchange carrier): A local telephone service company (local exchange carrier) that competes against the original regional Bell operating company in any LATA.

CRM (customer relationship management): A business practice, and systems or software programs that support the practice, that allows a business to track and manage its contacts and relationships with customers.

CSU (channel service unit): A device used to interface a customer's equipment to a carrier network service such as a T1. A CSU provides final termination for digital circuits and final regeneration of signal and deals with the clocking required to manage the individual channels. A CSU is usually required by a carrier before it will allow a T1 to be connected to a phone system or network router.

CTI (computer-telephony integration): The joining together of a computer processing system and a telephone system through a physical link (usually a cable connection) and logical connections (software that allows one system to share information with and exercise control over the other). A good example of the use for this technology is the "screen-pop" application. In the event of an incoming call, the phone system, receiving the phone number of the caller through ANI, passes the number to the customer database and orders it to assign the customer's record to the screen of the agent it is routing the call to.

CTI link: The physical connection between a phone system and the PC or server, usually a serial cable or ethernet LAN cable.

Customer assurance server: A term for a computer server–based system that allows recording and playback of agent calls. More advanced than standard, hard-wired monitoring systems, the customer assurance server may also be capable of making a live record of the activity of an agent's computer monitor simultaneously with calls.

Database hooking: The concept of one automated processing system (phone system, for example), sending a request into a database, to retrieve meaningful information about callers. Such a database request may be used by the phone system to determine how to route the call (an account in collections to the accounting department, for example) or would be used to retrieve useful information to play to a caller (account balance, recent transactions).

Dedicated long distance: When a carrier provides long-distance telephone service over a T1, it is considered dedicated service because the T1 is a direct connection between the carrier and customer, bypassing the local telephone company and dedicated solely to long-distance calling.

DID (direct inward dial): Telecommunications service that allows a LEC to provide a customer with a disproportionate ratio of telephone numbers to lines into a business. For example, a customer could be provided with numbers for every one of its twenty-five employees but only install four DID lines to carry calls on. When one of the numbers is dialed, the carrier sends, along with the call, digits to signal to the phone system whose number was dialed. The phone system, if so equipped, can interpret this DID information and route the incoming call to the correct telephone within the business, bypassing the need for a receptionist or attendant.

DID trunk: Any telephone line that is used to provide DID service. The analog version of DID lines are limited to carrying inbound calls only. DID trunks as channels on a T1 can be used for inbound and outbound calls if so programmed.

Digital (telephone signaling): A method of transmitting telephone calls and other telecommunications signals by converting them to digital information (1s and 0s) before transmitting the signals, then reconstructing the signal on the far end. Digital signaling has been applied to all aspects of telecommunications technology: telephone networks (SS7 and SONET protocols), carrier service lines (T1), and customer premise equipment (digital PBX and digital telephones).

Divestiture: The 1983 government action that deregulated the telecommunications industry and forced the break up of the Bell Telephone System. Once completed, divestiture left behind twelve regional Bell operating companies (local phone companies) that were restricted to doing business within certain geographic boundaries. Also spun off was AT&T (the long-distance and telephone equipment divisions of the Bell System), which created an open, competitive field of play for long-distance telephone service.

Dmarc (demarcation):   The physical location for any customer-provided service in which the PSTN interfaces to the building. Carrier responsibility for service usually ends here.

DNIS (dialed number identification service):   A feature of dedicated long distance that allows a carrier to provide, in essence, DID service on a dedicated long-distance T1. With it, a carrier could assign a customer multiple toll-free numbers across long-distance (T1) circuits. With a properly equipped phone system, the customer could determine, before the phone system decides where to route a phone call, which toll-free number was dialed by the customer.

DNS (domain name service):   Within the Internet, there are numerous DNS servers that act as interpreters, translating the domain names typed into browsers into the IP address numbers computers need to move information back and forth.

DSL (digital subscriber line):   A series of data telephone lines specially conditioned for use as a computer connection. This type of carrier line is often used to provide high-speed Internet connectivity. DSL has limitations, the most common being that the customer and carrier need to be physically located within a certain number of direct cable-feet for DSL to work at its highest rating. Many customers, limited by the copper wiring that serves their home or business, cannot use the technology.

DSLAM (digital subscriber line access multiplexer):   Installed in a carrier's nearest POP or CO, this device is used to interface DSL lines from customers to the carrier's data network.

A single DSLAM may provide the interface for dozens, even hundreds, of subscribers served by that POP.

DS0:   Analog, copper-based circuits become conditioned by the carrier for data and are certified to carry 56k or 64k of data. The circuit is terminated to a channel service unit (much like the CSUs used to terminate T1s).

DS1:   See *T1*.

DS3:   Usually provided on fiber-optic or coaxial wired cabling from the carrier, this traditional PSTN interface has a relative bandwidth and carrying capacity of 45 mb, and is multiplexed down into twenty-eight T1s. DS3s are used to provide multiple T1s on a consolidated circuit for high-use customers (large call centers) or to provide high-speed data interconnections for large customers and ISPs. DS3s are also commonly used by carriers to interconnect their switching offices.

DTMF (dual-tone multifrequency):   Touch tones. When pressing the keys of a push-button telephone, tones are produced that signal other telephone equipment the number the person intends to dial. To the human ear, the 1 and 4 sound the same. The distinction between individual digits for telephone systems is made by combining two cycling currency frequencies together. Phone system equipment has the capability to distinguish between the frequencies.

E&M (ear & mouth) circuit: A type of telephone line used to deliver various services such as DID, tie line, and foreign exchange service.

FCC (Federal Communications Commission):   The government agency responsible for developing and enforcing federal regulation of the telecommunications industry.

FRAD (frame relay access device):   An interface device, similar to a CSU, used to connect frame relay service to a customer's equipment (usually a LAN).

Frame relay: A data circuit. Used by companies to create networks to join the computer systems of multiple offices together or to create connections to other networks (such as the Internet). Frame is similar to private line data service in that it provides a link between two points. The difference is that frame relay is a service provided by carriers that allows access to their network for customers to use to transmit data in a specific (frame relay), packet-based protocol.

The price of the service is determined by the amount of bandwidth access wanted. When installed, a company has only a certain portion of the bandwidth of a circuit it orders guaranteed available. An example would be a company that orders a 256k circuit may have a committed information rate (guarantee) of just 128k. Data transmissions of more than 128k can only pass through the circuit if the extra bandwidth is available on the frame relay network. This oversubscription and packet-based switching allows carriers to provide and sell frame relay service at lower cost than dedicated circuits.

FRS (family radio service):   Using this publicly available radio frequency, manufacturers of two-way radios offer FRS-band radios; a technology limited to one-half watt of transmission power (restricting the range to less than two miles even under ideal conditions). This frequency carries no licensing fees and the radios cost as little as ten to twenty dollars.

FX (foreign exchange) line: This telephone company service allows a business to order a telephone number that originates in a calling area other than its own, which allows the business to receive calls on a local number in another neighborhood or city as if it were a local call. The impression given to callers is that the business they are calling is local to them. This will save the customer any toll that may be incurred in dialing from another city. An FX line may be used by the subscriber business to dial into the foreign exchange as if it were a local call as well, bypassing tolls if applicable.

GMRS (general mobile radio service):   Using this publicly available radio frequency, manufacturers of two-way radios offer GMRS-band radios. As with FRS, GMRS allows radios that transmit at two watts of power, extending the range to five miles under ideal conditions. GMRS is also a frequency open to general use, but the FCC asks for a licensing fee from users.

Ground start trunk: Similar to a CO line except that the technical protocol for initiating a call on the line (triggering the CO to provide dial tone in anticipation of a call dialed) is to establish a ground on the line, as compared with standard

CO lines that use the establishment and disruption of loop current to initiate and tear down calls.

Hold music: Music, provided through a telephone system, to be played to customers while they are on hold. Most business telephone systems are equipped with a music input. There are companies that exist to provide legal, copyrighted music and audio programs to be broadcast over business telephone systems. Some can even create "hype-on-hold" programs that blend music together with commercials for the business.

Hunt group: A set of telephone lines programmed in a sequence for the main number to roll to the next open line when busy. Also can mean a group of telephone extensions in a business telephone system programmed to hunt together.

Hunting: When a business has multiple telephone lines, the phone company central office can be programmed, when a caller dials a main or lead number, to roll the call to another line in the group until it finds one free. The order in which the lines are programmed to roll is called the hunting sequence. Usually the last line in the group is programmed to roll to the first line in the group (circular hunting) or to stop hunting at the last line in the group (terminal hunting). The same hunting concept can be applied to groups of extensions within a phone system.

Hybrid telephone system: A mid-size business telephone system, usually with additional capabilities over a key telephone system (greater size capacity or digital trunking capability [T1 and DID]).

IDF (intermediate distribution frame): A gathering point for the wired infrastructure in a building that is not the final destination for the wiring; it is just a place to gather, organize, and tie wiring back to the main distribution frame.

ILEC (incumbent local exchange carrier): The original telephone company that served the market as part of the Bell System. In many states, the incumbent may have the same name it did at divestiture or it may have been bought or consolidated with another company. The incumbent is still the company that controls the wired telephone infrastructure built into a city, however.

Inter (LATA, state) calling: Any toll calling, billed by your long-distance phone company, that terminates outside the state or LATA you are calling from but within the United States.

Interconnect (equipment vendor): A supplier, installer, and maintainer of business telephone systems and peripheral equipment. In this book, the term interconnect refers to mid-size vendors who are selling and to installation dealers for various manufacturers of business telephone systems and related equipment or services. An interconnect may also provide, in addition to its equipment business, other services such as computers and networking equipment and data and voice cabling, and be a reseller for local or long-distance telephone companies.

Internet: The Internet is nothing more than a great, world-wide, public interconnection of computer systems and networks. It's a network of servers, e-mail systems, databases, Web pages, and the users who are accessing them.

Internet Assigned Numbering Authority: The governing organization for the global Internet community that manages the distribution and public and private use of Internet protocol addresses by regional and national numbering authorities.

Intra (LATA, state) calling: Any toll calling, billed by the local phone company or your long-distance phone company, that terminates within the state or LATA you are calling from.

Intranet: A private Internet. Intranets allow partners, subsidiaries, and remote workers access to proprietary services and information offered by a company. An intranet looks and feels like the Internet by using browsers and Web pages to display information and interface with the users. Yet it is closed to public access and is only available to those on the WAN or those granted secured, protected access from outside the network.

IP (Internet protocol): The open language that computers use to communicate with each other on the Internet. Because it is the standard protocol, or communications language, for computers worldwide, many corporate local networks have adopted IP as their standard protocol as well.

IPSEC: One variation of software that encodes and decodes the information travelling between locations in a VPN. The software encrypts the information and keeps the communication private even though it travels across a public network.

ISDN (integrated services digital networking): A circuit provided by a local phone company using a protocol optimized for data transmission. ISDN comes in two versions: BRI, a channelized analog telephone line, that provides one control channel for signaling information and two bearer channels for carrying data or telephone calls. The second is PRI, a channelized T1 circuit providing a carrier channel and twenty-three bearer channels for voice or data. The ISDN protocol is capable of bonding single (64k) channels together to form larger data pipes for certain types of data call (such as video conference calls or Internet connections).

ISP (Internet service provider): A carrier that provides products and services to allow customers to access the Internet.

IVR (interactive voice response) system (or server): A telephony server that allows customers calling into a business access to the business database through a touch-tone interface. A good example is a banking system that allows customers to dial in to check the balance on a checking or other account.

IXC (Interexchange carrier): A long-distance telephone company; a phone company that carries telephone calls between LATAs. After divestiture in 1984, local telephone companies were barred from carrying traffic across LATA lines, leaving that business to long-distance carriers.

Key telephone system: A small business telephone system. "Key" originated from the term "key line appearance," which usually means that all the telephone lines working on the phone system appear as buttons on each of the telephones. A business with five lines and a key system would have five line buttons (line 1, line 2, line 3, etc.) on each telephone. Lines can be accessed directly. This is in contrast to a PBX where, usually, lines are accessed by pressing a 9—users are ignorant of which of the multitude of business lines attached to the system they have been assigned.

KSU (key service unit): A generic term for the main component of small business telephone systems; the box on the wall that houses the "brains" of the system—the interface modules for telephone stations and lines.

LAN (local area network): An intraoffice network of computers, servers, printers, and other peripheral devices. The interconnection allows the users connected on the network to share resources and information.

LATA (local access transport area): The regional boundaries dividing the country that the FCC drew to separate the operating boundaries of the local and long-distance telephone industries after divestiture. RBOCs were allowed only to carry service within the LATAs they were assigned. Long-distance companies were allowed only to carry calls between LATAs.

LEC (local exchange carrier): A local telephone company. Usually refers to the incumbent LEC, the original Baby Bell that has ownership of the public telephone network within a LATA.

Listen-only mailbox: A type of mailbox programmed on a voice mail system that plays a greeting but records no message. Listen-only boxes are used to automatically provide verbal information in lieu of employees reading it to the customer (such as directions to the office or upcoming show times).

Loop current: The electrical current on a telephone line that carries an analog voice telephone signal.

Manufacturer direct (equipment vendor): A supplier/installer of telephone equipment that is a wholly owned branch office or subsidiary of a telecommunications system manufacturer.

MDF (main distribution frame): A gathering point for the wired infrastructure in a building or campus. The final destination for all station and PSTN wiring. The dmarc is usually located at the MDF. The phone system is usually mounted at the MDF.

Monitoring unit (system): A hard-wired, stand-alone unit that, when installed on telephone lines of a business, provides a supervisor monitoring access to the conversations of the attached telephones.

NANP (North American numbering plan): The numbering plan for the PSTN in the United States and its territories, Canada, Bermuda, and many Caribbean nations. It was invented in 1947 by AT&T and Bell Laboratories and conforms to the International Telecommunications Union Recommendation E.164, which is the international standard for numbering plans.

Numbers under the plan are broken down into the following.

NPA (numbering plan area): commonly known as a long-distance area code.

NXX: The office code prefix (where N is any digit 2–9 and X is any digit 0–9).

XXXX: The four-digit office extension.

Night ringing bell: A chime device that is not a telephone, but that can be triggered by a phone system to ring when an incoming call comes to the system. Originally, bells were used by businesses after normal business hours who have employees who do not necessarily work by a telephone (such as night stockers at a grocery store or security guards in a building).

Optical carrier: Telecommunications transmission technologies using fiber-optic cables, on which can be placed PSTN or private access segments in varying capacities that give tremendous carrying capacity. The optical carrier standard OC3, for example, provides a carrying capacity of 155 mb per second.

OPX (off-premise extension) line: A service that provides a direct, permanent telephone line between a business and, usually, one of its remote offices. The remote location can be dialed as an extension of the original telephone system. The service provides a hot line between the two locations that can only be used for calls between.

Packet-based switching: A method of transmitting data by reducing it into packets (chunks) and enveloping it with information on where it is destined and where it has originated, across a public, shared network.

PBX (private branch exchange) telephone system: A business telephone system. Usually larger than a key or hybrid system, a PBX will offer most or all technology and telephone system options available from the manufacturer (compared with its key or hybrid offerings). The PBX version of a manufacturer's line of telephone systems is usually the one with the highest processing capability and the one with the most sophisticated set of features and options. The term

PBX is a throw-back from the original, manually controlled technology of the original Bell telephone network. Operators worked out of buildings called exchanges and, using cordboards, made physical connections for callers between telephone lines. If a business had enough telephones within it and it had its own cord board or switching system, it was called a private branch exchange.

PDA (personal digital assistant): A PDA is a hand-sized computer that runs simple applications (one example is a Palm Pilot).

The device itself is no more than a hardware platform (just as a PC or a Mac computer is). This platform runs an operating system, such as Palm OS or Windows CE or some proprietary OS depending on who manufactured the device. Software is then written to run on the OS. Applications taking advantage of the unique characteristics of the device (portability, low power requirements) offer everything from electronic calendars, contact databases, and simple games to Internet access, e-mail, custom business applications, and scaled versions of the most popular desktop software.

Phantom extensions: In many phone systems a "virtual" telephone extension number can be programmed. Such an extension is used to provide a telephone destination for calls that do not belong to one telephone device. The phantom can then be programmed to appear on a number of multiline telephone extensions on a phone system so those extensions can all share responsibility for answering calls coming into the phantom. This capability works well when used for groups of workers who are not a business's main receptionists and therefore don't normally answer all incoming calls.

PICC (presubscribed interexchange carrier code): A unique four-digit number assigned to each long-distance provider. The local telephone company programs these codes into the switch database records relative to a telephone service to indicate who the long-distance service provider is. When a long-distance call is placed, it is routed by the local carrier to the correct long-distance network.

POP (point of presence): The physical location of a carrier's network that serves as an interface to customers and the greater PSTN. This could be a CO, switching facility, or colocation of carrier network equipment inside another carrier's switching office.

Port: The name used for plug-in outlets on a telephony system or server where a physical connection to a telephone line, T1, telephone station, or voice mail port is made.

POTS (plain old telephone service) line: Another term for *CO line.*

PPTP (point-to-point tunneling protocol): One variation of software that encodes and decodes the information travelling between locations in a VPN. The software keeps the communication private even though it travels across a public network.

Predictive dialer: An outbound call-center phone system server that automatically dials telephone numbers then connects only answered calls to live agents.

Prepaid calling card: A credit card style card issued by a carrier and purchased by users on a retail basis that allows a user to access the carrier's network from any public telephone, place telephone calls, and have the charges for calls deducted from the balance of the card's original value.

PRI (primary rate interface): The T1 version of ISDN. Provides one carrier channel for signaling and twenty-three bearer channels for carrying traffic. Because it is a conditioned, data-ready telephone line, multiples of bearer channels can be bonded together to establish one data call (for example, a 512k call could be set up between videoconference equipment using eight channels).

Private line: A carrier service that provides businesses a permanent, "on-all-the-time" connection at a variety of bandwidths between two offices. Businesses that need to have interoffice computer systems communicate (or network two telephone systems together so they act as one) and make use of carrier-provided, dedicated tie lines.

PSTN (public switched telephone network): The huge network of telephone lines and switches owned by the combined local and long-distance telephone companies of the United States that is used to provide telephone service to the general public.

Push-to-talk: A hybrid service, push-to-talk devices work and act just as a mobile phone and come with all the features a normal cell phone would. In addition though, there's a walkie-talkie style function. With it, users can communicate, two-way, in much the same fashion as any two-way radio system. Nextel is currently the most popular provider of such service.

PVC (permanent virtual circuit): A logical address or pointer within a frame relay network that establishes a pathway for data to travel. Point A is assigned a PVC to point B. Data are now permitted to pass (at the CIR of the PVC) through the frame relay carrier's network between the two points.

As a service, PVCs are purchased in variable bandwidths as part of a frame relay service. The cumulative bandwidth of all PVCs at one location of a frame network makes up that location's committed information rate.

RAD (recorded announcement device): A recording device used to play messages in automated call processing systems. In an ACD system, RADs are used to play the in-queue messages.

RBOC (regional Bell operating companies): The original twelve local telephone companies created from the divestiture of the Bell Telephone System in 1984. The other entity created was the long-distance carrier AT&T.

Refurbished (telecommunications equipment): Used telephone equipment, usually cleaned and tested to still be in good working order.

Screen pop: The process, enabled by software, of making a customer record appear on an agent's desktop computer simultaneously with the delivery of a telephone call.

SDSL (synchronous digital subscriber line): A version of a DSL service in which the upstream and downstream data rates have the same bandwidth characteristics. SDSL provides data service on a standard telephone line but usually precludes the ability to simultaneously use the line for voice calls.

SMDR (station message detail recording [or reporting]): Most business telephone systems have, or can be equipped with, an output port that posts records about every call made to or from the system. These raw records usually indicate information such as the number dialed (on an outbound call) or the number dialing (on an inbound call for a phone system equipped to read ANI), the time, date, duration of the call, and the originating or terminating extension. These raw data can be captured by call accounting systems to provide a business with useful and relevant reports about telephone traffic and usage.

Static IP: An IP address permanently assigned to one specific router, server, or Web site location within a server that helps one computer find another one in the Internet. Static IPs are needed when a computer must always be reachable on the Internet by other computers.

Station card: A printed circuit board that resides inside a business telephone system and provides the physical connections for telephone extensions to the system.

Switched long distance: Service provided by a long-distance telephone company off the back of regular local telephone lines. Toll calls are "switched" to the carrier by the local phone company for delivery by the long-distance carrier to their destination.

Switches: A generic term for a device that makes telephone and data call connections. For a local telephone company, for example, the switch is located in the CO and provides the interface between the telephone and the rest of the PSTN. The term can also be applied to larger telephone systems.

Switching matrix: In this book, this term refers to the circuitry within a business telephone system responsible for establishing the connections between stations (telephones and other devices) and telephone lines. The same term could be applied to the component within other equipment (data routers or central office switches) that makes similar internal circuit connections.

T1: A single digital telephone circuit channelized into twenty-four equal segments. These segments can be used by local phone companies to provide twenty-four lines of local phone service, by long-distance carriers to provide twenty-four dedicated connections to their networks, or by data carriers to provide up to 1.544 megabytes of data pathways. T1 is the most basic and common carrier circuit used to provide many complex and advanced types of telecommunications services. T1 is a widely used circuit type in all manner of voice switches, business telephone systems, and data connectivity equipment.

T1 line card: The printed circuit board or circuit pack in a business telephone system or switch that establishes the physical interconnection between a T1 circuit from a carrier and the system.

TAPI (telephony applications programming interface): A software protocol developed by Microsoft that acts as an interface between specially equipped telephone systems and software applications that run under the Microsoft Windows family of personal computer operating systems.

Tariff: A legal filing, required from carriers by the FCC and a state's public utility commission, that defines a carriers standard products and pricing methods.

TCU (total cost units): TCUs (and similar billing schemes used under other names) are billing increments that, when used on a long-distance bill, look just like time but is a measurement of something else altogether.

A TCU is a special number used to represent a formula the carrier has applied to calculate the cost of a call. Instead of inflating the rate, the formula inflates the perceived length of the call (by multiplying the true call length by the formula) to make this new number look like it represents time.

In a TCU billing scheme, a thirty-second call may appear on a phone bill, as 3.3 TCUs and billed at the per TCU rate of five cents. The customer perceives the rate of five cents as a per minute rate; therefore a 16.5 cent call appears normal. But, at five cents per *minute*, the same call would have cost a mere three cents—that's a 550% mark-up!

Telecom Reform Act (1996): The legislative act that deregulated the local telephone business. In exchange for opening their local markets to competition, incumbent LECs are able to compete in the lucrative long-distance voice and data market.

Telemarketing: A mass-effort business marketing method using telephones to reach customers.

Telemarketing campaign: A planned telemarketing program, with specific goals, developed and implemented by a business or outsourcer.

Terminal hunting: A method of programming the hunting sequence of telephone lines or extensions in which the last member of the group does not hunt to the first, therefore terminating the cycle at the last number. A customer who calls into a busy terminal hunt group will be given a busy signal by the central office.

Tie line: Another term for private line, any telecommunications circuit that provides a direct connection between two points is called a tie line. In business, private tie lines can be used to link computer systems at two or more remote offices together. In a carrier's network, tie lines are used to transport traffic between switch offices and network nodes.

Tip & ring: The two sides (one side for current to flow into the telephone or device, one side for current to flow back to the central office) of an analog telephone circuit.

Toll-free service: Service provided by a long-distance carrier that allows a customer to issue a telephone number for people to call from toll areas in which the customer bears the toll for the call. Originally, all such numbers had the (NPA) designation of 800. Because of demand for the service, the NPA has been opened up for toll-free service to include 888, 877, 866, and 855.

Tree mailbox: A voice mailbox programmed to present callers with choices to make progress beyond the tree in different directions. One example would be a department routing mailbox ("press 1 for sales, 2 for engineering, 3 for administration . . ."). A tree mailbox does not record messages, it just provides routing.

Trunk lines: A term applied to many different telephone circuits. For carrier networks, tie lines and the connections to other carrier networks are called trunk lines. When connected to PBXs, CO lines and the channels of T1 circuits are sometimes called trunk lines. "Trunk" is considered a euphemism for a telephone line when it is connected to equipment rather than directly to telephones (such as a home telephone line).

There was a time when the distinction between an interoffice trunk and a line out to someone's house or business was important. Now, with all switching handled within sophisticated automatic switching equipment, the distinction of the term is irrelevant.

Trunk utilization reporting: A report, available with the use of some call accounting systems or as a service provided by a carrier, that gives information about the activity of a group of telephone lines. The most common use of such a report is for companies to see how many times all their lines were in use at the same time during the month, therefore showing how often their customers received busy signals.

Trunker (equipment vendor): A small company (many times just one or two people) that provides telephone equipment and service of business telephone systems.

TSAPI (telephony services applications programming interface): A software protocol developed by Novell that acted as an interface between specially equipped telephone systems and applications that ran under Novell's family of computer network operating systems.

T-span: Another term for *T1*.

Turn-key: A generic term for pricing in proposals that means all-inclusive. In telephone system purchase terms, it means a total price for the proposed system that should include all parts and labor needed to install the system so it performs as proposed.

Unified messaging (server): A voice mail system that has been developed, using computer-telephony integration, to provide access for users to voice mail, e-mail, and, sometimes, fax from common user interfaces (usually existing e-mail programs such as Microsoft Outlook or Lotus Notes). Most unified messaging systems also give access to the various message media they support through a traditional voice mail telephone interface.

Universal (uniform) call distribution: Programmed intelligence within a business telephone system to allow universal distribution of calls over a group of stations.

USOC (universal service operating code): Standard codes that local telephone companies assign to telecommunications service offerings used in carrier billing and switching systems. 1FB is an example of such a code. If a line has a USOC of 1FB in the carrier's billing and maintenance database, the carrier knows what service to provide out of the switch physically connected to a business (a single, flat business telephone line). The billing software then knows, by USOC as well, what to charge for that service.

UTP (unshielded twisted pair): The most common kind of copper telephone wiring. The term unshielded comes from the fact that UTP, although wrapped in a protective polyvinyl chloride layer, is not sheathed in a grounding foil (shielded) as is a shielded twisted pair. Within UTP wiring, pairs of insulated copper wires are twisted around each other.

VPN (virtual private network): VPNs create a WAN using the Internet as the backbone. Each location establishes a connection to the Internet and communicates to the other locations using an encrypted version of the universal, global, network protocol, IP.

VPN appliance: An access or interface device, much like a router or CSU, which sits on a LAN and provides tunneling (encryption and logical connections) through the Internet in support of a VPN application.

Voice mail: A computerized system that can play and record messages and greetings.

Voice-over IP: The application of several technologies (IP, packet-based switching, digital telecommunications transmission) that allows telephone traffic to be carried across data networks using IP.

Voice-over IP, in its application as products to be sold to consumers, really means two things. The first is the interconnection of telephone equipment within an office using the existing data LAN as the distribution. For this to work, the telephone stations at the users desk and the KSU that run them, have to communicate within the LAN's data streams in the LAN's protocol languages.

The other meaning relates to providing gateways between remote offices to make voice telephone calls across whatever WAN technology is in place. Again, the voice traffic must be embedded in the data protocol language (IP) of the WAN to be transmitted between sites.

WAN (wide-area network): Using carrier technology, companies with multiple locations interconnect their office LANs so employees can share the information and resources across geographically dispersed locations.

WAP (wireless applications protocol): A protocol suite used by mobile phones that includes a language (WML) for displaying Web sites that have been developed to allow a properly equipped wireless phone to be used, for example, as a Web browser.

Zero plus dialing: A long-distance carrier service in which, by dialing "0" before a long-distance telephone number, a carrier operator or automated system allows the caller to bill a call to a credit card, collect to the called party, or back to the home telephone service.

Commonly available at hotels, the service is traditionally and notoriously expensive compared with other methods of billing for long-distance telephone service when travelling (cell phone, calling cards, toll-free numbers).

Appendix ONE

Telecom Industry Publications

The following is a list of magazines and publications that can help you immerse yourself in the business of telecom.

Art Sobczak's TelE-sales
13254 Stevens Street
Omaha, NE 68137
(402) 895–9399
www.businessbyphone.com

Call Center Focus
CMP Europe Ltd.
+44 (0) 208 987 7698
www.callcentre.co.uk

Call Center Magazine
CMP Media, Inc.
12 West 21st Street
New York, NY 10010
(888) 824–9793
www.callcentermagazine.com

Call Center News Service (Call Center Savvy)
Dawson Publishing
(718) 788–6220
www.callcenternews.com

CC News — The Business Newspaper For Contact Center And Customer Care Professionals
United Publications
106 Lafayette Street PO Box 995
Yarmouth, Maine 04096
(207) 846–0600
www.ccnews.com

Communications Convergence
CMP Media, Inc.
12 West 21st Street
New York, NY 10010
(888) 824–9793
www.cconvergence.com

Communications News
Nelson Publishing, Inc.
2500 Tamiami Trail N.
Nokomis, FL 34275
(941) 966–9521
www.comnews.com

Customer Interface Magazine
Advanstar
201 Sandpointe Avenue, Suite 600
Santa Ana, CA 92707
(714) 513–8829
www.c-interface.com

Customer Support Management
Intertec Publishing, a Primedia Company
11 River Bend Drive South
PO Box 4949
Stamford, CT 06907–0949
(203) 358–9900
www.customersupportmgmt.com

Direct Magazine
Intertec Publishing, a Primedia Company
11 River Bend Drive South
PO Box 4265
Stamford, CT 06907–0265
(203) 358–9900
www.directmag.com

Operations & Fulfillment
Intertec Publishing, a Primedia Company
11 River Bend Drive South
PO Box 4949
Stamford, CT 06907–0949
www.opsandfulfillment.com

Tele.com
CMP Media, Inc.
12 West 21st Street
New York, NY 10010
(888) 824–9793
www.teledotcom.com

Total Telecom
Tower House
Sovereign Park, Market Harborough
Leicestershire, LE16 9EF, UK
+44 (0) 1858 438 847
www.totaltele.com.com

Wireless Week
Reed Business Information
P.O. Box 266008
Highlands Ranch, CO 80163–6008
(303) 470–4800
www.wirelessweek.com

Appendix TWO

Telecom Industry Organizations

The telecommunications business is well represented by trade organizations. Effective telecom managers take full advantage of the opportunity these groups and organizations represent to help them grow stronger in their chosen responsibilities.

What each of the following entities focus on within that sphere is sometimes apparent by their name; sometimes not. From this list though, you'll find groups that feature research and reference materials, groups that focus on networking and fellowship with others in your position, and organizations that provide tools to locate manufacturers, consultants, and suppliers.

Also included are user groups for some of the major brands of telephone equipment.

American Teleservices Association
1620 I Street NW, Suite 615
Washington, DC 20006
(202) 293-2452
www.ataconnect.org

Association for Telecommunications Professionals in State Government
P.O. Box 11910
2760 Research Park Drive
Lexington, KY 40578-1910
(859) 244-8186
www.nastd.org

Call Centre Management Association
GPO Box 1552P
Melbourne VIC, Australia 3001
011-61-1300-301-390
www.ccma.asn.au

Central Station Alarm Association
440 Maple Avenue East, Suite 201
Vienna, VA 22180
(703) 242-4670
www.csaaul.org

Customer Care Institute
17 Dean Overlook NW
Atlanta, GA 30318
(404) 352-9291
www.customercare.com

The Direct Marketing Association, Inc.
1120 Avenue of The Americas
New York, NY 10036-8700
(212) 790-1500
www.the-dma.org

Help Desk Institute
6385 Corporate Drive, Suite 301
Colorado Springs, CO 80919
(800) 248-5667
www.helpdeskinst.com

Incoming Calls Management Institute
PO Box 6177
Annapolis, MD 21401-0177
(410) 267-0700
www.incoming.com

Industrial Telecommunications Association
1110 North Glebe Road, Suite 500
Arlington, VA 22201-5720
(703) 528-5115
www.ita-relay.com

International Alliance of Avaya Users
(800) 344-6489
www.inaau.org

International Customer Service Association
401 North Michigan Avenue
Chicago, IL 60611
(800) 360-4272
www.icsa.com

International Nortel Networks Meridian Users Group
9441 LBJ Freeway, Suite 502
Dallas, TX 75243
(877) 446-6624
www.innmug.org

North American Mitel Users Group
C/O DCI Marketing
2727 W. Good Hope Road
Milwaukee, WI 53209
(414) 228-4310
www.mitel.com/user_communities/index.cfm

Siemens International Users Group
1671 Center Point Parkway, Suite 113-352
Brimingham, AL 35215
www.snug.org

Society of Consumer Affairs Professionals in Business
801 North Fairfax Street, Suite 404
Alexandria, VA 22314
(703) 519-3700
www.socap.org

Telecommunications Industry Association
2500 Wilson Blvd., Suite 300
Arlington, VA 22201
(703) 907-7700
www.tiaonline.org

Appendix THREE

Consulting Resources

Should you need to find a good consultant beyond qualifying potentials from your local telephone listings, try this helpful resource.

Society of Telecommunications Consultants
P.O. Box 416
Fall River Mills, CA 96028
(800) 782-7670
www.stcconsultants.org

Index

Page references followed by "f" indicate a figure.